CONSTRUCTING THE PERSUASIVE PORTFOLIO

Constructing the Persuasive Portfolio teaches you the art of designing a compelling and effective architectural portfolio. Margaret Fletcher categorizes the architectural portfolio design process into a step-by-step method that you can manage and understand. The full-color book provides 400 portfolio examples from 55 designers and includes annotated case studies along with more than 50 diagrams. With a set of 48 design actions that are marked throughout, the book offers best practices for a variety of design problems to simplify troubleshooting for the designer. You will learn how to:

- identify your audience;
- collect, document, and catalog your work;
- organize your portfolio;
- visually structure your portfolio;
- design your layout; and
- manage both printed and digital portfolio formats.

As your ultimate persuasive tool, your portfolio is the single most important design exercise of your academic and professional career. *Constructing the Persuasive Portfolio* shows you everything you need to know to create your portfolio. It is the only portfolio design book you will ever need!

Margaret Fletcher is an assistant professor of architecture in the College of Architecture, Design and Construction at Auburn University in Auburn, Alabama, USA.

CONSTRUCTING THE PERSUASIVE PORTFOLIO
the only primer you'll ever need

Margaret Fletcher

Routledge
Taylor & Francis Group

NEW YORK AND LONDON

First published 2017
by Routledge
711 Third Avenue, New York, NY 10017

and by Routledge
2 Park Square, Milton Park, Abingdon, Oxon OX14 4RN

Routledge is an imprint of the Taylor & Francis Group, an informa business

© 2017 Taylor & Francis

The right of Margaret Fletcher to be identified as author of this work has been asserted by her in accordance with sections 77 and 78 of the Copyright, Designs and Patents Act 1988.

All rights reserved. No part of this book may be reprinted or reproduced or utilized in any form or by any electronic, mechanical, or other means, now known or hereafter invented, including photocopying and recording, or in any information storage or retrieval system, without permission in writing from the publishers.

Trademark notice: Product or corporate names may be trademarks or registered trademarks, and are used only for identification and explanation without intent to infringe.

Publisher's Note
This book has been designed by the author and prepared from the provided camera-ready copy.

Library of Congress Cataloging in Publication Data
Names: Fletcher, Margaret, 1969–
Title: Constructing the persuasive portfolio : the only primer you'll ever need / Margaret Fletcher.
Description: New York : Routledge, 2016. | Includes index
Identifiers: LCCN 2016014152| ISBN 9781138860964 (hardback : alk. paper) | ISBN 9781138860971 (pbk. : alk. paper) | ISBN 9781315716176 (ebook)
Subjects: LCSH: Architecture portfolios—Design. | Architectural services marketing.
Classification: LCC NA1996 .F58 2016 | DDC 720.2—dc23LC record available at https://lccn.loc.gov/2016014152

ISBN: 978-1-138-86096-4 (hbk)
ISBN: 978-1-138-86097-1 (pbk)
ISBN: 978-1-315-71617-6 (ebk)

Acquisition Editor: Wendy Fuller
Editorial Assistant: Grace Harrison
Production Editor: Alanna Donaldson

Typeset in Helvetica Neue, Futura and Gill Sans.

For Product Safety Concerns and Information please contact our EU representative: GPSR@taylorandfrancis.com
Taylor & Francis Verlag GmbH, Kaufingerstraße 24, 80331 München, Germany.

To Mom,
I know what you're thinking. . . "mirabile dictu!"

Contents

01
the work before the work
01

02
designing portfolio systems
20

- viii Introduction
- x **Design Actions**

02 Identifying the Audience
- 04 *Identify the Audience*
- 05 *Flexibility of Portfolio and Content*

06 Collect, Document and Catalog the Work
- 08 *Collect the Work*
- 08 *Document the Work*
- 17 *Catalog the Work*

22 Planning the Work
- 24 *The Design Narratives*
- 26 *Flexibility of the Portfolio System: Print Portfolio and Digital Portfolio*
- 27 *Designing the Content and Designing the Container*
- 28 *Determining the Size and Orientation of the Portfolio*
- 29 *Components of a Portfolio*
- 32 *Storyboarding*

34 Strategies for Portfolio Organization
- 36 *Organizing the Content Narrative*
- 42 *Organizing the Visual Narrative: Using Visual Components of Graphic Layout as Organizational Structure*

64 Systems of Visual Structure
- 68 *Grid and Alignment Systems*
- 75 *Designing the Active Area*
- 79 *When to Break the Rules*
- 84 *Visual Relationships between Objects on a Page*
- 90 *Visual Pace*

03 designing the graphic layout 92

- 94 **Representation Strategies: Graphic Design Basics**
  - 94 *Visual Order and Visual Hierarchy*
  - 108 *Typography*
  - 115 *Graphic Punctuation*
  - 116 *Graphics: How Far Is Too Far*
- 120 **Project Narrative Visual Representation**
  - 122 *Determining Holes in the Project Narrative*
  - 122 *Representing Work: Does Additional Material Need to Be Produced?*
  - 123 *How Many Projects Should Be Included?*
  - 124 *Visual and Verbal Representation of Design Thinking*
  - 128 *Architectural Symbols and Conventions for Presentation Drawings*
- 144 **Text in Your Portfolio: What it Says and How it Looks**
  - 146 *What it Says: The Value of Words*
  - 147 *How it Looks: The Graphic Presence of Text in a Portfolio*
  - 148 *Content and Visual Goals of Text in a Portfolio*
  - 150 *Architecture Specific Text Issues*
- 156 **Editing and Reviewing Your Work**
  - 158 *Visual Review Process*
  - 158 *Editing Checklists*

04 determining portfolio format 160

- 162 **The Printed Portfolio**
  - 164 *Print Portfolio Types*
  - 165 *Portfolio Dimensions and Orientation*
  - 165 *Deciding on a Production Method*
  - 166 *Printing Options*
  - 166 *Binding the Portfolio*
  - 170 *Material Choices*
- 172 **The Digital Portfolio**
  - 173 *Determining Digital Portfolio Goals*
  - 174 *Digital Portfolio Types*
  - 177 *Issues Presenting Architectural Work Digitally*
  - 178 *Basic Web Guidelines*

05 case studies 180

- 182 **Case Study 01** *Will Gregory*
- 194 **Case Study 02** *Adam Kernes*
- 202 **Case Study 03** *Wei Xia*
- 208 **Case Study 04** *Ryan Tyler Martinez*
- 218 **Case Study 05** *Derek Pirozzi*
- 226 **Case Study 06** *Jia Joy Hu*
- 232 **Case Study 07** *Nikki Hall*
- 236 **Case Study 08** *Annie McCarthy*

- 241 **Illustration Credits**
- 242 **Acknowledgments**
- 244 **Index**

Introduction

Your portfolio is one of the most important design exercises of your career. It is the document that not only represents all of the hard work you've accomplished but also serves as an indicator of how you consider the world around you. Think about this: the work that is in your portfolio will follow you for the rest of your life. Over the years, you'll redesign it, update it, add new projects and remove old ones. There will be a continual framing and re-framing through the different phases of your design life. How you represent yourself and your work is incredibly important.

A portfolio is a design exercise and should be treated as such. This design problem embodies both the act of planning and the act of doing. Designing and producing a portfolio often seems foreign simply because it has not been your area of study—architecture has, landscape architecture has, or urban design has! Here's the good news: you don't need to be a graphic designer to create a successful portfolio. You do, however, need to understand the complex design systems at work in a portfolio to be able to visually communicate the ideas that have formed and shaped the work you've designed. Remember, through your portfolio you are not only being evaluated on your formal design work; you are also being evaluated on the design of your portfolio and how you've used this opportunity to frame your ideas.

It is not enough to just show beautiful images of compelling design artifacts, though those items should be included. A successful portfolio demonstrates how you think and how you work. The organizing systems used to regulate your portfolio will support these visual descriptions. Your portfolio will clearly demonstrate your ability to explore your own creativity in meaningful ways.

A significant factor of being a successful designer is having the ability to parse through an incredible amount of information and discover interrelated themes. It is a skill unique to design culture and exists in the realm of design thinking and design knowledge. It is important for you to understand how you, yourself, think so that you can demonstrate it to others. The portfolio should be designed to display this design thinking. If we understand the complexities of how we think, we can begin to understand and define how we might represent

Introduction

and explain all of the diverse knowledge that has gone into each design project.

Architecture, landscape architecture, urban design and the like are professions where the study and representation of the thing becomes a thing in of itself. As a designer works through complex problems with a multitude of constituent components, modes and means of visual representation act to record those design ideas. The artifacts we create become a scalar physical manifestation of a design that cannot come to fruition until the piece is actually built full scale with real materials. This is where it gets interesting; the idea of "real materials" is strange because the artifacts we make are also built with "real materials" albeit representational materials. The idea that our design models are artifacts that represent something else is easy to reconcile. This idea is also true for every single representative object—drawing, diagram, sketch, model, prototype—that is produced through a design investigation. The work is always a representation. But even though it is a representation of something else, it still maintains presence as a thing in of itself. Your portfolio operates in this same manner; it is the ultimate representational artifact.

When we understand this conundrum of representation, it becomes even more important that the visual representations are true to the ideas of the designer. Keep in mind that some artifacts are created to figure something out, or to describe something or simply to represent something; all of these visual representation types need to reveal the value of the artifact relative to your design ideas. This act will convey meaning to your audience. Only when you are able to assign the value of the artifact relative to the design ideas you are trying to represent, can the visual representation of your design ideas emerge. Identify your ideas so you can begin the process of representing them. Of course, that's easier said than done. In working we develop ideas. We express these ideas through representational activities. One does not necessarily come before the other. The design process is circuitous in that we develop ideas that are then represented through the very artifacts that were used to generate the ideas in the beginning.

It is no wonder that portfolio design is so demanding and important. It is the visual and verbal representation of work that by its very nature is incredibly difficult to represent. Understanding and breaking down your own design thinking can frame the representation in your portfolio. The complexities embedded in your design work need to be elucidated through the design of your portfolio. Don't forget that while you were designing each project, you were designing an argument to support that project. The same mentality needs to be used to develop and represent a persuasive argument that supports your portfolio design.

Designing visual artifacts that represent ideas is not a radical or new concept but it is a particularly clear process and one that is easy to follow if you are able to parse your projects into digestible and discernible bits to establish their particular design meaning. This book will help you align the ideas and systems that go into the creation and design of a portfolio.

My ultimate goal is to enable you, the designer, to understand all of the visual and organizational systems that work together within the portfolio. Understanding these systems will help you formulate a persuasive and purposeful presentation of your work.

There are so many things to consider when you are designing and creating your portfolio—so many things that an entire book has been written about it! However, even though there is an extraordinary amount of information to consider, when you break it down into tasks that you can accomplish one by one, the enormous job of designing and creating a portfolio can be accomplished without an extraordinary amount of stress.

Margaret Fletcher

Constructing the Persuasive Portfolio: the only primer you'll ever need

Design Actions

Identifying the Audience

① *Know the requirements of your intended audience and stick to those parameters.* — page 04

② *Understand it is best to prepare flexible content and a flexible portfolio design to support a variety of portfolio outputs both printed and digital.* — page 05

Collect, Document and Catalog the Work

③ *Collect all physical artifacts to be documented for possible inclusion in your portfolio. Store physical artifacts properly.* — page 08

④ *Perform both reference documentation and presentation documentation.* — page 08

⑤ *Digitally clean and edit all of the digital representations of your work.* — page 15

⑥ *Store all digital material in an organized cataloging system.* — page 18

Planning the Work

⑦ *Learn and understand the difference between content narrative, visual narrative and project narrative. Make purposeful decisions for each.* — page 24

⑧ *Develop a flexible portfolio system.* — page 26

⑨ *Design the content and design the container.* — page 27

⑩ *Determine size and orientation of the portfolio.* — page 28

⑪ *Identify portfolio components that need to be included.* — page 29

⑫ *Develop an organizing storyboard.* — page 32

Strategies for Portfolio Organization

⑬ *Organize the Content Narrative: Decide if projects will be organized in an order or by category or some combination.* — page 36

⑭ *Portfolio Components: Decide which portfolio components will be used as an organizing strategy. Portfolio components to consider:* — page 42

   table of contents
   section divider spreads
   headers and footers
   page numbers
   graphic icon systems

⑮ *Project Components: Decide which project components will be used as an organizing strategy. Project components to consider:* — page 58

   parallel project introduction material
   consistent graphic indicators

Systems of Visual Structure

⑯ *Decide on underlying structure: grid or alignment system or both.* — page 66

⑰ *Design the active area.* — page 75

⑱ *Design the visual relationships between objects on a page.* — page 84

⑲ *Design the visual pace of the portfolio.* — page 90

Graphic Design Basics

⑳ *Establish visual order and visual hierarchy.* — page 94

㉑ *Get a handle on graphic rules of typography and implement them.* — page 108

㉒ *Learn correct graphic punctuation and put what you've learned to good use.* — page 115

㉓ *Don't screw it all up with goofy graphics.* — page 116

Design Actions

Project Narrative Visual Representation

(24) Determine the project narrative for each project being considered for inclusion. page 122

(25) Decide if you have representational artifacts to match all of the ideas from the project narrative. page 123

(26) Decide which projects should be included in your portfolio. page 123

(27) Determine the appropriate order for each project narrative. page 124

(28) Apply hierarchical relationships to support the project narrative. page 126

(29) Understand best practices for typical architectural symbols and conventions and apply them. page 128

(30) Use labeling systems appropriately. page 131

(31) Make sure your presentation drawings are legible at the scale of the portfolio. page 139

(32) Correct issues with image quality in your portfolio. page 143

Text in Your Portfolio

(33) Improve your word selection throughout the portfolio. page 146

(34) Review and implement writing tips. page 146

(35) Understand and implement the content and visual goals of text in your portfolio. page 148

(36) Get straight how you are approaching architecture specific text issues in your portfolio. page 150

Editing and Reviewing Your Work

(37) Perform a thorough visual review of your portfolio. page 158

(38) Review your portfolio page by page against the graphics editing checklist. page 158

(39) Review your portfolio page by page against the copy editing checklist. page 159

The Printed Portfolio

(40) Understand different print portfolio types and determine which ones need to be produced from your designed portfolio system. page 164

(41) Review and implement portfolio dimensions and orientation guidelines. page 165

(42) Decide on a printing method. page 166

(43) Decide on a binding type. page 166

(44) Decide on cover material and design. page 170

(45) Decide on paper type. page 171

The Digital Portfolio

(46) Match your goals and objectives for creating a digital portfolio to the value of each digital portfolio option before embarking on a separate digital portfolio exercise. page 173

(47) Review and implement issues related to presenting architectural work digitally. page 177

(48) Review and implement basic web guidelines. page 178

The Work Bo

fore the Work

02 Identifying the Audience
Identify the Audience
Flexibility of Portfolio and Content

06 Collect, Document and Catalog the Work
Collect the Work
Document the Work
Catalog the Work

The Work Be

Design Actions

(1) *Know the requirements of your intended audience and stick to those parameters.* page 04

(2) *Understand it is best to prepare flexible content and a flexible portfolio design to support a variety of portfolio outputs both printed and digital.* page 05

fore the Work

Identifying the Audience

When first embarking on the creation of a design portfolio, one of two situations will be present: either it will be known the exact purpose for the portfolio—graduate school application, design firm application, etc.—or it's simply time to get started on a portfolio because one will be needed some day soon. In either case, it seems like a good idea to get started! Chances are, the work for your portfolio will begin long before the actual portfolio is needed. That's because all of the material created while learning to become an architect will become the content for the future portfolio. There are many issues to consider when designing and creating a portfolio—but let's start at the beginning.

Identify the Audience

The more you know about the organization you are applying to, the better your portfolio will be received. It sounds obvious but it is surprising how many people skip this simple yet vital step. While it is important to target a specific place that matches your interests, design skills and goals; it is also important to do enough research on an organization to determine the application requirements and match them precisely.

Different Audiences

There are a wide variety of audiences that require a portfolio and it is guaranteed they will all have slightly different formats for the application submission process. Below are several examples of different types of audiences. Each type demands a slightly different focus for the portfolio design.

Professional Portfolio: This portfolio type is typically used for a professional job search.

Award Portfolio: This portfolio type could be either academic or professional and requires a very focused and specific presentation.

Academic Portfolio: This portfolio type can cover a wide range of applications including but not limited to: a year-level progress portfolio, graduate school application portfolio, scholarship portfolio, etc.

Each of these portfolio types could vary in terms of output, tone, project range, length, focus, format, etc. and should be designed accordingly. One portfolio cannot fulfill all of the portfolio formats needed in a lifetime! It is imperative to understand who the audience is and what they require prior to completing the design work on that specific portfolio.

Find Out What They Want: Do the Research

Generally when submitting a portfolio, it means that something specific is being applied for. We have already established that there are many different types of portfolio applications for many different types of organizations. It is incredibly important to do the research and figure out the precise requirements for submission and follow these instructions exactly. The first thing to do is to look up format and content requirements; these are typically the most stringent of the requirements in terms of length and accepted format.

One hundred and fifty of the top national and international architecture firms were contacted to determine trends in submission format. 75% of responding firms requested an initial digital submission with a printed portfolio expected at the in-person interview. It was also discovered that each organization has a slightly different submission process. There is not a one-off solution for every organization. That would be too easy! To generalize the requirements; a resume, a cover letter, a set of digital work samples—PDF format, often with a file size requirement that is relatively small—and a print portfolio will always be needed. This list should be considered as a base set of materials. 33% of responding firms required a hard copy of portfolio materials to be mailed prior to being granted an interview. Suffice it to say, it is no longer permissible to ignore either print or digital formats; both types will be needed.

Portfolio Review Process

It has been acknowledged that each organization is going to require a slightly different type of portfolio submission. It is also true that each organization is going to review the material in a slightly different way. While it may be impossible to determine how a portfolio will be reviewed prior to submission, it is a good idea to understand all of the different possibilities. Through our research, it was determined that about half of the firms contacted review portfolios through a small committee while the other half have a single point of contact to initiate the review process. In most cases, all portfolios have to go through several hands before candidates are asked in for interviews. For digital submissions, the vast majority of firms, 85%, review portfolios on a computer monitor. Other options for reviewing digital portfolios were on large format TV or projected on a large screen. Only 10% of firms indicated that they actually print out the digital submissions for review.

So why do different organizations require different formats? I wondered the same thing; so I asked. Most firms replied that due to the volume of applications, a small-format digital submission was simply most practical. These submissions are manageable to review through committee since the material is very easy to distribute. Other firms indicated that they would only accept a printed portfolio, even as the initial application. For these firms, they felt it demonstrated that the applicants were serious about the application simply because it takes a greater commitment from the applicant to prepare a printed submission. These firms also felt strongly that the printed portfolio is a clear indicator of the care an applicant takes in the selection of materials and assembly of their portfolio. For them, it makes it easier to determine potentially successful candidates based on the quality of the printed material.

When all is said and done, it is true that the success of the portfolio is dependent primarily on the material available to put in it. However, there should be purpose and intent behind what is included and how it is presented. Part of this purpose and intent must reflect what the organization being applied to wants to see. Don't forget this!

Flexibility of Portfolio and Content

Ultimately the portfolio will become the most important tool of persuasion to achieve your specific goals. Knowing what these goals are as the portfolio is being designed is indeed helpful but, sooner or later, the portfolio will be used for a variety of application types that can't be imagined at the beginning of the process. The best way to attack this problem is to remember to keep the portfolio format and content very flexible. Being prepared for this and understanding how the portfolio systems work to accommodate these requests will make life easier in the long run. The goal is to design one portfolio that can be output in multiple ways.

The portfolio content also needs to be incredibly flexible. The best way to achieve this is to have everything digitally organized in a logical fashion and to maintain a variety of digital formats such that the original format of the material does not get overwritten.

There are several different types of typical portfolio formats to be aware of. The flexibility of the portfolio systems should be able to accommodate any of the types listed here. There are two main portfolio categories: print portfolios and digital portfolios.

Print Portfolio Types

A print portfolio is just what it says: printed on paper. There are many different types and scales of printed portfolios. Typical print portfolio types include: cut sheets (unbound project sheets), a leave-behind or mailer portfolio (a truncated version of the full portfolio), full printed portfolio and the interview portfolio (physically bigger portfolio to be presented to a group).

Digital Portfolio Types

Digital portfolios have a variety of formats as well. There are digital formats that are full design exercises in their own right and digital formats that are merely digital outputs exported from print portfolio files. Web portfolios fall into several different categories: a self-coded website, pre-coded portfolio template gallery website, blog website and web-based book portfolio. The most requested digital format is a PDF (Portable Document Format).

The Work B...

Design Actions

(3) *Collect all physical artifacts to be documented for possible inclusion in your portfolio. Store physical artifacts properly.* page 08

(4) *Perform both reference documentation and presentation documentation.* page 08

(5) *Digitally clean and edit all of the digital representations of your work.* page 15

(6) *Store all digital material in an organized cataloging system.* page 18

Before the Work

Collect, Document and Catalog the Work

No matter what is decided regarding portfolio format, style or purpose; there is always work that needs to be done prior to embarking on the full design of a portfolio. It is important that the portfolio pre-work is flexible and can serve a variety of portfolio needs. After all, it's best to only prepare material once and be able to use it forever. In order to successfully accomplish this, there are a few things to be aware of. This section describes everything that needs to be done before beginning the work of actually designing the portfolio. Some of this work is quite tedious but it will make the future much easier if the effort is put in correctly at the beginning.

The most important thing to do to ensure portfolio success is to properly collect, document and catalog all of the work. As mentioned above, this set of tasks is extremely tedious and time consuming. It is one of those tasks best tackled with work done daily—or at least weekly or it might even drop to monthly—but no matter what; do not neglect this task. If you wait until it is needed, it will be too late.

The process of collecting, documenting and cataloging work in an effective and efficient way is imperative to the success of the portfolio. All three of these processes are relatively time consuming but can be accomplished with a plan, a system and a commitment to the work from the beginning.

The good news is that no matter what type of portfolio is being designed, the preparation work is largely the same. So, get started!

Collect the Work

When collecting material for an architectural project, think of things in a very thorough manner. It is impossible to know now what exact documentation will be needed in the future. This documented material will be referenced time and time again, in 6 months, 2 years or 20 years. It will be the primary means to figure out exactly what a project was about and what was actually accomplished. This documentation should include basics such as copies of the original problem statement, sketches, study models, process material, class notes, a list of team members, etc. Actually, it should include everything that was developed for the project, not just the final representational objects.

It is a substantial task to collect all of this material for each and every project worked on but it is imperative that the documentation is complete. Develop the habit of doing the collecting, documenting and cataloging of the work on a daily or weekly basis. Once a system is developed, it will become easier to be efficient with these tasks so that it does not become a burden.

If work done daily isn't going to happen, divide the year into segments and collect project artifacts for a massive documentation session that happens several times a year. If this is going to be the plan, store project artifacts in a safe place so they don't get damaged while in the collection phase. Sketches on trace should be stored flat and not folded; it is virtually impossible to remove folds or wrinkles in digital scans of trace. Sketches in a sketchbook are relatively safe as long as they are stored properly and labeled. Drawings on vellum or mylar can be rolled and stored in a tube; again folds are very difficult to remove from digital scans. These drawings can also be stored flat. Both study and final models should be stored in sturdy boxes with lids. Boxing these models will prevent them from getting crushed or dirty. It is imperative that all of the project artifacts are well cared for. While it is admittedly a lot to collect and document, it is important to be thorough and include as much material as possible in the documentation for potential inclusion in the portfolio.

Document the Work

In general, the tasks of collecting and documenting work go procedurally together. It is essential that there is a robust yet simple method to organize both the physical artifacts and the digital copies of this material. Over time, the physical artifacts may be lost or thrown away; therefore the digital representation of this work and the organization of the digital files becomes radically important in the documentation process.

Some documented material — reference documentation — will only be used as a visual reference for the particulars of a project. Some documented material — presentation documentation — will be edited and prepared for direct inclusion in the portfolio. It is crucial to have both types of documentation for each project.

Collect and document at least the following material produced as physical artifacts for each project:

1. Photograph all model studies / prototypes / final iterations.

2. Scan all large format drawings.

3. Scan sketches and process or analytical materials.

4. Scan problem statements — for reference, not for inclusion in the portfolio.

5. Write complete descriptions of both the design process and design intent.

6. Obtain digital images from classmates or instructors of reviews, discussions, special events, or even just time spent in studio.

All design material that is already in digital format should be filed accordingly alongside the newly created digital files from the material listed above.

Reference Documentation

Reference documentation is documentation performed simply to remember the basics about a project. It is done so that information about a project, the specifics of its development and the construction of its relevant physical artifacts, are properly recorded. It is impossible

two types of project documentation

reference documentation

Reference documentation is documentation performed to remember the basics about a project and includes items such as: elevation and plan view images of all models, copies of the problem statements, copies of studio readings, your specific notes on the project, and notes on the order in which the design developed.

presentation documentation

Presentation documentation could be anything that is intended to show the best aspects of a project: model images from flattering angles—both process models and final models—descriptive diagrams, final orthographic drawings; typically anything and everything that might be considered for inclusion in the portfolio.

There are two completely different types of project documentation that should be done for each project.

---

to anticipate now what might be needed in 10 years; so the job of reference documentation is to be completely and entirely comprehensive. One situation that comes up more often than anticipated is having to rebuild a model in order to generate a new set of images that fulfill a specific set of needs. If reference documentation of the model exists—elevation images of all sides, plan view images, etc.—it is much easier to recreate the model.

Reference documentation also includes items such as copies of the problem statements, copies of studio readings, your specific notes on the project, and notes on the order in which the design developed.

Presentation Documentation

While there are many types of documentation that qualify as presentation documentation, in general it is defined as documentation performed in anticipation of inclusion in the portfolio. Examples of presentation documentation could be anything that is intended to show the best aspects of a project: model images from flattering angles—both process models and final models—descriptive diagrams, final orthographic drawings; typically anything and everything that might be considered for inclusion in the portfolio.

Best Practices for Project Documentation

This discussion is by no means a complete guide to documenting architectural projects but is intended to provide enough information to give the designer a solid direction on how to do this work. The better the original documentation, the better the portfolio, the better the chance of achieving whatever goals are being aimed for with the portfolio work. It is a reciprocal relationship. Proper documentation is vital to the success of the portfolio. It is important that this work is completed with a certain degree of tenacity and gusto. It is very likely that the documentation will need to be done and re-done and re-done again until the digital representations of the project artifacts are truly successful. Be prepared to be patient. It takes quite a bit of work to get this right.

Photography

As a basic rule of thumb, photograph any artifact that is three dimensions; scan anything that is two dimensions. There are exceptions to this rule, but we'll get to that later; just remember this basic distinction.

Photographing in the Photography Studio
There are going to be many different types of project models that will need to be documented. The best scenario for photographing these models is to have a photography studio to work in. However, it is possible to set this up outside of a photography studio. To do this, gather the following: a backdrop of non-reflective black or white paper or fabric, a table, proper lighting, tripod and camera. If the model being photographed is made with lighter colored materials, use a black backdrop. If the model being photographed is made with darker colored materials, use a white backdrop. Non-reflective backdrops will help keep the lighting focus on the actual model and will prevent a lighting hot spot from appearing on the backdrop of the image. Museum board or a felt-type fabric work fine.

For lighting, ideally a spotlight is needed to act as the sun and a fill light is needed to act as ambient light. For the spotlight, use any movable light source. The fill light is a little more difficult to set up. This light needs to be diffused light. In the photography studio this is accomplished with a translucent white filter placed over the light source. It is also possible to use white umbrellas placed over the lights—these soften the light and spread it so it does not travel in a direct line to the object. Alternatively, try reflecting the light off something white so it disperses and does not travel in a direct line to the model. When working with more than one light source, it is crucial not to get a dual shadow—shadows coming from more than one direction. Watch out for this when setting up the lighting.

The next most important thing to keep in mind regarding lighting is that the light must be white light. Avoid yellow light or blue light in the photography studio. Since incandescent bulbs are a thing of the past this may not be as much of a problem as it was, but modern bulbs are sold with different light qualities to mimic different lighting conditions. Anything but white light will add additional color tones to the model and will appear in the final image. This erroneous color will ultimately have to be edited out of the digital images. Trust me on this point: it takes a lot more time to edit the color digitally than it takes to get the correct white bulb prior to photographing the work.

The next item that is needed is a Digital SLR camera. Ask at school; there may be a good digital camera that can be checked out of the media center on campus. It is not necessary to be an expert with a digital camera to get a quality image. Believe it or not, auto settings without the flash will produce good results. A phone camera is not ideal for this situation. It could possibly be acceptable if it really is all that is available. However, do not resort to a camera phone if there is a Digital SLR camera available. The portfolio is only as good as the material that is put in it. That means both the quality of design, as well as the quality of the documentation.

Maintaining a steady camera will greatly increase the sharpness and quality of the images; use a tripod.

Photographing Outdoors
It is entirely possible and sometimes quite effective to photograph models outdoors. If the project location happens to be in a similar geographic location as your actual physical location, the sun can be used to document the lighting condition on the model at specific times of day through different seasons. In this case, use the sun as the primary light source. There is plenty of reflected ambient light as well so no worries there either. A good camera and tripod are still needed. One of the challenges of photographing outdoors is the background. It is important to figure out what will appear in the background of the model in the image. Often there is a problem with the scale of objects in the background, as they appear much larger relative to the scale of the

Photographing work at your desk can be an effective way to communicate your work methods. Project by Andrea Moore-Lewis.

architectural model. Set up the image so objects in the background appear in the same scale as the model. Of course, it is also possible to take advantage of the outdoor sunlight and still use a studio backdrop to prevent the scale issues of the natural background.

Photographing at Your Desk
There are some situations when photographing models at the work desk makes sense. Most of the time, this situation is to show comparison images of a model in developmental progress. Even though photographing outside a studio setting, this is not an excuse to take a poor quality image. Photographing at the desk means the photographer needs to be extra careful about what's in the periphery of the image. Make sure there is a similar background for each image such as the same cutting mat, drawing surface, etc. It is not necessary to clean the desk completely before each photograph, as that would defeat the purpose of shooting at the desk.

However, slide the visually distracting objects—Diet Coke can, hot-pink water bottle, and car keys—out of the frame before taking the image.

A Note on Photography Angles
When photographing models, images taken at a flat angle, such as an elevation, are usually going to be the least flattering because they have the tendency to visually flatten the three-dimensional object. Elevation images are often necessary to explain certain characteristics of a project but it is difficult to achieve a visually interesting image. If an elevation is absolutely necessary, pull the camera and tripod further back from the actual model and use the zoom feature on the camera to get a closer framing of the image. This process will reduce the key-stoning distortion of the image of the elevation and will help improve the quality of this relatively flat image.

Constructing the Persuasive Portfolio: the only primer you'll ever need

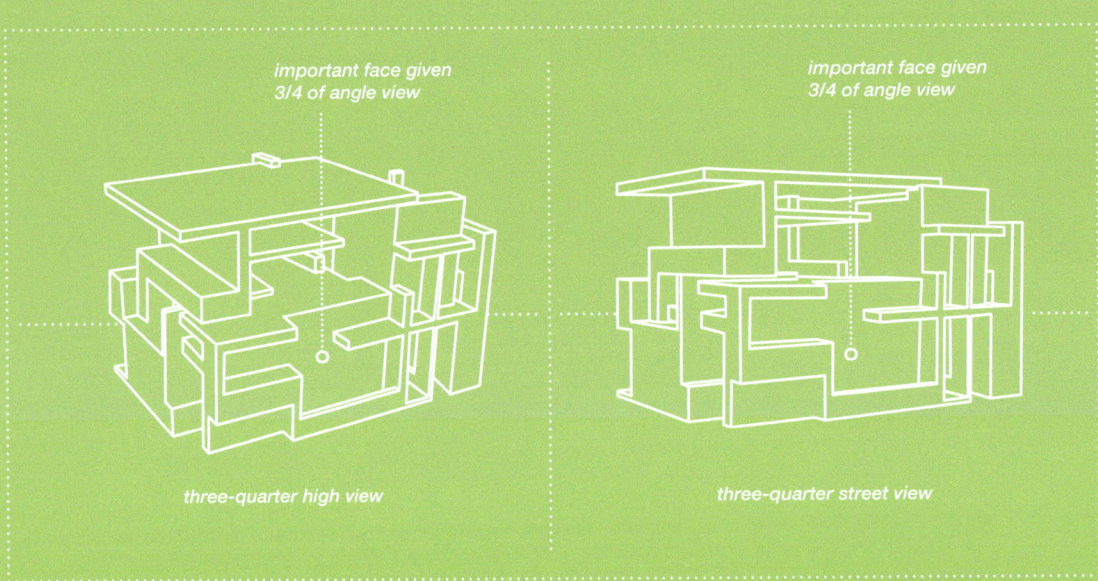

Architectural models often look their best when photographed at an angle. These examples of two different three-quarter views are usually successful for any model. Drawing from project by Madeline Gonzalez.

An image taken at an angle is often the easiest way to achieve a compelling view of the project. These images are referred to as three-quarter views because the model is rotated such that one side of the model is given greater emphasis than the other but both sides are visible. The two most successful three-quarter views are the three-quarter street view taken from the point of view of a pedestrian, and the three-quarter high view taken with the camera angle set higher than the roof so that it is visible in the image. With any three-quarter view, make sure to give the long edge view to the more important face of the model. Remember, there are not many opportunities for conveying the spatial qualities of a project; choose image angles purposefully.

Photographing Two-Dimensional Work
Scanning is the best way to digitally represent flat work. The only instance when a piece of flat work should be photographed is if it is too large to be accommodated on a scanner. The best way to do this is to pin the work up on a wall, light the entire piece with diffuse light and pull the camera and tripod away from the wall and use the zoom feature on the camera to get the framing correctly centered on the two-dimensional object. This process will reduce the key-stoning distortion of the object in the image and will help improve the quality of this relatively flat image.

Scanning

Digital scanning is the preferred method of translating two-dimensional physical work to digital representation. It is an incredibly easy task and does not require the same amount of skill as photography. There are a handful of tips to keep in mind when scanning that will make the digital images the best they can be.

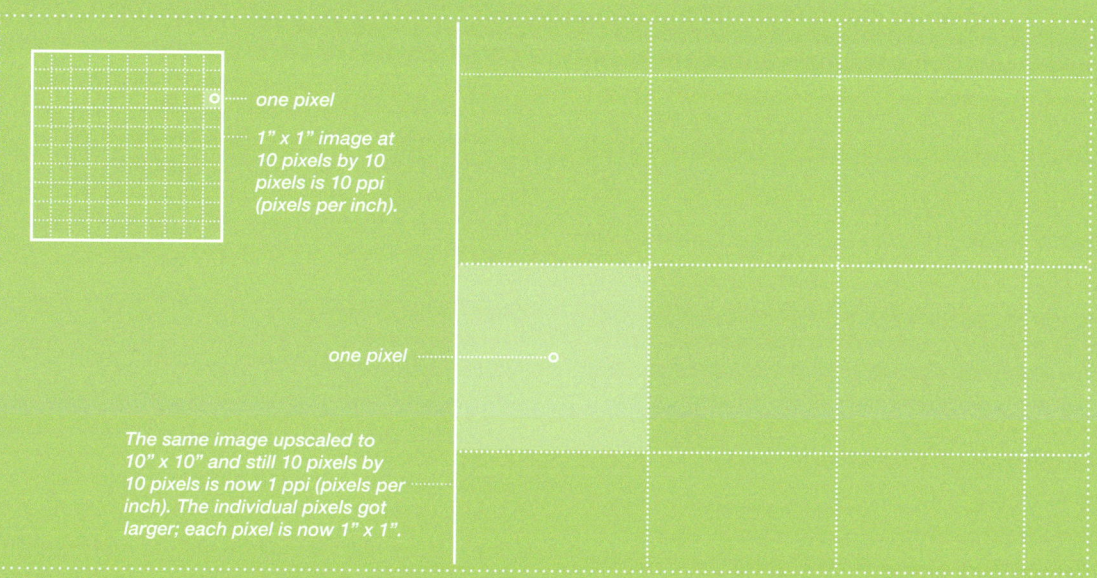

It is important to understand the relationship between resolution, scale and pixels per inch. When an image gets physically larger, its pixels also grow larger. You can't add pixels; the file has its maximum number of pixels when it is created.

Image Resolution

Digital images in raster programs—such as Adobe Photoshop—are made up of pixels. Each pixel is square-shaped and is assigned a specific color. There are a certain number of square pixels arrayed horizontally and vertically that make up a raster image.

Resolution is described as the relationship between pixels and the dimensions of the image and is measured in ppi—pixels per inch. Once a digital image is created, the relationship between pixels and the size of the image remains in a relative and proportional relationship for the life of the image. The physical size of the image can be adjusted or the number of pixels per inch can be adjusted but since these two numbers work proportionately together; if one is adjusted, the other is automatically adjusted.

So if an image is 100 ppi and measures 1" x 1", this image has 100 pixels across and 100 pixels down arrayed in a standard grid. If the image is printed at 1" x 1", it maintains its resolution of 100 ppi—that's 100 pixels per linear inch. If the image size is changed from 1" x 1" to 10" x 10" and printed at this new size, the resolution of this printed image is 10 ppi—the image still has only 100 pixels across and 100 pixels down but now it is arrayed over 10" in both directions, thus reducing the resolution when it is printed to 10 pixels per inch.

Print Resolution

Image resolution only becomes a significant issue when images are printed. As mentioned above, resolution is described as pixels per inch and is the relationship between pixels and the physical size of the image. Physical size of the image comes into play when the image is printed. This is important because at some point in time, the portfolio will be printed and all of the resolution issues for the images need to be resolved long before the print button is selected.

There are varying standards for acceptable print resolution. Acceptable print resolution means the image will not appear pixelated—individual pixels are visible—when printed. Publishing companies will request between 300 ppi and 500 ppi for images at the actual size they will be printed. 300 ppi at the actual size the image will be printed is perfectly acceptable; aim for this.

Scanning Best Practices
Below is a list of best practice scanning tips to help with the scanning task.

1. Maintain an unedited digital archive file of each scan. This archive file should be kept unaltered to be used in the future as needed. All of the scans need to be edited but do the editing in a "save as" file and maintain the original archive file for posterity. In the future, the file will be needed in this unedited state. Trust me on this.

2. It is best to scan all two-dimensional work in color. A digital file can be changed from color to black and white but a black and white scan cannot be changed to color. To preserve the most amount of digital information as possible, scan in color and maintain that file as the archive file.

3. Scan drawings with a higher resolution than it is anticipated needing. If the scanner will accommodate a higher resolution file, go ahead and scan higher than 300 ppi. But remember this will be a rather large file and digital storage room will be needed to keep the unaltered archive file. When it comes time to use the image, adjust the resolution in the edited file, not the archive file, such that it will be 300 ppi at the actual size it needs to be printed in the portfolio.

4. Drawings on translucent paper—trace, vellum, mylar, etc.—should be scanned with a piece of white opaque paper behind them to produce a relatively bright background for the scan. This trick will help improve the overall quality of the scan since it will be easier to adjust the background to white without losing a significant amount of line work in the digital file.

5. Opaque drawings with a special edge—the deckle edge of Arches Watercolor paper for instance—should be scanned with black paper behind them. Digitally crop outside the paper edge to preserve the legibility of the deckle edge in the digital scan.

6. Scans from a sketchbook should be scanned with the full edge of the book visible in the scan. There are occasions when it is best to show sketches within the object of the sketchbook in the portfolio. The sketchbook edge can always be cropped out later but it is impossible to put the edge of the book back in the digital image unless it is there from the beginning.

Small Format Scanning
It is relatively easy to find a small format flatbed scanner. Most libraries or college media centers have an abundance of these machines. They are typically 11" x 17"; occasionally a small format flatbed scanner can be found that measures 13" x 19". Use these scanners for any small two-dimensional items. Be careful that the glass of the scan bed is clean before putting any material on it. If the object being scanned is thick—such as a sketchbook—and the scanner lid won't close, place sheets of white paper on top of the object prior to scanning. This paper will add a white background to the scan and will make it easier to digitally edit.

Large Format Scanning
For drawings that are larger than a flatbed scanner, a large format scanner is needed. These scanners are typically a roller-type scanner which means the material being scanned needs to be flexible so that it can bend around the rollers as it moves through the scanner. There are a few things to be cautious of when using these scanners. First, there is a tendency for dirt to get caught in the rollers of the scanners as they are used. This dirt will transfer to a drawing if precautions aren't taken. Don't trust anyone that says a scanner has been recently cleaned. The best way to protect a drawing is to get a sheet of clear acetate that is larger than the drawing and put it on top of the drawing prior to scanning. There is no need to attach the acetate to a drawing, just place it on top and feed it through the scanner. In this manner, the drawing is completely protected from dirt during the scanning process.

The other potential pitfall to this type of scanner is that some scanners have rollers that have teeth to grab and move the paper. These teeth can imprint on paper and leave a serrated, indented line across the drawing. It's best to run a test sheet through the scanner prior to putting an original drawing into the machine so there are no surprises when the drawing is scanned.

Best Practices for Digital Image Editing

⑤ For each digital image to be included in the portfolio there will need to be some sort of digital editing performed. Since these files are raster images, the editing needs to happen in a raster program such as Adobe Photoshop. It is not necessary to be a master of Photoshop to be able to perform image-editing tasks. There is a set of basic operations that work best for editing digital images in Photoshop and they are all relatively easy to learn.

The most common task in editing digital files is correcting the background of model images. All model images must have their backgrounds cleaned of any dirt, dust or non-intentional background elements. If the models were photographed in a photography studio, there is a good chance that there are some lighting hot spots—brighter areas due to direction of lighting—reflecting off the backdrop. If this is the case, the editing goal is to reduce the background to a flat condition with consistent tone of its colored state. So if the background drape is black, the goal is to digitally adjust the background to appear as flat black. If the background drape is white, the goal is to digitally adjust the background to appear as flat white.

There are many other tasks that need to be performed when editing digital files. Below is a list of Photoshop tools and functions and examples of when it is appropriate to use them in the digital editing process. It should be noted that there are many, many ways to perform the same editing task in Photoshop and with each software release, more and more options become available. Don't worry about knowing all of the ways to do something, just figure out what works best and stick with it. The only things to be wary of are shortcuts that reduce the quality of the digital editing. If the editing method is faster but doesn't look as professional, then it is not worth the time savings. Quality work takes time and effort.

1. Marquee Tool: The marquee set of tools is used to select a specific set of pixels. Each tool selects pixels framed in a specific shape unique to each tool; the rectangle marquee tool is often the most practical. Use this tool to select areas of the background to edit erroneous items from the image.

2. Polygonal Lasso Tool: The polygonal lasso tool is another tool used to select a specific set of pixels. The polygonal lasso tool allows a much more specific selection of pixels by letting the designer essentially draw the shape of the area that should be edited. The polygonal lasso tool draws with straight lines. This tool requires shape closure. After the desired area has been selected, mouse over the first point made and a small circle will appear at the selection site. This circle is an indication that the shape can be closed. Left click with your mouse and the shape will be closed and all pixels within will be selected.

3. Crop Tool: The crop tool is used to crop out portions of the image that should not be included in the digital file. The crop tool is especially handy when it comes to editing scanned drawings. Usually there are extra non-drawing areas in a scanned image that need to be removed. Use the marquee tool to select the area that should be retained. Then navigate to the top tool bar and select image / crop and the non-selected areas will be deleted from the file.

4. Brush Tool: The brush tool is used to change the color of pixels. Typically this tool is used after a set of pixels has been selected with the marquee tool or the polygonal lasso tool. Once pixels are selected, choose a color and use the brush tool to "paint" all of the selected pixels with the chosen color. The size of the brush can be adjusted; this affects the number of pixels painted at once. The opacity of the paint can be adjusted; this affects how translucent or opaque the color is applied. And the flow can be adjusted; this affects how fast the color comes out of the brush much like aerosol spray paint.

5. Clone Stamp: The clone stamp effectively picks up a selected area of the image and duplicates exactly that selected area in another location. This tool is typically used to replace a flaw in an area that has similar properties to another area on the image.

6. Eraser Tool: The eraser tool is used to erase pigment on pixels. With this tool pixels are erased to transparency revealing the designated background color.

7. Foreground and Background Color Function: All images have a designated foreground and background color. When painting, drawing, etc. the selected foreground color is used. The background color is revealed when the foreground is erased.

8. Image Rotation: The image rotation tool rotates an entire image based on set parameters: 180 degrees, 90 degrees clockwise, 90 degrees counter clockwise. Or this tool rotates the image based on a specific degree setting and is called "arbitrary" in the tool function. This tool is incredibly helpful when trying to rotate a scanned image into an orthogonal position. It is located at the top tool bar, select image / image rotation.

9. Image Size: Image size is the tool used to make resolution adjustments. With this tool the image size (width and height) and resolution (pixels per inch) can be adjusted. It is located at the top tool bar, select image / image size.

10. Canvas Size: With this tool the canvas size (width and height) can be changed without scaling the image. The canvas size tool adds physical area to the image. It also has a positioning function that determines where the original portion of the canvas remains. This tool is particularly helpful when extending the black background of a model image to fit the proportion of an image requirement in the portfolio. It is located at the top tool bar, select image / canvas size.

11. RGB, CMYK and Grayscale Color Models: The different color models are used for different purposes. RGB—red, green, blue—is a screen color model only. CMYK—cyan, magenta, yellow, black—is a print color model only. Grayscale is used when all color information can be discarded from an image. Grayscale color model produces a much smaller file size than either RGB or CMYK color models.

12. Brightness and Contrast: The brightness and contrast tool is an effective way to make simple adjustments that alter both the intensity of lightness and the contrast between tonal values in a digital image. Use it sparingly. It becomes very obvious if these settings are pushed too far. This tool is located at the top tool bar, select image / adjustments / brightness contrast.

13. Levels: The levels tool adjusts the values for whites, blacks and midtones in a digital image. Adjust the white and black points first, then use the midtone adjuster. The levels tool is a great way to make tonal adjustments on line drawings and can be a big help reducing a background to white while still maintaining crisp, dark lines. This tool is located at the top tool bar, select image / adjustments / levels.

14. Color Balance: The color balance tool is used to adjust the balance of colors in the shadows, midtones or highlights of a digital image. Use this tool when there is an obvious color imbalance—too much of one color—in the digital image. This often happens in scanned images where there is a magenta cast over the entire image. The overcast of magenta can be corrected by increasing the color cast of green. The process is similar to adding a color filter over the entire image. This tool is located at the top tool bar, select image / adjustments / color balance.

15. JPEG, TIFF or PSD File Formats: There are several file format options available when working in Adobe Photoshop. It is a good idea to understand the difference between some of the more common file formats.

A TIFF (Tagged Image File Format) is a file format that is non-compressed and retains the majority of its raster file information. It is often an industry standard for graphic artists. The primary drawback with using a TIFF is that since it does not discard digital information through compression, it can be a rather large file.

A JPEG (Joint Photographic Experts Group) is a raster file format that indicates there has been some compression—loss of digital information—associated

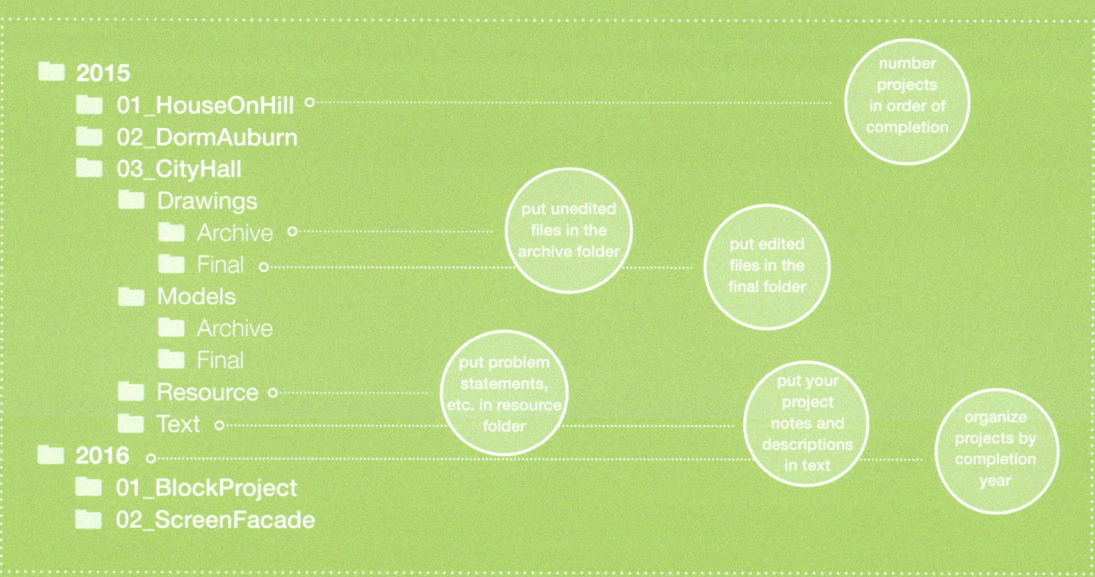

One of the most valuable things you can do is to properly establish and maintain a digital filing system for your portfolio documentation.

with the file. JPEGs are one of the most common file formats used because the degree of compression can be adjusted. This ability to adjust the compression rate allows the user some control over the trade-off between image quality and file size.

A PSD (Photoshop Data File) is the native file extension for Adobe Photoshop documents. However, this file format should only be used if extensive edits have been done resulting in multiple layers. It can be used to store archive images maintaining all file layers without flattening them into one layer. This enables the user to revisit, re-edit or change the image layer by layer. This file format type has a large file size since it maintains all of the separate editable layers.

Catalog the Work

The task of digitally cataloging work is almost as important as actually documenting it. If there isn't a logical digital storage system in place, it becomes difficult to find any of the images needed for the portfolio. Developing this system at the beginning is the best practice. Whatever system is used should be flexible enough to accommodate different types of work and work situations as the designer moves forward in their design education and career.

Digital File Organization

Only the designer can determine what is the best system for digitally storing their work. Years of experience have revealed several obvious strategies that work well for the ease of finding material.

Constructing the Persuasive Portfolio: the only primer you'll ever need

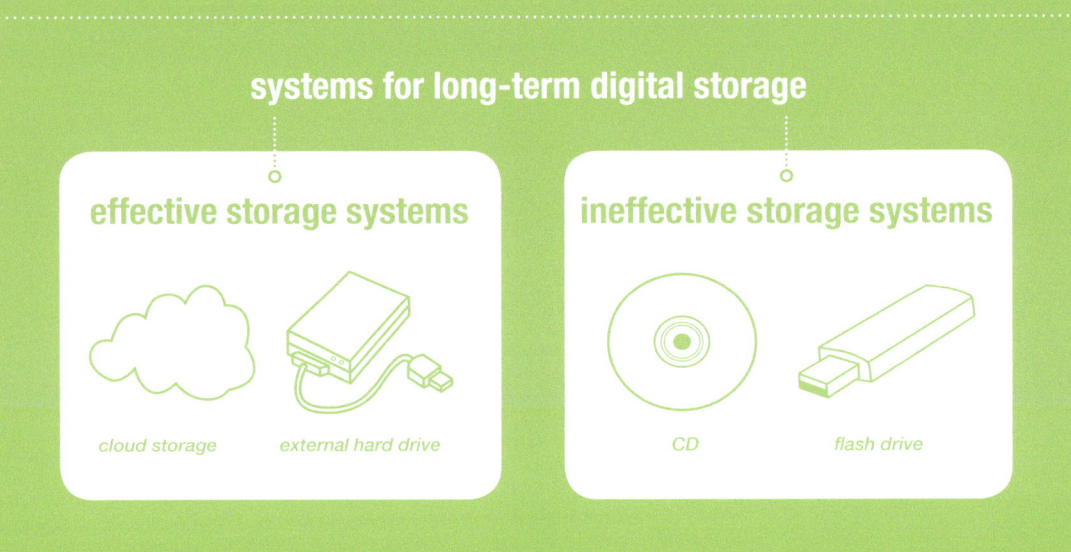

For long-term digital storage needs, choose cloud storage or an external hard drive. Do not use a CD or a flash drive.

(6) Separating files into folders by the year the work was completed is the easiest way to keep things organized. In 20 years, you may not remember the title of a project but you will still have a pretty good idea of when the work was completed.

Adding projects in the order they were completed is the next step in the file organization and should be the next level in the file structure. Use "01, 02, 03, etc." instead of "1, 2, 3, etc." so that the projects will stay in order if there are more than 10 projects completed within a year. Also include a short title for the project so it is easily identified.

At this point in the file structure, some sort of separation of file type is needed so that a more specific file search can be performed. "Models," "Drawings," "Resource" and "Text" should suffice as a basic set. Images of models go in the "Models" folder. Scans of drawings go in the "Drawings" folder. Any information such as problem statements, timeline notes, etc. should go in the "Resource" folder. Reflective writing on your design process or major ideas behind a project should be stored in the "Text" folder.

It is also important to establish a system that allows for the retention of both unedited digital files and edited digital files. Folders called "Archive" and "Final" work fine. The original unedited digital images should be stored in the "Archive" folder. The edited digital images should be stored in the "Final" folder. Do not overwrite the original digital images; keep two copies, both the unedited version and the edited version. In 20 years you will have different needs for the images and, frankly, better digital editing skills. The original files will definitely be needed.

File Nomenclature

File nomenclature is the practice of naming digital files. There are effective ways and not so effective ways of doing this. This is likely the one area where the designer is going to completely, totally drop the ball. In an ideal world, file names would look something like this: lastname_projectabbreviation_imagetype.jpg. So fletcher_houseonhill_finmodel01.jpg indicates that the author is Fletcher, the project is House on Hill, the image is of the final model and it is the first image of the final model. It is more likely that file names will look something like this: modelfinal_FINfin_done.jpg.

Even though it would be best to use an appropriate file nomenclature system, because of the fast-paced nature of design work, it will prove elusive. If it is possible to only do one thing, get the file structure correct.

One last thing: do not use dashes or spaces in the digital file names. Use the underscore if separate characters are needed in the file names. This rule applies to the file structure as well as the file name. This practice is a holdover from days of Unix systems where a "space" in the file name could not be read. Today the practice is still in use for ease of moving files between different computer platforms; the underscore avoids using what may be an illegal character within different operating systems.

Systems for Long-Term Digital Storage

One of the most frustrating aspects about maintaining a digital archive of work is that technology changes so quickly that inevitably the designer will be saddled with the task of upgrading digital image storage at some point. Count on it; it will happen. However, there are some solutions that are better than others.

The absolute worst system to use to store or back up digital material is on either a flash drive or a CD. Flash drives should only be used for their original purpose: to temporarily store or transfer files. The life of a flash drive is approximately two years or less. A CD is not much more stable than a flash drive and has a storage life of about five years. Neither one of these systems provides the longevity needed for long-term storage.

However, there are two relatively effective options available right now. One is to use cloud storage and place files online as a more permanent backup solution. The other effective solution is to place digital files on an external hard drive. A hard drive will degrade over time instead of just failing—as a flash drive will do—so that some data is always recoverable.

Just remember, any media can deteriorate and nothing is completely fail proof. Always keep multiple copies of backups and perform annual checks to make sure the backups are still working.

Designing Por

...folio Systems

22 Planning the Work
   The Design Narratives
   Flexibility of the Portfolio System: Print Portfolio and Digital Portfolio
   Designing the Content and Designing the Container
   Determining the Size and Orientation of the Portfolio
   Components of a Portfolio
   Storyboarding

34 Strategies for Portfolio Organization
   Organizing the Content Narrative
   Organizing the Visual Narrative: Using Visual Components of Graphic Layout as Organizational Structure

64 Systems of Visual Structure
   Grid and Alignment Systems
   Designing the Active Area
   When to Break the Rules
   Visual Relationships between Objects on a Page
   Visual Pace

Designing Po...

Design Actions

(7) *Learn and understand the difference between content narrative, visual narrative and project narrative. Make purposeful decisions for each.* page 24

(8) *Develop a flexible portfolio system.* page 26

(9) *Design the content and design the container.* page 27

(10) *Determine size and orientation of the portfolio.* page 28

(11) *Identify portfolio components that need to be included.* page 29

(12) *Develop an organizing storyboard.* page 32

Portfolio Systems
Planning the Work

One of the easiest ways to coordinate the different necessary systems within the portfolio is to categorize these systems into narratives, understand them separately and then capitalize on their overlaps.

This section concentrates on three specific types of narrative systems that need to be strengthened and made apparent throughout the design of the portfolio. The three types of narratives are: visual narrative, content narrative and project narrative. All three of these systems should be considered as organization systems for the portfolio. Visual narrative and content narrative consider broad issues that bridge across the design of the entire portfolio. Project narrative specifically refers to the narrative within individual projects. However, there must be a conscious attitude toward the idea of project narrative across all projects in the portfolio. In other words, for project narrative focus at the individual project level as well as at a larger context across all projects in the portfolio.

The Design Narratives

It's important to work on all three narratives—visual, content, project—simultaneously as the design progresses. It might seem like the portfolio process is linear, but it is really a back and forth design effort between the interrelationships of these three narratives.

To better understand the three types of narratives, let's look at the basic definition of a narrative. A narrative—in this context—is a purposeful and designed relationship between elements that are constructed to be understood together.

Visual Narrative: Goals and Purpose

Keeping the definition of narrative in mind and incorporating the definition of visual—all things seen— think of the visual narrative as the deliberate, designed visual relationships between elements in the portfolio composed to be understood together and considered across the entire portfolio. The visual narrative is visual storytelling, so there must be a story to tell. Ideas describing the detailed components of a visual narrative are written in subsequent sections of this book. For now, let the following topics give some indication about what types of elements fall under the purview of the visual narrative: visual organization cues, headers and footers, parallel use of project introduction pages, grid and alignment systems, consistent graphic indicators, consistent visual order, consistent visual hierarchy, consistent typeface usage, etc.

Content Narrative: Goals and Purpose

The content narrative for a portfolio is the thoughtful, purposeful inclusion of projects, project types and project themes that best convey the designer's position relative to both meaning and skill and is to be considered across the entire portfolio. Resolving the content narrative early in the design process will readily help determine the content focus of the portfolio and will automatically help determine which projects should be included, emphasized, or left out altogether. All content should support the content narrative. Think of the content narrative as a purposeful and meaningful organization or categorization of all of the projects included in the portfolio.

Project Narrative: Goals and Purpose

First and foremost, the project narrative in the portfolio relates to each individual project. It is the specific visual and written material required to convey the thinking behind the work.

Projects assigned for coursework are assigned with a specific pedagogical agenda. When constructing the project narrative for use in the portfolio, it does not need to be the same as what was assigned in class. In fact, your specific project narrative should be authentic to what you found interesting through the experience of your own design work.

Make sure the focus is on the conveyance of this thinking behind the work; don't leave anything unsaid and believe it will be obvious to the reviewer. To do this, make a list of all the ideas to be conveyed for each project and make sure each of these ideas can be represented with a visual artifact. Once there are visual artifacts to represent all of the ideas in the project narrative, use text elements to support the ideas conveyed through the visual artifacts.

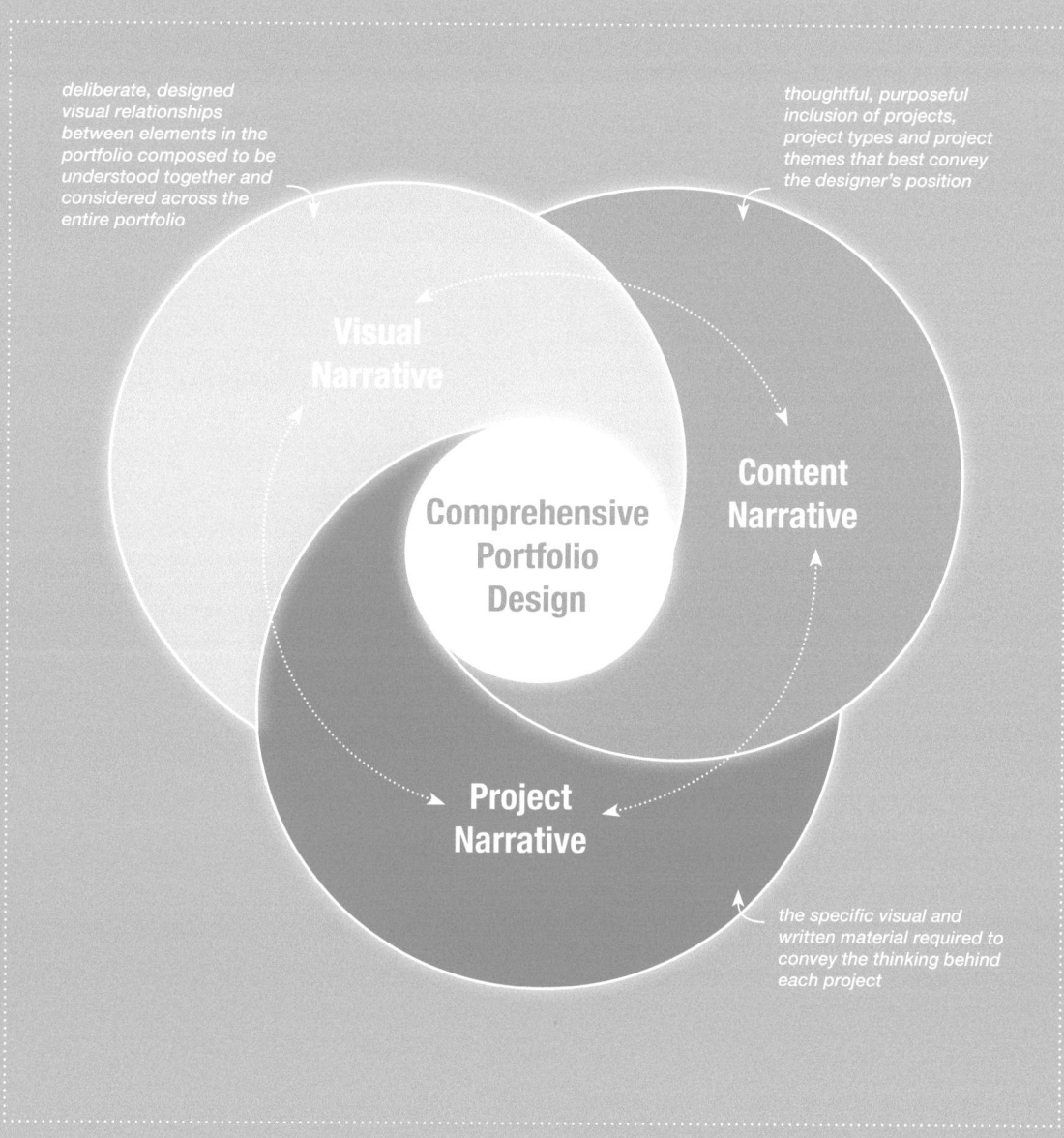

If you learn nothing else; learn this. There are three design narratives that must be considered as systems that work independently and as systems that work in conjunction with one another.

Flexibility of the Portfolio System: Print Portfolio and Digital Portfolio

(8) There are quite a few decisions to make before beginning the actual work of designing a portfolio. The urge will be to dive right into layout design. But, be warned, there are a handful of major decisions to be made in the beginning; this section outlines those issues. A little up front planning and actually understanding what should be accomplished will go a long way toward design process efficiency, effectiveness and ultimate success.

It's no secret that all application submissions are different processes and require different portfolio submissions—some require the submission of cut sheets sent through the mail, some require full printed and bound portfolios, some want a PDF uploaded or emailed, and some want a link to a website. The job of the portfolio designer is to design one portfolio that works in all scenarios and it's actually relatively easy to accomplish. The most complicated output should be the one primarily designed, which in the case of a portfolio is the print version. With a well-designed print portfolio, spreads can be output and printed as individual cut sheets; the portfolio could also be printed for hard copy submission, or could be exported to any variety of PDF resolutions for digital submission and uploaded to a website such as ISSUU for a web portfolio.

It's important to develop a flexible system in whatever portfolio format is selected. There will be many situations where it is required to add or remove projects to accommodate different audience needs. There will also be scenarios where the format of the portfolio needs to be incredibly flexible—digital or print and even certain numbers of pages or page size and orientation. Most organizations have submission requirements that are unique to that particular organization; these guidelines must be followed to the letter!

The following are flexibility instances common to design portfolios; be prepared to do any of the following things as the circumstance of a portfolio can change at a moment's notice.

1. The portfolio needs to be organized such that projects can be added and removed easily. For instance, if the design structure is fully understood it can easily be applied to new projects as they are added to the portfolio. Also, the portfolio should be set up properly in Adobe InDesign to take full advantage of the flexibilities built into that software. For instance, automatic page numbers and header and footer material need to be correctly set up in the Master Pages of the InDesign document.

2. The portfolio design needs to support a range of output formats. We've already discussed that it will be likely that at different times it will be required to output the portfolio in different ways. Be prepared for this and understand how the portfolio systems work to accommodate these requests; it will make life easier in the long run.

A Note on Software

Portfolios should be designed in book layout software such as Adobe InDesign or similar. Use programs such as Adobe Photoshop for editing image raster files (pixel-based), Adobe Illustrator for vector (line and tone) drawings and Microsoft Word for text information.

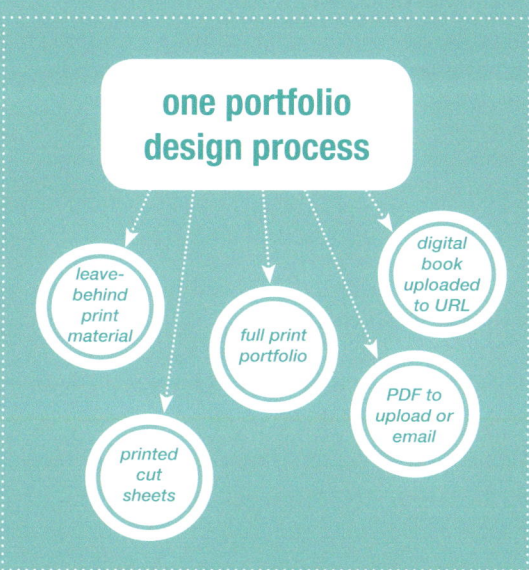

Put your effort into designing one portfolio system that will support a variety of outputs both print and digital.

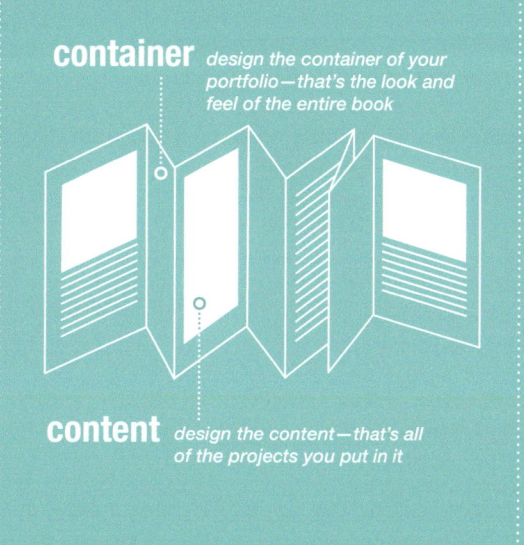

Understand that there are several design tasks going on in portfolio design operating at different scales.

Designing the Content and Designing the Container

When thinking of all the material that needs to be included in the portfolio, it is a daunting task to understand everything that should be accomplished. One way to tackle such a large project is to understand all of the different components required to design the portfolio and how those components ultimately fit together. Recognize that each of these different components requires a slightly different design attitude.

There is a range of design tasks when beginning the design of the portfolio and there are clear distinctions between these tasks. The largest of these is the distinction between designing the contents of the portfolio and designing the system of the portfolio itself, known as the "container."

Both of these tasks require an attitude toward design that will ultimately affect the look and feel of the portfolio. It can actually be a little confusing to try to separate these very distinctive design tasks at the beginning. But these ideas will become clearer as the work progresses through the design of the portfolio.

Just remember these two different design tasks: design the content—this is the content narrative and the project narrative, representational work associated with architectural projects—and design the container for the content—the visual narrative that is the entire system of the portfolio.

Determining the Size and Orientation of the Portfolio

Size and Proportion of the Portfolio

The best general rule to follow regarding size is to make the portfolio physically able to be filed. It may sound like a mundane way to make this decision but if submitting a print portfolio to a business, they need to be able to file it. It could be a commercial office or an academic institution, but in either case, the portfolio submissions will end up in a file cabinet and therefore need to be sized to fit in that file. Some students say, "Ah ha! I have a great idea: I'll make my portfolio oversized so it can't be filed and then it will have to sit on a desk which means it will get looked at over and over again." This will not happen. Oversized portfolios that can't be properly stored are a nuisance in an office—particularly one that needs its layout space such as a design office—and will be discarded. That means your brilliant idea just landed you in the trash bin. So, size it so that it can be filed. In the US that means letter-sized, in Europe it means A4.

Here's the next problem: most graphic designers know that Letter or A4 is actually not the greatest proportion to work with for page design. This fact leads the designer to the issue of determining a trim size—dimensions to trim the book to—for the portfolio. If considering an online printing service, such as Blurb, start by looking up what sizes they print and use their InDesign templates from the beginning. It is much more difficult to start with a letter-sized portfolio and convert it to a different size—just think about all the margin settings and white space relationships—than to start with the final size from the beginning. If the portfolio is designed to a size using a specific template provided by an online printing service and it is decided not to use them, it's not a problem—just go ahead and print the portfolio at a local print shop and have it trimmed down to whatever size is needed.

If the goal is to design a portfolio that operates as both a print portfolio and a digital portfolio, it is still a good idea to design to the print size needed. For digital portfolio output, the screen is much more accommodating to variations in dimension.

Orientation of the Portfolio: Horizontal Format or Vertical Format

There are also decisions to be made in the beginning about the orientation of the portfolio. Is it going to be vertically oriented—portrait—or horizontally oriented—landscape? As always, there are pros and cons to each layout scenario and there are no easy answers. However, there are some issues that can help guide the designer through this decision.

1. Review all of the material available for inclusion in the portfolio and determine if it is predominantly vertical or predominantly horizontal.

2. Review your specific typical layout style. Are the layouts usually organized around a series of images in a horizontal arrangement or a vertical arrangement?

Frankly, either horizontal or vertical format is fine. There are advantages and disadvantages associated with each format orientation.

Predominantly Horizontal Images

With a horizontally formatted portfolio, horizontal images can be displayed much larger on the page than if a horizontal image was placed on a single vertical page. A horizontal image, however, can span full bleed across two vertical pages to accommodate the enlargement of a horizontal image in a vertically formatted portfolio. So that solves the horizontal image in a vertical portfolio issue. However, in a horizontally formatted portfolio, using a horizontal image across a double spread means that the image needs to be very long and narrow to get any advantage to image size across a double page spread. In a horizontally formatted portfolio, there can also be two horizontal images side by side, one on each side of the spread. Both images can remain quite large. In a vertically formatted portfolio, while it is possible to have two horizontal images side by side on each spread, they can't be any wider that the width of the vertical page.

So for horizontal images, both a vertically formatted portfolio and a horizontally formatted portfolio can accommodate these images albeit in different ways.

Predominantly Vertical Images
Vertical images in a vertically oriented portfolio obviously work fine. A single vertical image is easily accommodated on each side of the spread. However, placing a vertical image in a horizontal portfolio limits the height of the image to the height of the page. There is no way to accommodate a large vertical image in a horizontal portfolio.

All the information described above is to say this: either a horizontally or vertically formatted portfolio will work. The vertical format offers more options if there is a mixture of both vertical and horizontal images. The horizontal format works best if the majority of the material is horizontal as this format does not have great options for using vertical images in a large format.

One last thing: what if the designer has both vertical and horizontal images and says, "I'm just going to put them in the portfolio however they fit best and have the portfolio reviewer rotate the book back and forth!" That's a really, really bad idea. In fact, it's a disaster! It tells the reviewer that either the designer can't really figure out how to put a layout together—a skill that is practically required in all academic and professional settings—or the designer is just lazy. Either way—unskilled or lazy—the designer doesn't come out looking great.

Components of a Portfolio

There are many different parts to a portfolio. Each part has to be handled slightly differently and these parts have sets of components that need to work in conjunction with one another. In this section there is a discreet list and description of all the major components of a portfolio and the nature of things to be thought about when designing them or determining whether or not they should be included.

Typical components of a normative book are: cover, front matter, content pages and back matter. By their very nature, portfolios are different altogether from typical books. However, there are cues to be taken from book organization and applied directly to the design of a portfolio. In fact, these design cues borrowed directly from traditional publication design can inform the design of the portfolio to become more graphically legible by paying attention to standard publication conventions.

The following sections are basic components of a book to be considered through the lens of portfolio design. See pages 56–57 for a diagram of these components.

Cover

The cover of the portfolio sets the tone for the entire experience of reviewing a portfolio. There are two completely different schools of thought on what to do with the cover design: one is to produce a completely understated cover perhaps with just the designer's name and contact information, the other is to provide an example of the caliber of work that will be included within the portfolio itself. Both strategies have merit and the decision should be made relative to the designer's overall design attitude about his / her work and the intended portfolio audience.

Front Matter

The front matter section of the portfolio could include the following sections and should be presented in this order:

Half Title Page

Title Page

Introduction or Foreword

Table of Contents

This introductory sequence of pages establishes the pace and tone for the portfolio and should not be ignored. The introductory sequence shifts the viewer from whatever tasks they were completing prior to reviewing the portfolio into a focused mode, ready to review the work. It sets expectations and can alter the attitude toward the work.

Half Title Page and Title Page
The half title page and title page are much less complex than the introduction / foreword or the table of contents and provide visual breathing room before moving into more specific content found in the portfolio.

The half title page for publications is usually just the title. In the case of a portfolio, it could be the author's name. The title page should include the full title of the portfolio, author's name, specific audience (if appropriate), and year of the portfolio.

Introduction or Foreword
The introduction or foreword is written in paragraph format and usually describes the purpose of the portfolio. This section could also include any additional information the author wants the reviewer to know. For portfolios, the introduction or foreword could include information such as: where the designer studied, what year level the designer has completed, any special programs the designer has participated in, etc. Consider the introduction as a place to set the story and provide any necessary background details.

Table of Contents
The table of contents page plays a vital role in the organization and therefore usability of the portfolio. For purely practical reasons, the table of contents tells the reviewer what is included in the portfolio and where it is located in the portfolio. This is the most straightforward way to use a table of contents and if that's all that it does, it is still an incredibly valuable tool. However, there are many other ways to make the table of contents page valuable both visually and informatively. The table of contents can be used as an introductory space to begin to categorize the work around certain areas of study. For instance, instead of just listing names of projects in chronological order, they can be cataloged around major themes in the design work. A strategy such as this delivers additional information to the reviewer; any time this can be accomplished is a positive decision and should be done.

As an organizational system, the table of contents is a one-page location that contains the most information about the contents of your portfolio. A strong table of contents contains the following information:

Project list including geographic locations
    Shows a range of project types
    Shows a range of project scales
    Shows a range of geographic conditions: urban, rural, coastal, mountainous, etc.

Number of projects included

How many pages are allotted for each project

How the projects are organized
    Chronological
    Reverse chronological
    By project type
    By design theme
    By development: academic work, professional work or personal work
    Or some combination of the above

Content Pages

Content pages are very easy to describe. These are the pages that directly contain the design projects. There are several types of content pages to be aware of and to design.

Section Divider Pages
Section divider pages include visual material that indicates the start of a new section within a portfolio. These pages could be very simple color blocks with basic text or could be a collection of project images from projects found within that section.

Project Introduction Pages
Project introduction pages include project content material and signal the start of a new project section. Typically these project introduction pages operate in a parallel fashion throughout the entire portfolio—the same typefaces, information and design for all pages dedicated to project introduction.

Basic Content Pages
Basic content pages include project content material and make up the bulk of the portfolio.

Back Matter

The back matter is a section of a book that typically includes several types of sections such as afterword, endnotes, bibliography, glossary, appendices, etc. This type of material is seen as supplemental to the contents of the publication.

The back matter of a portfolio can include the following sections and they should be included in this order:

Project Chronology

Resume or Curriculum Vitae

Colophon

Project Chronology
The project chronology section of a portfolio simply lists all of the projects that have been completed, or participated in, to date. Not all of these projects need to be included in the portfolio. The project chronology list describes the depth of experience by the designer and should include at least the project title, project location, project development type—academic, professional, personal—and year completed. This list will put all of the design work into context with one another.

Resume or Curriculum Vitae
There is a difference between a resume and curriculum vitae (CV) that is very easy to understand. Basically a resume is concise—typically one or two pages—and is geared toward professional accomplishments and applications. A CV is a relatively detailed outline of all of life's accomplishments to date. It is often geared toward academic accomplishments and applications.

A resume will typically include:

Name and Contact Information

Education and Qualifications

Work Experience

Honors and Awards

Academic or Professional Memberships

Skills

References

A CV will typically include:

Name and Contact Information

Education and Qualifications

Research Areas of Interest

Grants

Honors and Awards

Publications and Presentations

Employment and Experience History

Scholarly or Professional Memberships

Colophon
The colophon section of the portfolio is a brief paragraph outlining the design choices that have been made in the design and production of the portfolio. It typically includes typefaces used, paper selection and printing method. Colophon is derived from Latin and translates to "finishing touch." Describing the design choices made to complete the portfolio is the final location to indicate the care with which the portfolio has been created.

Storyboarding

The practice of visual storyboarding is extremely helpful in developing an overall design strategy and provides a very easy way to keep track of the project goals and how many of them have actually been accomplished.

A hard copy, sketched storyboard works as a constant visual reminder of where the designer is within the overall project. Many designers find it absolutely necessary to have a physical, visual reminder on hand at all times. In some ways, it acts a bit like a sketchbook does for design ideas—it is easily portable and can be used at any time in case an idea strikes.

Modern page layout software, such as Adobe InDesign, provides a facsimile of a visual storyboard in its "Pages" view. This view, much like a sketched visual storyboard, shows a smaller scale view of all the pages at once and makes it easy to see if legible visual patterns are being established where they are intended.

The visual storyboard can also provide a clear overview of all of the page designs so that the visual pace of the portfolio can be designed and developed. It is important to manage the overuse of certain design arrangements from spread to spread. Portfolios that have the same design layout on multiple pages begin to feel redundant to the reviewer and can cause the eye to read the pattern of the images instead of seeing the actual content of the images. Visual variety as one moves through the portfolio is necessary to keep the reviewer engaged in the visual content.

The storyboard is the first place to experiment with the order of projects included in the portfolio as well as how many pages are allocated and necessary for each project. Taking a broad overview while making these decisions infuses the actual page-to-page design with a sense of direction. A good storyboard will change as often as needed while designing the portfolio with the actual content material that is available. It is possible to end up with 10 or more sketched storyboards before the portfolio is actually completed. It can be an incredibly useful tool to keep organized, creative and on track.

Try this:

1. Copy the storyboard template (mock up a horizontal storyboard template if needed).

2. Block out spreads for all of your projects to determine how many pages are allocated for each project.

3. Sketch ideas for content on each page.

4. Experiment with different visual densities of layouts to adjust the visual pace.

5. Experiment with different numbers of pages for each project considered for inclusion to reflect their importance within the content narrative.

Designing Portfolio Systems—Planning the Work

Vertical storyboard template.

Designing Por

Design Actions

 Organize the Content Narrative: Decide if projects will be organized in an order or by category or some combination.   page 36

 Portfolio Components: Decide which portfolio components will be used as an organizing strategy. Portfolio components to consider: page 42

    table of contents
    section divider spreads
    headers and footers
    page numbers
    graphic icon systems

 Project Components: Decide which project components will be used as an organizing strategy. Project components to consider: page 58

    parallel project introduction material
    consistent graphic indicators

Portfolio Systems
Strategies for Portfolio Organization

Thinking though several large-scale organizational strategies at the beginning of the portfolio design project will help in making decisions about the focus of the design work on a project-scale basis. In other words, making some big decisions up front will allow informed, detailed decisions to be made regarding issues of individual project representation.

There are two important types of large-scale portfolio organization systems to understand and make decisions about at the onset of a portfolio design project. These systems are content organization systems and visual organization systems. Content organization systems—the content narrative—are those that literally relate to how the included projects are ordered or cataloged. Visual organization systems—the visual narrative—are the repetitive visual systems of order employed to give organizational clues to the audience. Making decisions about both content organization systems and visual organization systems is required to design a successful portfolio.

The organization of material in the portfolio ultimately determines how all of the work is understood as a collective body of work. It is important to recognize that the understanding of the design work is completely dependent upon how it is presented. There are numerous opportunities to convey meaning beyond just the display of project work. How the material is organized in the portfolio is one of the largest factors in this conveyance of information.

design a system of organization for your projects

through a purposeful project order

For this organization system, arrange projects through a purposeful project order. Projects could be organized in chronological order, reverse chronological order, or by placement of strongest work.

through categorization of project type

For this organization system, arrange projects through a purposeful cataloging system. Projects could be organized and cataloged by project type, project theme, or by academic or professional work.

One of the most pertinent decisions regarding the organization of your portfolio is the order in which projects are included.

Organizing the Content Narrative

There are actually many ways to organize the project material in a portfolio. Below is a list of ideas to help identify how the order of work might best be presented.

(13) Think about this organization in two ways: an order to things—literally a linear progression of some sort—or a categorization of projects—organized by type. It is probable that more than one of these ordering systems needs to be incorporated. If that is the case, make sure to prioritize decisions based on a primary ordering system and a secondary ordering system. For example, it could be decided to catalog projects by project type, and then, within each project type, the projects are ordered in a chronological fashion.

Order of Inclusion of Projects

Chronological
With this ordering system the first things accomplished are included first and the last things accomplished are included last.

Pros: This method of organization has the potential to show a clear trajectory through the designer's education and can show how much progress has been made in improving design skills.

Cons: This method can backfire if the very first project ever completed happens to be the weakest project in the entire portfolio. Should the first impression of the work be the weakest project included in the portfolio?

Reverse Chronological
This ordering system is the opposite of the first example and is where the most recent work is included first and it works backwards from there through time.

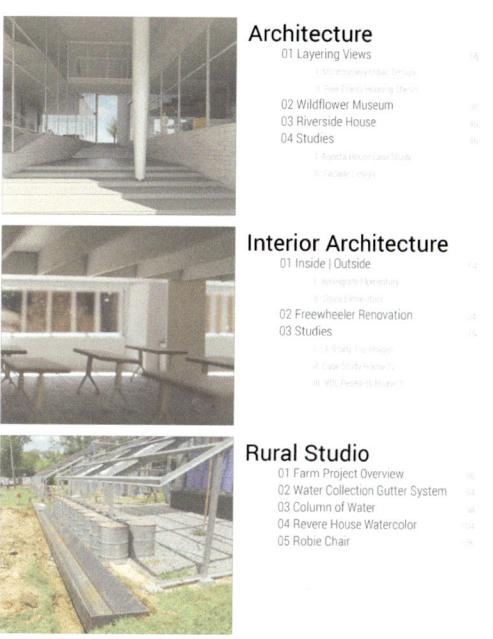

Table of contents organizes portfolio and projects by type. Portfolio design by Cynthia Baker.

Pros: This method of organization starts with the most recent work, therefore it stands to reason that it is a representation of the strongest, most comprehensive design efforts.

Cons: Since reverse chronological ends with the oldest project, there is a significant chance that the last project is the weakest since it occurred earlier in the design education. As much as it is a brilliant idea to start with the strongest work, it is a bad idea to end with the weakest. The weak project will be the last thing the reviewer remembers about the portfolio. Not the best idea, right?

Placement of Strongest Work
The last organizational strategy to think through focuses on the idea to start with the strongest project and close the portfolio with the second strongest project. All of the remaining projects should be organized between these two bookends.

Pros: The strengths of this organizational strategy are obvious—make the first impression of the work the best it can possibly be. And, leave them with a good last impression as they conclude the review of the portfolio.

Cons: The only drawback to this organizational strategy is that it requires a little extra work on the designer's part to make sense of this new order. This system will need to be combined with another one to add a cohesive sense of ordering purpose to the portfolio. For instance, it may be necessary to overlay a project type organization system or academic and professional categorization system to support the selection of placing the strongest work first.

Categorization

Project Type
This cataloging system categorizes design work by project type. For example, collect all of the urban

Constructing the Persuasive Portfolio: the only primer you'll ever need

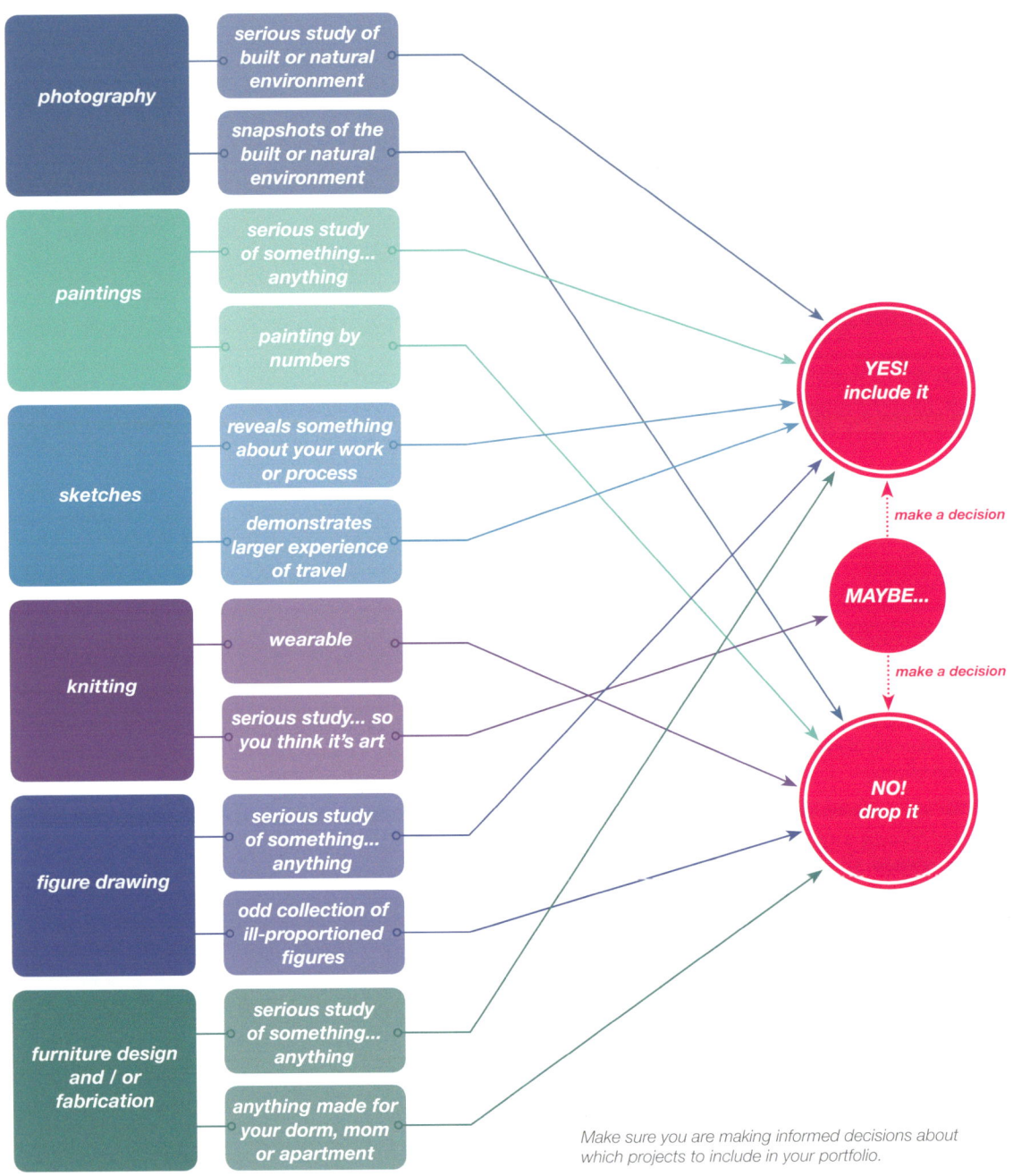

Make sure you are making informed decisions about which projects to include in your portfolio.

projects into one section of the portfolio, or collect all of the high-rise projects together.

Pros: This categorization system gathers similar project types together to present a super-set of common ideas. It can also provide a very clear categorization system that is easily legible in the table of contents to set the tone for the understanding of the entire portfolio. This method completely shuffles when each project was created and replaces the importance of when the work was done with what was accomplished with the work.

Cons: This method completely shuffles when each project was created and replaces the importance of when the work was done with what was accomplished with the work. Wait?! That's the same statement that is listed under "pros" above. How can that be? The truth is, if this cataloging method is used, a more robust way of presenting the project completion time frame has to be developed. It's not that big of a deal but something to definitely keep in mind.

Design Theme
A similar categorization strategy is to organize projects in the portfolio through a design theme that has developed over a course of study. The pros and cons are almost identical to those discussed with "categorization by project type." However, it should be noted that this categorization strategy begins to demonstrate to the reviewer that the designer is looking at the thinking behind the design work in a more thoughtful manner and taking opportunities within all of the work to delve deeper into a particular area of study to solve specific design challenges. The pros and cons listed here should be taken in conjunction with those listed for "categorization by project type."

Pros: This categorization strategy can really separate one portfolio from another. It is imperative to present these themes in a thorough and sophisticated way. It is not enough to just say there are design themes running through the work, it must be visually demonstrated through the included studies, diagrams, drawings, images and verbal descriptions.

Cons: One of the only negatives to be mindful of with this type of categorization is that it has the potential to produce a narrowed reading of the work included in the portfolio. Make sure the reviewer comes away from the portfolio with the thought: "Now there's a designer who has been making more of their education by working beyond the assignments to pursue what truly interests them!" However, this reading of the work should be avoided: "I can't believe they only learned one thing! And to top that off, it sure is a lazy presentation of that one thing!"

Academic Work versus Professional Work
Professional experience should be presented separately from academic work within the portfolio. It is acceptable to have completely separate sections in the portfolio to accommodate these two categories or any of the ordering systems or categorization systems described above, but make sure to have a strong visual indicator of which work is academic and which work is professional.

"Other" Design Work
Often students will come to me and say they have some work that they have produced outside of the studio that they would like to include in their portfolio and are wondering if it is appropriate to do so. This is frankly a tough question to answer without actually seeing the work. See the diagram on the left for some guidelines to help determine if the work is appropriate to include. A general rule of thumb is that the work that is included must be a serious study. It can't just be the sweater you knit for your cat—even if it is a really complicated sweater.

One image explains how intensively the sketchbook is being used. Portfolio design by Ciera Shaver.

Designing Portfolio Systems—Strategies for Portfolio Organization

Photography section of portfolio demonstrates the keen visual eye and compositional skills of the photographer and is not just an inclusion of snapshots. Portfolio design by Saurabh Mhatre.

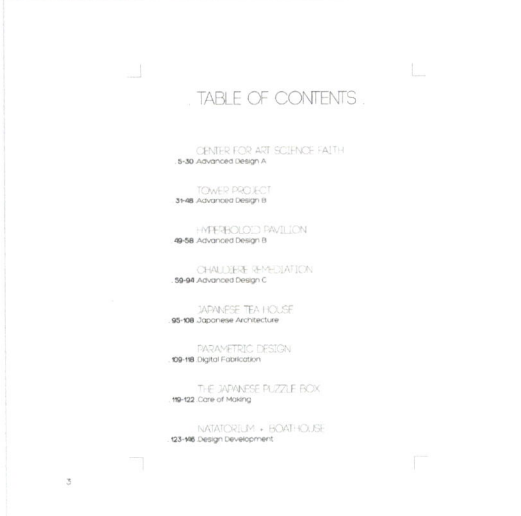

Organizing the Visual Narrative: Using Visual Components of Graphic Layout as Organizational Structure

Topics related to the visual organization systems in a portfolio are just that—visual clues that organize material. Successful visual organization systems don't necessarily need to be completely understood to be valuable visual tools. They just need to appear in a similar fashion again and again so that the visual system becomes legible over the space of the entire portfolio.

The list below outlines areas to focus on to develop the visual narrative through a variety of organization systems. Additional visual organization systems will likely be developed in the process of designing the portfolio. It should be noted that there are different scales of visual organization systems within the portfolio itself: some systems are portfolio-wide systems and relate to the overall visual narrative of main portfolio components—page numbers, headers, footers—and some systems are project specific and relate to the visual aspect of the content narrative for project components—parallel visual use of images and text.

Visual Organizational Strategies of Portfolio Components

Visual organizational strategies for portfolio components stretch across the portfolio system as a whole and work together to make the organizational strategies being employed readily visible and understandable.

Table of Contents
The table of contents can be used as a visual strategy for portfolio organization and sets the tone of the portfolio organization from the very beginning of the portfolio. While it is not always completely necessary to include a table of contents in the portfolio, it is a good plan to make a first impression on the reviewer regarding the contents they are about to review.

At the bare minimum, a table of contents lists project names and page numbers. However, there is an organizational opportunity available that can change the table of contents from just a list or a page finder to another clue regarding the way the designer defines the body of work.

The organization and categorization strategies listed previously in the section titled Organizing the Content

Designing Portfolio Systems—Strategies for Portfolio Organization

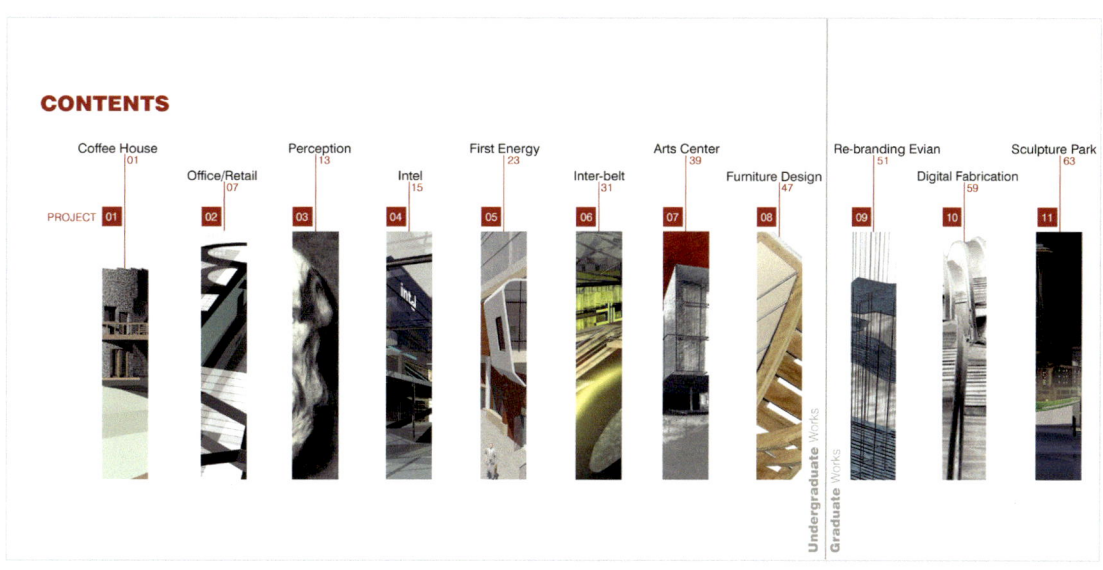

Table of contents that uses imagery as graphic organizer. Note the vertical division that separates undergraduate from graduate work. Portfolio design by Sean Burns.

Project imagery is used as graphic organizer for the table of contents. Portfolio design by Nico Forlenza.

opposite: Typographical range is used to visually organize the table of contents. Portfolio design by Joshua Riek.

following page: Infographic-style table of contents sets up color families to identify portfolio sections. Portfolio design by Shawn Backstrom.

Constructing the Persuasive Portfolio: the only primer you'll ever need

ARCHITECTURE IS A DIALOGUE SIMULTANEOUSLY INFORMED BY AND INFORMING PEOPLE AND PLACE. THIS RECIPROCAL NATURE FOSTERS GROUNDS FOR PERPETUAL EVOLUTION.

OUR GENERATION ENTERS A DIGITALLY DRIVEN WORLD WHERE BOUNDARIES BETWEEN DISCIPLINES ARE EVAPORATING.

THE ENIGMATIC IS NOW PRAGMATIC.
THE HYPOTHETICAL IS REAL.
SOCIETY ACCELERATES AT A BREAKNECK PACE.

I HAVE APPROACHED MY UNDERGRADUATE EDUCATION IN A SIMILAR VEIN. OVER FOUR YEARS I HAVE DEVELOPED WORK SPANNING MULTIPLE MEDIUMS:

ARCHITECTURE // GRAPHIC DESIGN // FILM
ACADEMIC // PROFESSIONAL // PERSONAL
LOCAL // REGIONAL // INTERNATIONAL

THROUGH ALL VENTURES I HAVE STRIVED TOWARD RECIPROCITY, SEEKING CONNECTIONS THAT LINK SEEMINGLY DISPARATE EXPERIENCES INTO AN EVER-EVOLVING DIALECT.

INHERENTLY YEARNING.
CONTINUOUSLY SEARCHING.
NEVER STAGNANT.

ALWAYS RECIPROCUS.

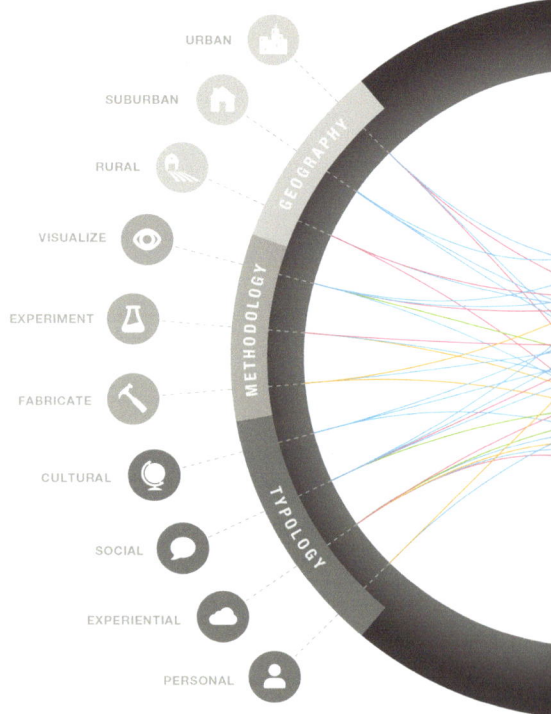

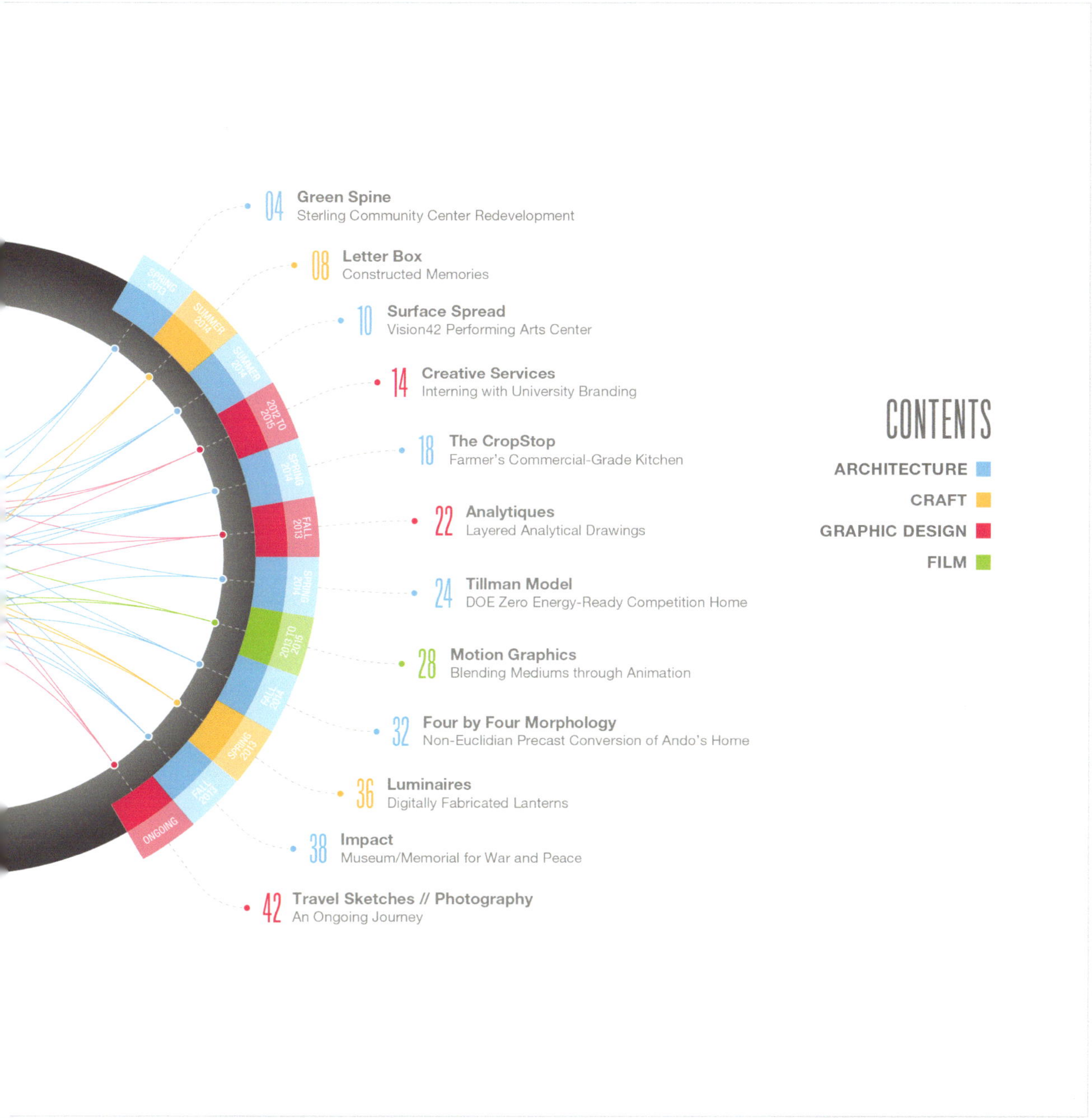

Designing Portfolio Systems—Strategies for Portfolio Organization

CONTENTS

ARCHITECTURE
CRAFT
GRAPHIC DESIGN
FILM

04 **Green Spine**
Sterling Community Center Redevelopment

08 **Letter Box**
Constructed Memories

10 **Surface Spread**
Vision42 Performing Arts Center

14 **Creative Services**
Interning with University Branding

18 **The CropStop**
Farmer's Commercial-Grade Kitchen

22 **Analytiques**
Layered Analytical Drawings

24 **Tillman Model**
DOE Zero Energy-Ready Competition Home

28 **Motion Graphics**
Blending Mediums through Animation

32 **Four by Four Morphology**
Non-Euclidian Precast Conversion of Ando's Home

36 **Luminaires**
Digitally Fabricated Lanterns

38 **Impact**
Museum/Memorial for War and Peace

42 **Travel Sketches // Photography**
An Ongoing Journey

 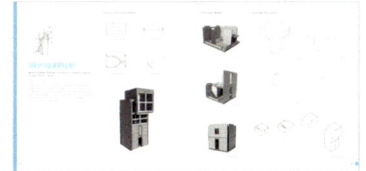 

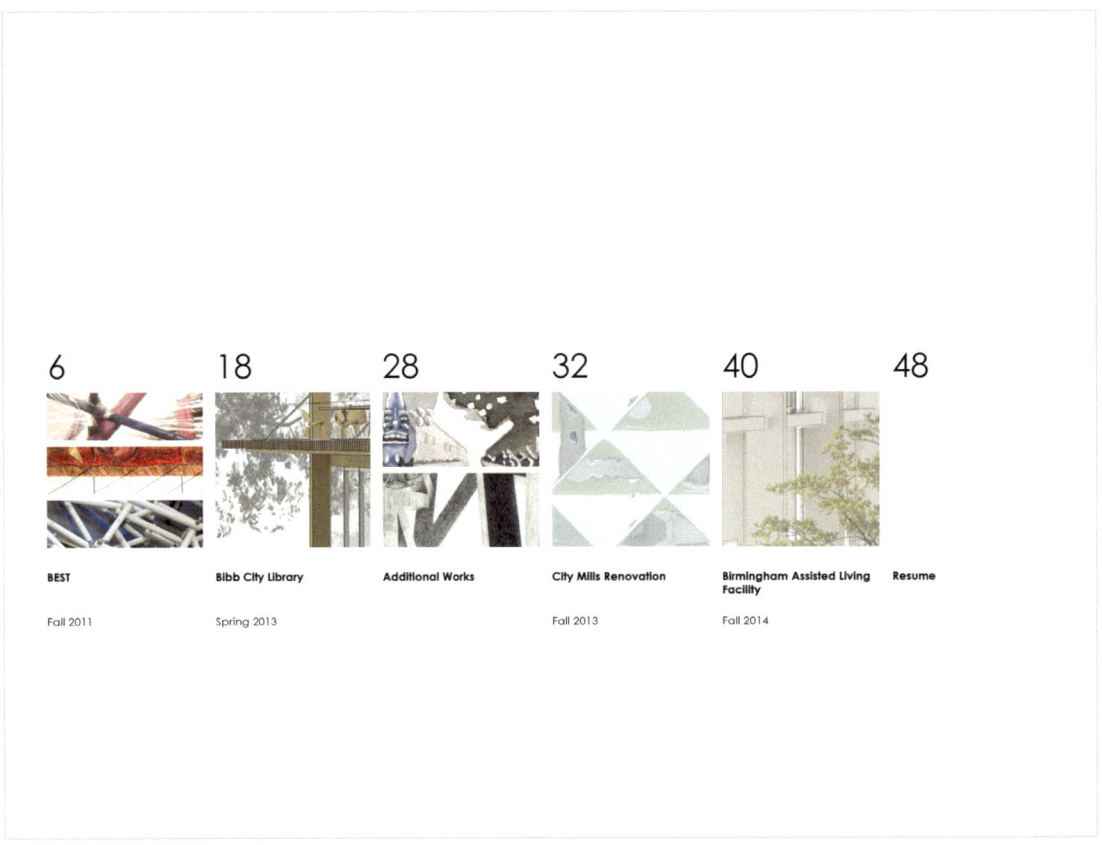

Abstracted project imagery is used as graphic organizer for the table of contents. Portfolio design by George Criminale.

Narrative should begin to elucidate some ideas about how to organize a table of contents. One of the visual goals with the table of contents is to make obviously legible a subset of information about the work.

For instance, it may be important to convey how many years the designer has been studying architecture or working in the profession. To convey this point, make the dates of the work one of the most visibly legible parts of the table of contents.

If the project type categorization or over-arching themes in the work are significant ideas, make the categories the most visually legible parts of the table of contents.

Designing Portfolio Systems—Strategies for Portfolio Organization

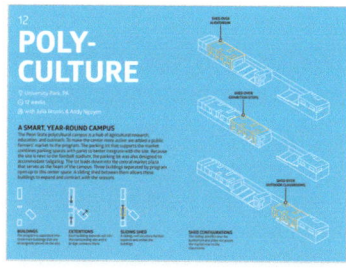
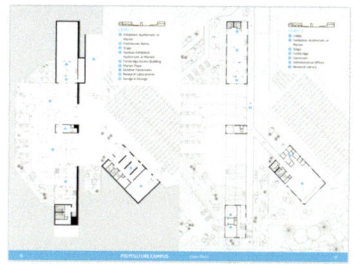
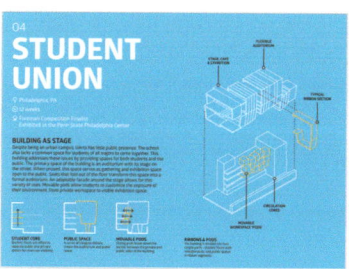
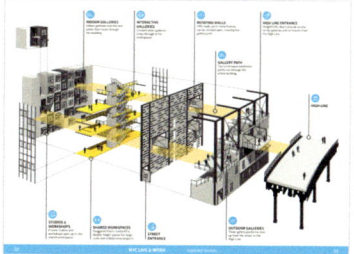
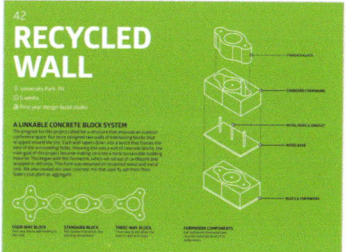

Color systems are established in the table of contents to organize project types throughout the portfolio. Portfolio design by Vonn Weisenberger.

A table of contents can operate as a design opportunity. This design opportunity could be a typographic strategy and / or an image-based strategy.

A typographic strategy should establish the look and feel that is carried throughout the remainder of the portfolio and is based on typographic style and hierarchy. If established at the table of contents, this typographic style and hierarchy can establish cues for the visual legibility of the remainder of the portfolio.

An image-based strategy for the table of contents can also be a powerful tool and works in conjunction with the typographic strategy discussed above. Including images of projects on the table of contents page gives another level of visual information about the projects to come and a visual teaser of the great work to follow.

It is very important, however, when working through these design opportunities to remember that the most important thing the table of contents does is pass on information about the organization of the contents of the portfolio. If that visual legibility is lost, then the value of the table of contents page is lost.

There are quite frankly many different types of information that can be conveyed in a table of contents and all are viable solutions.

Section Divider Spreads
Section divider spreads are another visual organization tool that is a portfolio-wide decision. The purpose of a section divider spread is to clearly and visually begin a new section within the portfolio. It offers the reviewer a moment of pause when transitioning from one topic to another. Section divider spreads reinforce any sections that have been developed as part of the organization or categorization strategy developed in the table of contents. They should be used to cause the reviewer to stop, pause, shift gears and clearly understand the overarching theme of the section they are about to view.

These pages work to separate large categories within the portfolio. They must work visually together as a set so they are legible together but they must also convey the individuality of each section they are defining.

Section divider pages can be graphically quite simple—such as a full spread color block with a simple section title—or quite complex with sample images of each project that will be included in that particular section. In order for the section divider pages to be read as a separate set of pages within the portfolio, there does need to be some graphic difference from the way more normative project content pages read against the section divider pages. Usually this is achieved through a change of visual pace—often with less visual clutter found on the divider pages.

The options are endless but, above all else, make sure these section divider pages achieve their primary goals:

1. Graphically set off a new section.

2. Announce clearly what that new section is.

3. Provide a graphic pause within the pace of the entire portfolio.

Headers and Footers
The header and footer material is an often overlooked but vitally important aspect of a portfolio. It acts as the primary visual way-finding system and provides clear access to all of the sections found in a portfolio. It is important to understand how to use headers and footers visually and how to use them in meaningful ways.

Headers and footers are one of the single most important organizing components to add to the portfolio. They are very easy to implement and should be considered at the beginning of the design process so their location can be accommodated within each spread.

Items that can be included in the header or footer are:

Page numbers

Author's name

Subject matter—project type or categorization

Date of completion

Project name

Basically anything that will help identify what page the reviewer is on, what section of the portfolio they are in or who did the design work.

Visually, headers and footers work with the margins to establish the active area of the page. They provide a visual edge adjacent to the actual page edge of each layout. It is not necessary to include both a header and footer if there isn't content to support them. Keep these things in mind:

1. The right-hand side of a spread usually contains the most important way-finding content. For example, this could be the section and project title: Architecture—Operative Conditions of a Field Study Hospital.

2. The left-hand side of a spread usually contains more overview-type content. In a literary book, this could be something like the title of the book. In the case of a design portfolio, this is where the designer's name could be located if it is decided to include the name on each page of the portfolio.

3. Pay attention to the hierarchical relationship between all typefaces on the page. The header and footer material is at the bottom of the hierarchy list and should be visually present but subservient to all other visual material on the page. This means it will either be smaller and lighter or visually separate and distinct or some combination thereof.

4. The header and footer material should be pushed to the outer margin of each page. Visually this content needs to be aligned or visually attached to something

Designing Portfolio Systems—Strategies for Portfolio Organization

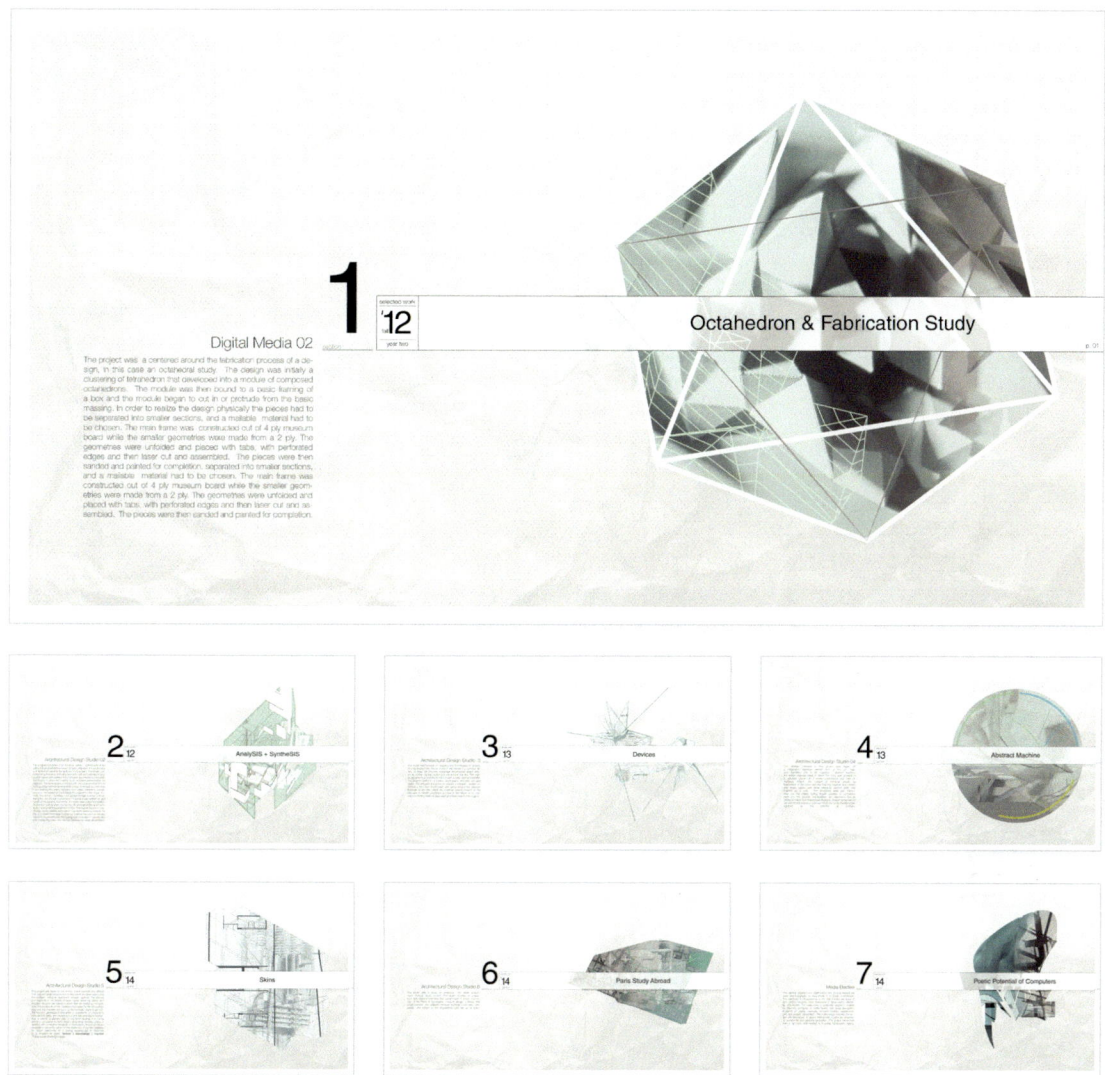

Project introduction pages act as section dividers to announce the beginning of new project sections. The pages show abstracted project imagery, project title, description and year of completion. Portfolio design by Marrisa Jena Meeks.

Constructing the Persuasive Portfolio: the only primer you'll ever need

Designing Portfolio Systems—Strategies for Portfolio Organization

above and opposite: Project introduction pages act as section dividers to announce the beginning of new project sections. The pages show project imagery, project title, description and year of completion as well as any awards given to the project. Portfolio design by Derek Pirozzi.

Constructing the Persuasive Portfolio: the only primer you'll ever need

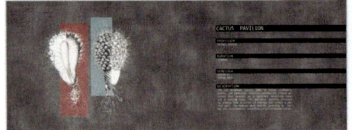

Designing Portfolio Systems—Strategies for Portfolio Organization

URBAN STRATEGIES

PROFESSOR
SARAH GAMBLE

DURATION
3 WEEKS

SEMESTER
DESIGN IV
SPRING 2014

DESCRIPTION
South Lamar is a central transportation hub that is home to multiple neighborhoods and many housing complexes. The current state of this street is unsafe and unslightly for residents and visitors. Plan Radii utilizes a system that ensures all residents and visitors on South Lamar close proximity to transporation, food, and recreation. This system will increase the amount of energy efficient transportation methods while making the corridor safer and more desirable to inhabitants. The plan uses form codes in order to improve the development along the corridor and to increase the safety and walkability of the road.

 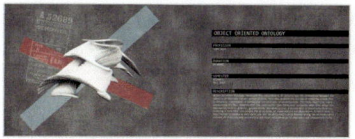 

above and opposite: *Project introduction pages act as section dividers to announce the beginning of new project sections. The pages show abstracted project imagery, project title, description and year of completion as well as duration of the project. Portfolio design by Alena Savera.*

and that something is the actual page. If header and footer content has visually floated away from the outer margin, it will appear ungrounded and will neither define the active area nor act as a way-finding system because it will be visually lost amongst the other visual content on the page.

5. Headers and footers should contain consistent titles that are pulled from other sections of the portfolio. For instance, if the portfolio is organized by project type and one of these types is named "Urban Collisions" in the table of contents, then the title "Urban Collisions" must be used exactly as it is listed in the table of contents within the header / footer.

Page Numbers
Page numbers are included within the header and footer system. Since some portfolios have only page numbers as their header and footer, page numbers warrant a separate discussion. Below are guidelines regarding page numbers to be mindful of as the header and footer system is being designed.

1. Page numbers are always odd on the right-hand page and even on the left-hand page for a double page spread.

2. Single page spreads, as might exist in a single-layout style digital portfolio, should have the pages numbered normally without worrying about right- and left-hand sides.

3. Page numbers should always be located at the outermost edge of the header and footer content. They are the ultimate way-finding tool and need to be visually located in the most prominent and commonly found location. Don't make someone search for the page numbers; that defeats the purpose. They should always appear at the outside edge of a page. Don't bury them within the header or footer.

4. Page numbers do not necessarily need to stylistically match the typeface in the rest of the header or footer.

Page numbers start with the first real page of content, typically this is after the table of contents. The first real page of content is always numbered "1" and is always on the right-hand page. Odd numbered pages are always the right-hand page of a spread and even numbered pages are always the left-hand page of a spread. If there is a reason to start pagination at the table of contents page, set it up as page "1" and hide the page number. There is typically not a page number visible on the table of contents page. However, now the first left-hand page will be numbered "2" and the subsequent right-hand page will be numbered "3."

Typically in the table of contents, page numbers reference actual content pages instead of the section divider spreads. But remember that the pages that do not actually receive visible page numbers are still counted as pages when the pagination is entered in the table of contents.

There are several page types that do not typically have full headers and footers located on them or can have a modified header or footer. In this case, modified means page number only. These page types are:

Front Matter: To be a stickler, front matter typically gets only roman numerals as page numbers for a header or footer and nothing else, but in a portfolio this might seem like overkill since there are not that many front matter pages included. My advice is to leave all headers and footers off the front matter material.

Section Divider Pages: There is no need for header or footer material on section divider pages. These pages are intended to visually divide sections of the portfolio and it would be redundant to list the section being reviewed on a page spread that only exists to announce what section is being reviewed.

Blank Pages: Blank pages are just that—blank, with no content on them. It is entirely acceptable to either include header or footer information on these pages or delete it completely. This will be a visual choice.

Typeface Use Consistency
Maintaining typeface consistency throughout the portfolio is of the utmost and primary importance. Once typeface styles have been assigned to each type of text—titles, subtitles, body text, captions, diagram titles and call-outs, header and footer—stay spectacularly consistent throughout the entire portfolio. If a part of the

Designing Portfolio Systems—Strategies for Portfolio Organization

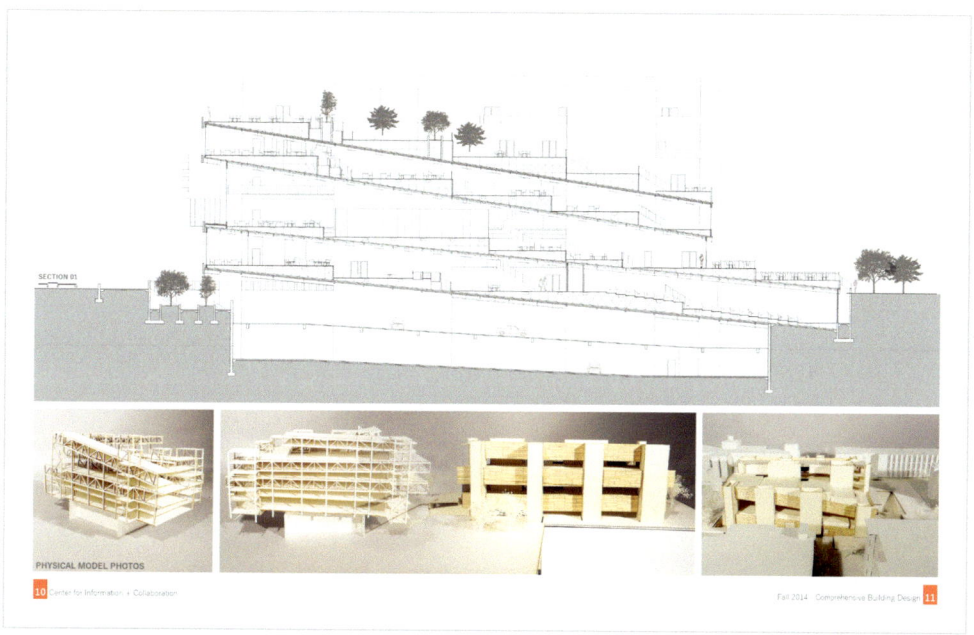

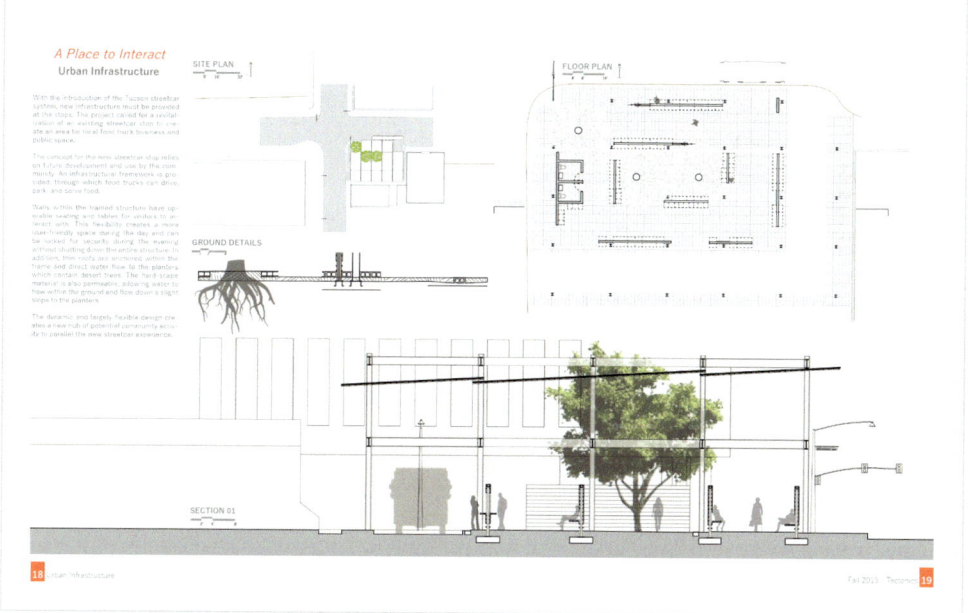

Page numbers are styled with clarity regarding typeface hierarchy, are located on the outside edge of the page and with odd number always on the right-hand page. Portfolio design by Nikki Hall.

Constructing the Persuasive Portfolio: the only primer you'll ever need

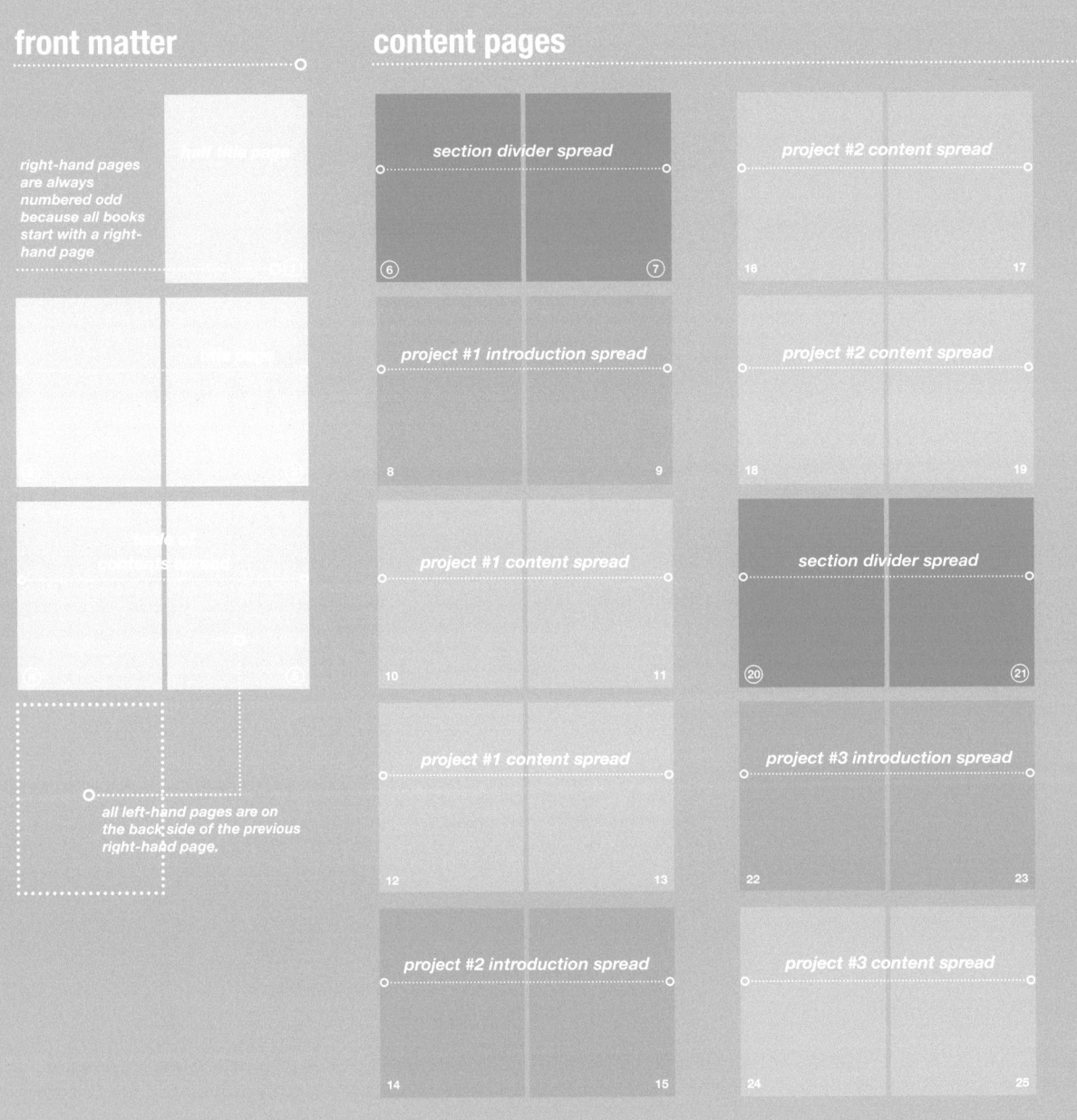

Designing Portfolio Systems—Strategies for Portfolio Organization

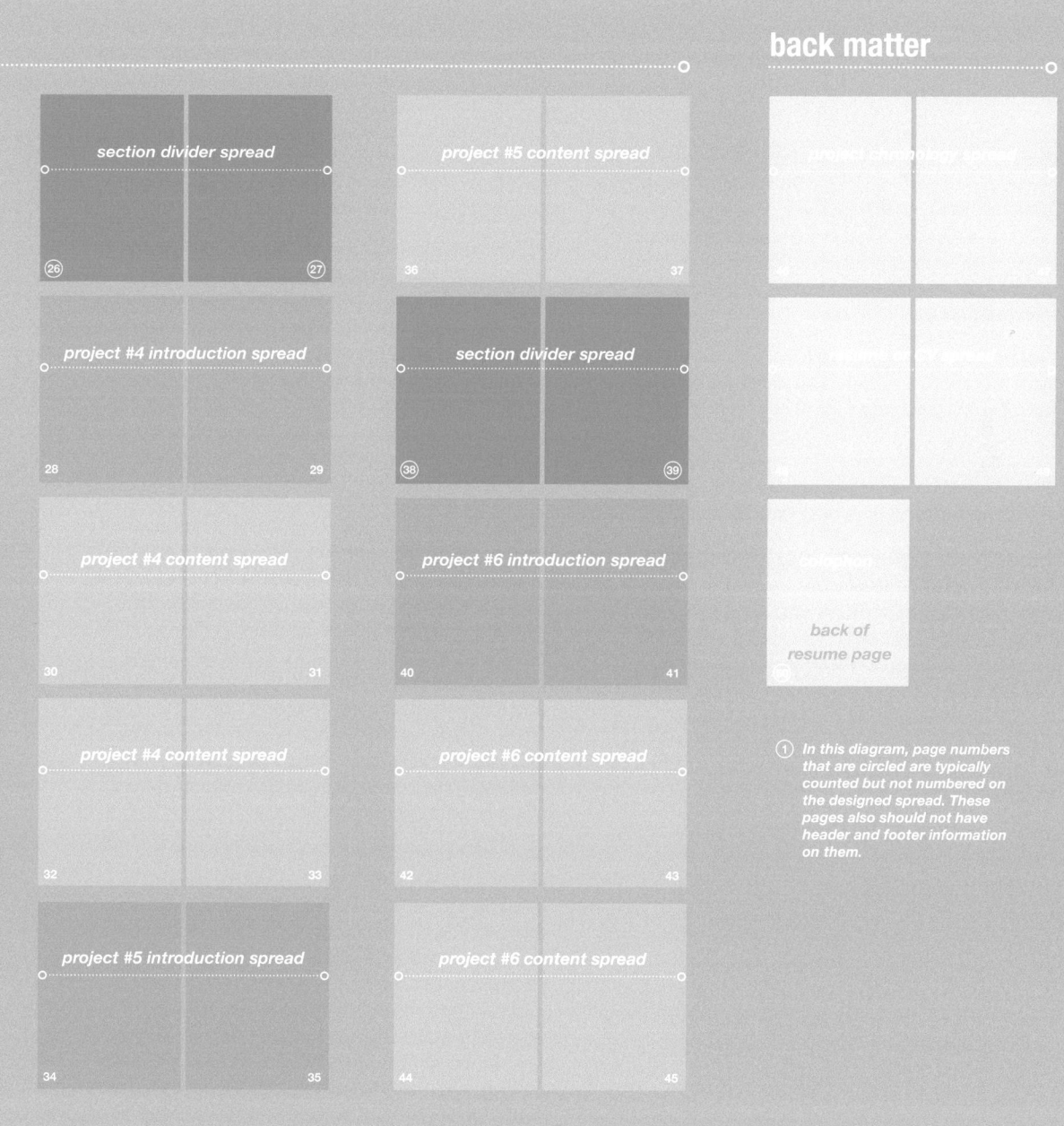

① In this diagram, page numbers that are circled are typically counted but not numbered on the designed spread. These pages also should not have header and footer information on them.

typeface system has to be changed to fit a particular need on one project, it actually means that the system does not work and it needs to be rethought and reworked throughout the entire portfolio.

Graphic Icon Systems
Graphic icons are symbol signs designed to convey common principles throughout the portfolio—these could be related to the organization and / or categorization systems established through the table of contents or begin to relate conceptual ideas from project type to project type. These icons must be designed so their meaning is obvious.

Graphic icon systems can be tricky—there are some significant pitfalls that should be avoided. First and foremost, the graphic icon must add value to the conveyance of information. It cannot be visually distracting to the content on the page. Weigh these two things against one another when designing graphic icons and determine whether or not to include them.

Visual Organizational Strategies of Project Content Components

Part of the struggle of visually organizing a portfolio is having a cohesive strategy that works for the entire portfolio and also works for the individual projects. Here's the problem that comes up frequently, and luckily, it is a relatively easy one to solve. Okay, here it is: "I've got all the projects that I want to include in my portfolio in the layouts, but they look sort of messy and it's hard to tell what's what."

This problem seems complex and time consuming to solve but it's really not. In the section called Project Narrative Visual Representation, there is a lot of information describing how to work through project content issues—which projects to include, in what order, etc. To answer this question through the lens of visual organization strategies for an entire portfolio, there are a couple of simple ideas to apply that will solve this issue of project legibility.

Parallel Use of Project Introduction Material
Project introduction pages work on two different scales; they act as a way-finding system related to all projects included in the portfolio and they provide vital, pertinent information for each individual project. With that in mind, it is important to make sure that whatever system is developed for the project introduction pages works for both the overall portfolio visual narrative as well as the individual project narratives.

Project introduction pages contain all of the important statistical information needed to convey the most pertinent facts about each project included in the portfolio. Visually the information needs to be organized so that it appears similarly again and again throughout the portfolio so the reviewer can instantly recognize it as the beginning of a new project section. This instant project-start recognition can and should be achieved through both the visual nature of the imagery and the organization and styling of the typography.

Image Components: Each time a new project spread begins, use the imagery with the greatest amount of visual impact to launch the project section. This imagery could be a model image, or an incredibly explanatory diagram, or an atmospheric rendering—anything is possible. The goal is to grab the viewer's attention immediately from the beginning and pique their curiosity about the work accomplished on that particular project. Gone are the days when each project needed to begin with precedent studies and a site plan; these are not necessarily the best tools available to convey design ideas with the greatest amount of impact.

Text Components: There are common descriptive components of each project that can be used to organize a set of introductory material to visually start a project spread. These descriptive components are usually at a minimum: project title, location and a brief description. But it can include much, much more. Consider for a moment the information you know about all of your projects. Now consider how very little the reviewer knows about these projects—absolutely nothing, right? Writing everything out in paragraph form will generate an essay that few reviewers will find the time to read.

Designing Portfolio Systems—Strategies for Portfolio Organization

[LANDSCAPE ARCHITECTURE] | 07 | Jamaica Bay Flux City: Urbanization Driven by Land-Water Ecological Linkages
Flux City. Landscape Architecture Design IV. Harvard GSD
| 2014 | Faculty: Chriss Reed | David Mah
Critics: Ed Eigen | Nina Marie Lister
Team Work: Flavio Sciaraffia, Sourava Biswas

PORTFOLIO
Selected Projects in Architecture, Landscape, Urban Design, Design Research and Critical Mapping
Flavio Sciaraffia Márquez

Graphic icons are used to identify project types throughout the portfolio. Graphic icon key has been cropped from full portfolio page to show detail. Portfolio design by Flavio Sciaraffia Márquez.

Constructing the Persuasive Portfolio: the only primer you'll ever need

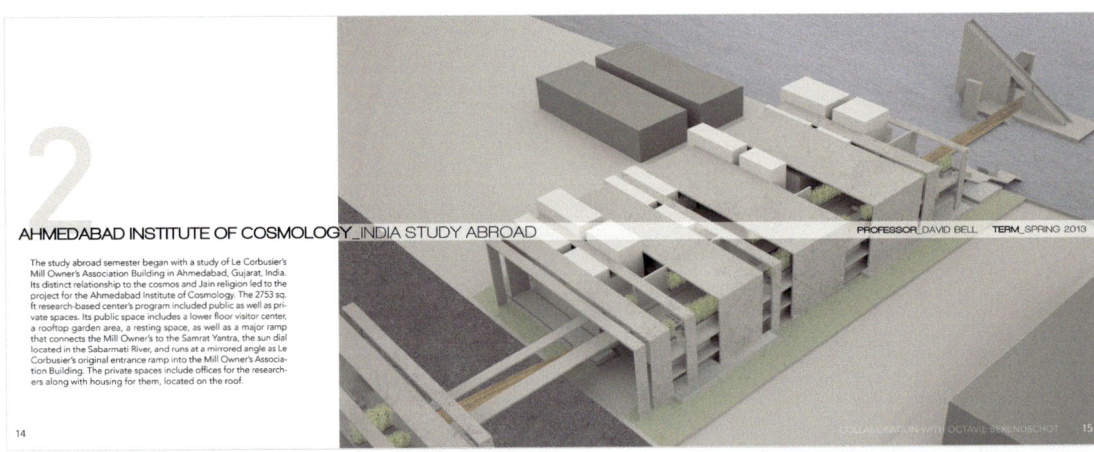

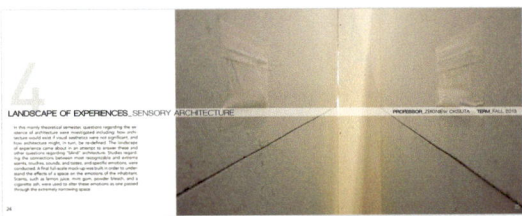
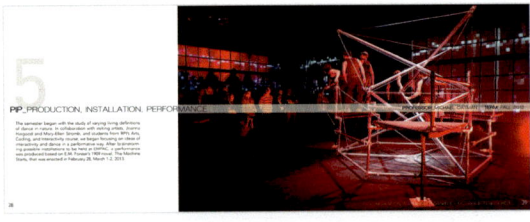

The best strategy is to make an incredibly informative and pointed list of facts about the project that can be used as a visual information system and apply this system across all of the projects in the portfolio. This list is very effective because it is brief and easy to read and becomes part of the system of information available about each project.

This descriptive material should be visually organized in a way that is recognizable as the start of a new project and flexible enough to be used with all of the projects. Here are some ideas to help think about the possibilities:

Title

Location

Project type with brief description

Main programmatic components

Organizing principles of the design (basically telling the reviewer in a couple of words how to review the project)

Size (square feet or square meters)

Year of completion—this could literally be the year or perhaps the year level in school or both

Your role on the team if it was a team project

Brief project description

Designing Portfolio Systems—Strategies for Portfolio Organization

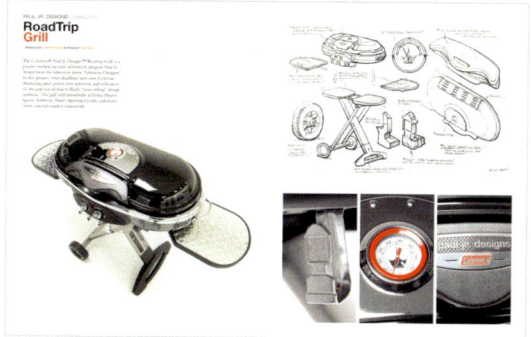

Project introduction pages with parallel project information. Portfolio design by Oliver Vranesh.

opposite: *Project introduction pages with parallel project information. Portfolio design by Erin M. Butler.*

Constructing the Persuasive Portfolio: the only primer you'll ever need

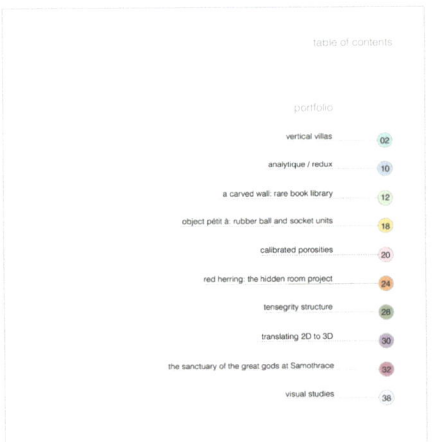

Consistent Graphic Indicators

Consistent graphic indicators are those things that happen repeatedly throughout the portfolio and mean the same thing each time they are used. Typical consistent graphic indicators are the table of contents, header and footer material, page numbers, section divider spreads, typeface use consistency, and project introduction pages. It is imperative that the graphic styles that have been set up in this portfolio material remain consistent throughout the entire portfolio.

There can be more visual cues throughout the portfolio that fall into the category of consistent graphic indicators; whatever they are, make sure they are addressed in a thoroughly consistent manner.

Designing Portfolio Systems—Strategies for Portfolio Organization

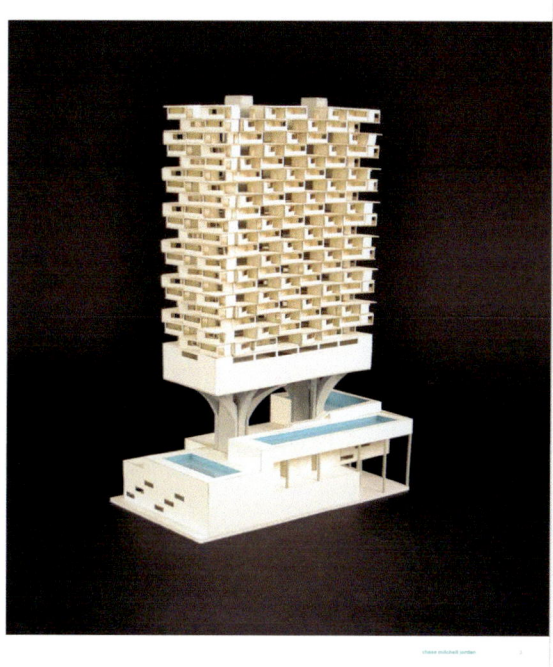
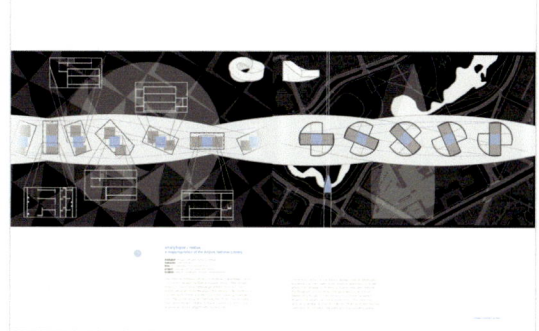
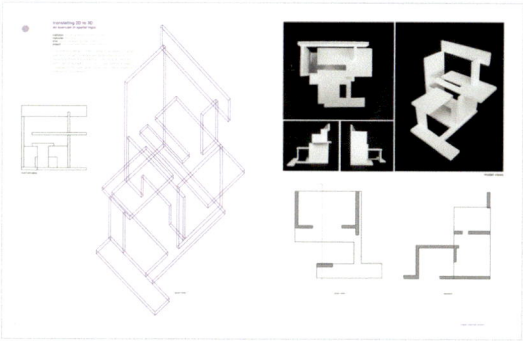

above and opposite: *Consistent graphic indicators are used to mark the beginning of each project and are flexible enough to be moved wherever they need to be on the page to balance the layout. Portfolio design by Chase Jordan.*

Designing Po[rtfolios]

Design Actions

(16) *Decide on underlying structure: grid or alignment system or both.* page 66

(17) *Design the active area.* page 75

(18) *Design the visual relationships between objects on a page.* page 84

(19) *Design the visual pace of the portfolio.* page 90

Systems of Visual Structure

The most important organizational systems to understand are the physical structures called grid and alignment systems. These systems relate specifically to how your images and text spatially relate to one another, and how images and text spatially relate to the page.

Having a series of systems through which all of the physical content is visually organized across all spreads throughout the entire portfolio is vital for the visual consistency of the work. This visual consistency makes it easier for the reviewer to focus on the work rather than on a confusing and changing alignment system. These grid and alignment ordering systems are the primary way to visually stitch all of your work together; it is another way to elevate the portfolio from a bunch of projects on pages to a choreographed collection of work.

There are several values that are achieved through the visual organization achieved by designing and following a series of grid and alignment systems consistently on all layouts:

1. It makes it easier for the reviewer to understand the conceptual underpinnings of the work. The reviewer will spend time actually looking at, understanding and absorbing the design work rather than spending energy trying to figure out what's going on with the visual organization of the material.

2. It will make it easier to make decisions about what to include and how to include it if there is a system to work within. As with any design problem—and the portfolio is a design problem—having a series of constraints to push against always makes it easier to make decisions and move the work forward.

3. Grid and alignment systems add to the visual way-finding systems that are being set up throughout the portfolio and, if done properly, will enhance the legibility of the work.

Luckily, there are a variety of systems to use to achieve visual organization—grid and alignment systems, visual organization systems and content organization systems. It would make things easier to be able to say that certain systems are more important to employ than others. Then it would be obvious what to do first. But the truth is, they all work in conjunction with each other to achieve the visual structure needed to consistently organize a portfolio—this describes the work of the visual narrative.

Constructing the Persuasive Portfolio: the only primer you'll ever need

Single Column Grid

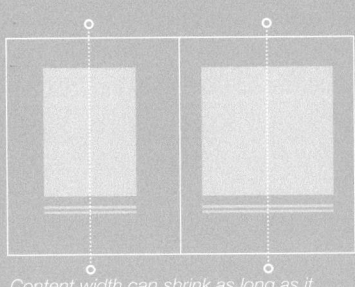

Single column grid operates around the center line for each page.

Content width can shrink as long as it stays true to the center line.

Content can split vertically as long as it stays true to the center line.

Multi-Column Grid

Basic two column grid.

Two column grid with content variation.

Two column grid with content variation.

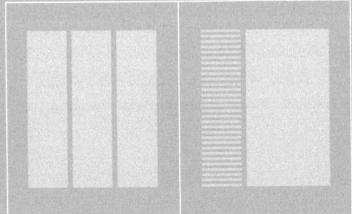
Basic three column grid.

Basic four column grid.

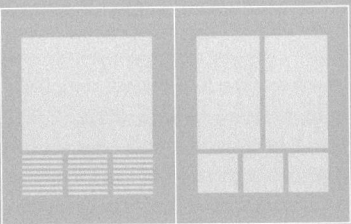
Combination of single, two and three column grids.

Designing Portfolio Systems—Systems of Visual Structure

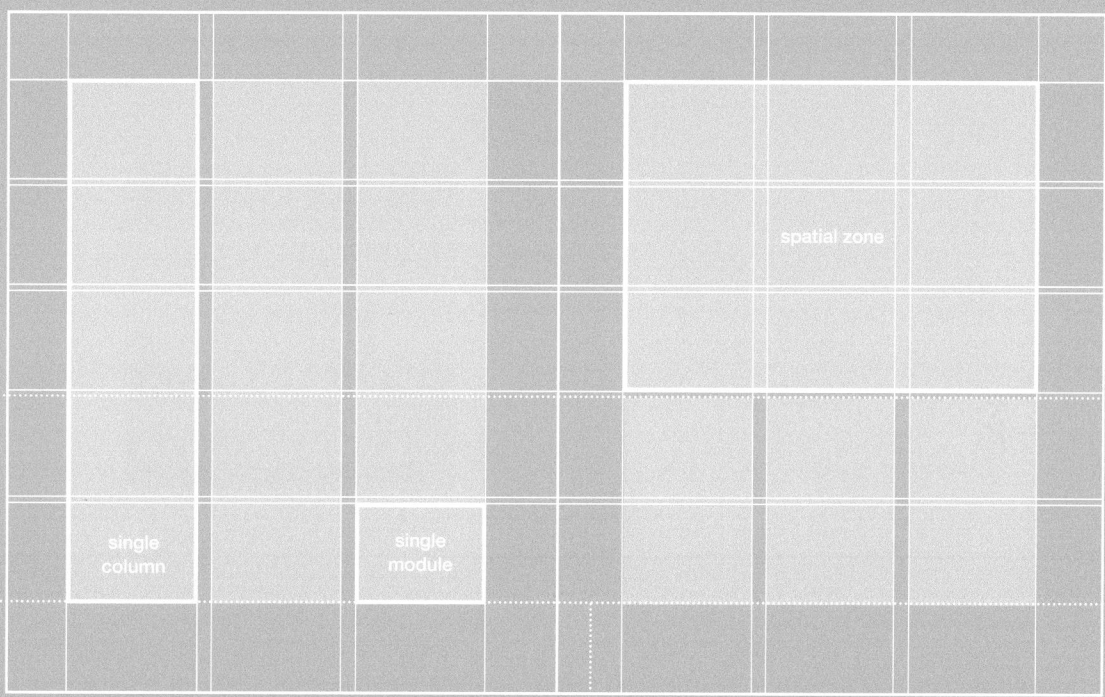

A compound grid uses vertical columns and horizontal hanglines and baselines to create modules. These modules can be combined to establish different spatial zones throughout the grid system.

○ *Baseline: items align and sit on the baseline.*

Hangline: items align and hang from the hangline. ○

How to Develop a Structural System for Your Portfolio

Determining what type of underlying structural system to use for organizing the material in a portfolio can be an exhausting task. Believe it or not, a degree in graphic design is not necessary to be able to use a grid or structural system. Understanding fundamental principles of a structural system, committing to paying attention to this structural system and admitting that one is needed is all that is required.

Review these different grid systems against the material available for your portfolio and make a best guess of which grid to begin with. As you can tell from this series of diagrams, all of the grid systems are relatively flexible and it's easy to combine several grid systems together to create additional flexibility to the grid structure. Keep in mind, baselines and hanglines are incredibly helpful when combining grid systems; they help the combined systems work seamlessly together.

Grid and Alignment Systems

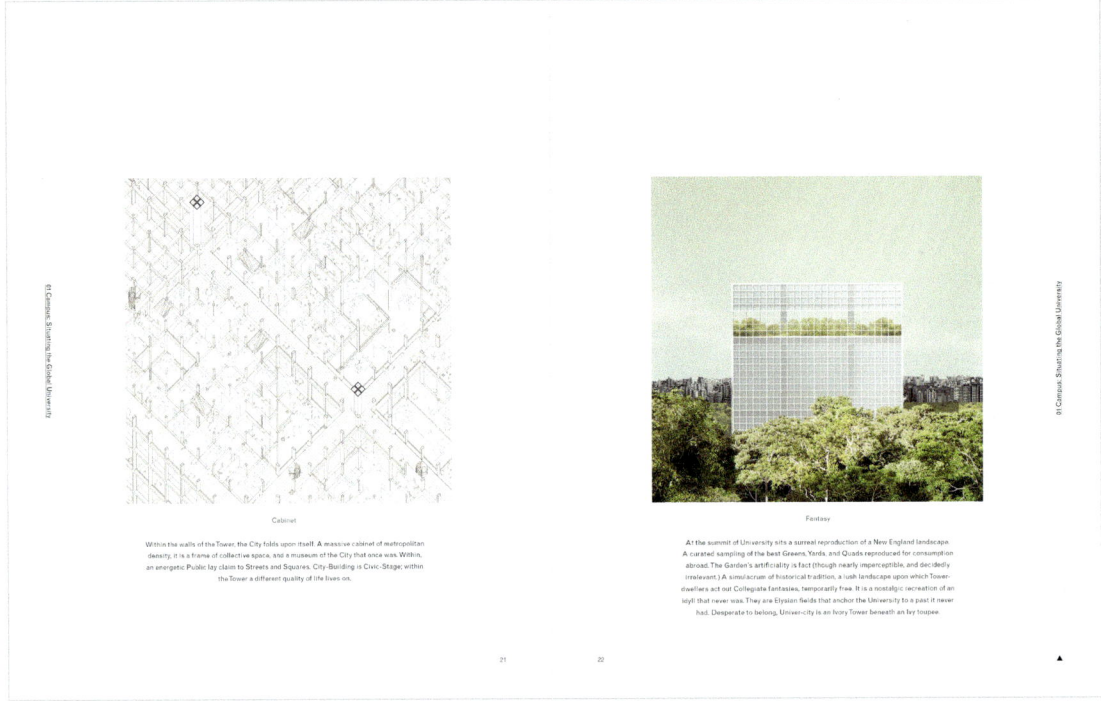

There are many different types of grid systems that designers use for page layout. The following are descriptions and examples of each. The intention of these descriptions is to increase understanding of each system, how it might work in any given situation and how to work within the designed flexibility of each structure.

The basic elements of a grid system are page margins, hanglines, baselines, the actual grid, defined spatial zones and the grid modules. Each one of these elements exists in each grid or alignment system; the proportion of the relationships just change. Different spatial zones are defined through the aggregation of a collection of individual grid modules. Packing modules together to create these spatial zones provides a much more flexible application of any grid or alignment system. Ultimately all the grid or alignment system does is provide an underlying structure to help visually organize graphic content. Don't let the grid bind the content unnecessarily to a structure. The content won't always fit to the grid. That's when it's time to break the grid and adjust things as needed.

Column Systems

Single Column Grid—also called Manuscript Grid
A single column grid is the simplest form of a grid and can actually carry quite a bit of visual power. Typically this type of grid is used to emphasize predominantly visual image content. Due to the simple nature of this grid, the folio material on the page—header, footer, page number—as well as particular attention to the page margins is of vital importance.

Designing Portfolio Systems—Systems of Visual Structure

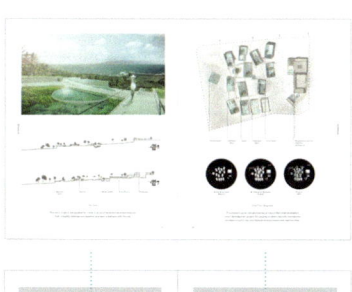
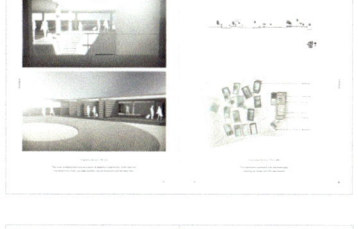
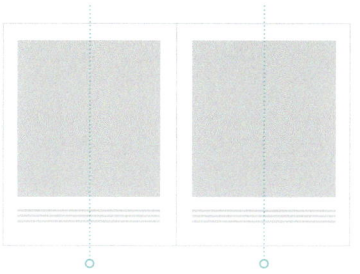
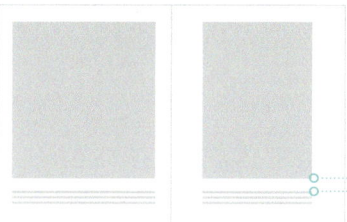

above and opposite: *Single column grid establishes centerline organization. Use of baseline and hangline organizes variant content across multiple pages. Portfolio design by Phillip Denny.*

baseline
hangline

centerline organization

Constructing the Persuasive Portfolio: the only primer you'll ever need

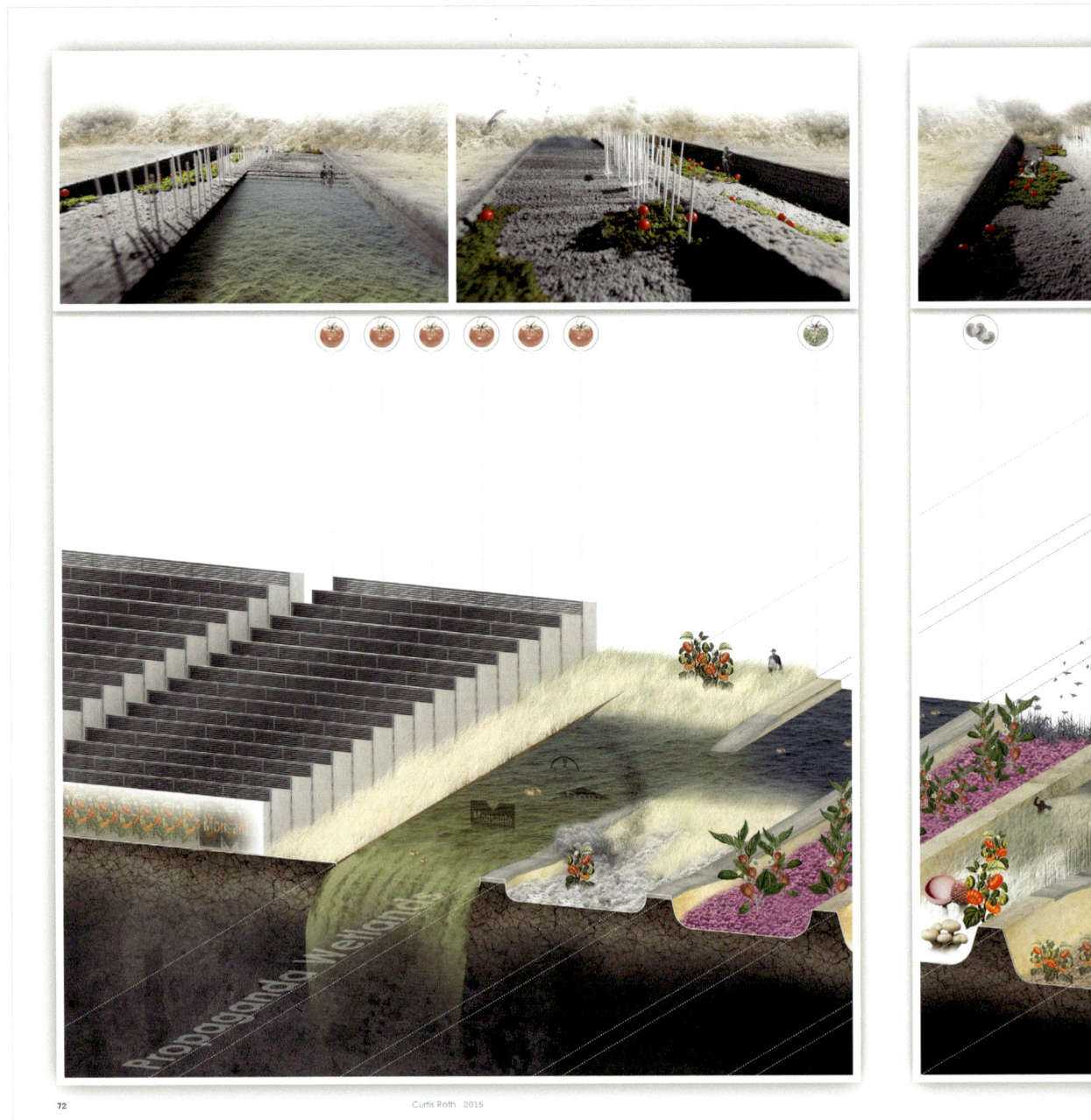

Designing Portfolio Systems—Systems of Visual Structure

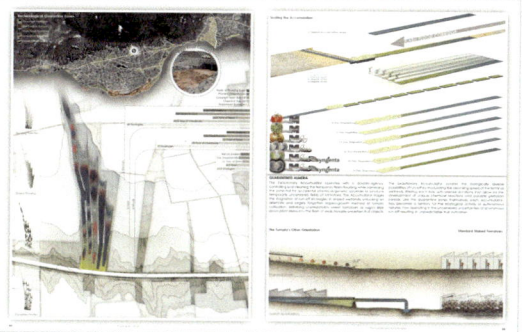

Multi-Column Grid
A multi-column grid can include any number of columns and is particularly helpful with a large variety of content types. This type of grid is commonly used for architectural portfolios due to the flexibility of the grid and the wide range of content types found within an architectural portfolio.

Modular or Compound Grid
A modular or compound grid system combines a horizontal and vertical grid system. The resultant orthogonal grid creates modules that can be combined in a horizontal or vertical direction. This type of grid is also incredibly flexible and an easy choice for the wide range of content types found within an architectural portfolio.

Two column grid provides flexibility of multi-column grid with minimal visual clutter. Portfolio design by Curtis Roth.

Constructing the Persuasive Portfolio: the only primer you'll ever need

Designing Portfolio Systems—Systems of Visual Structure

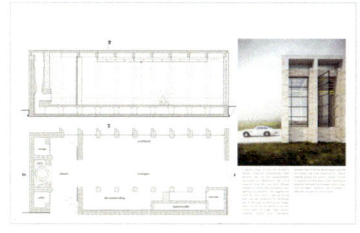
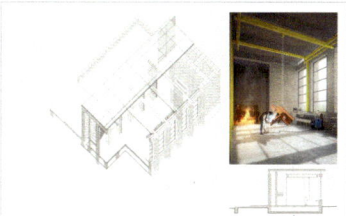

above and opposite: *Modular variations on a six column grid. Use of baseline and hangline organizes variant content across multiple pages. Portfolio design by Eric Barr.*

Alignment Systems Within the Grid

There are multiple ways to think through alignment systems within an overall grid structure. The important thing to remember is that items placed in adjacent relationships within a system will be read as a set of information. Align certain elements such that they are purposefully read together as a set.

The most interesting aspect to understand about any grid structure for a portfolio is how to modify the grid for a flexible arrangement of material. Any grid system can essentially merge grid cells together to create super-cells that still adhere to the original grid structure. Fundamentally, grids consist of edge alignments and alignment relationships more than anything else and can be incredibly flexible if they are thought of as systems to maintain edge alignments rather than boxes that need to be filled with visual content.

Hanglines and Baselines as Organizing Elements Throughout the Portfolio

Hanglines and baselines are implied horizontal lines that extend through all pages in the portfolio and act as organizing elements. Content hangs from the hangline and sits on the baseline.

A Note on Text and Column Width

Keep in mind the guidelines for the character maximums and minimums in a line of text when employing your grid system. The characters in a text column should fall somewhere in the 45–75 characters per line range. If the line of characters is shorter than that, the content is too visually choppy. If the line of characters is longer than that, then the content is too long for the eye to follow and understand where each line begins and ends. Either extreme leads to a legibility issue with the understanding of your text content.

Getting Started

Initially it can be quite difficult to determine exactly what grid system should be used to design your portfolio. Being familiar with the content available for the portfolio before beginning to design the grid system is important. For instance, if all of the images are strong vertical images, a different grid will be used than if the images are predominantly horizontal.

The truth of the matter is that there is likely a mix of everything! However, there will be patterns that emerge through the layouts as the work begins that will lend themselves to certain grids. In fact, some designers suggest that the layouts should be started with a general grid in mind, but then actual content will determine how the grid develops as the work progresses.

One of the easiest ways to begin is to look through existing portfolio examples, or admired publications, and make sketches of the underlying structural grid that is being used. This is actually a great way to make design determinations about the edge margins, headers and footers—all the design decisions required for a portfolio. There is a certain look and feel to all well-designed publications that can be elusive to a non-graphic designer. Most student portfolios feel unorganized because there isn't a strong point of view when it comes to the layout design.

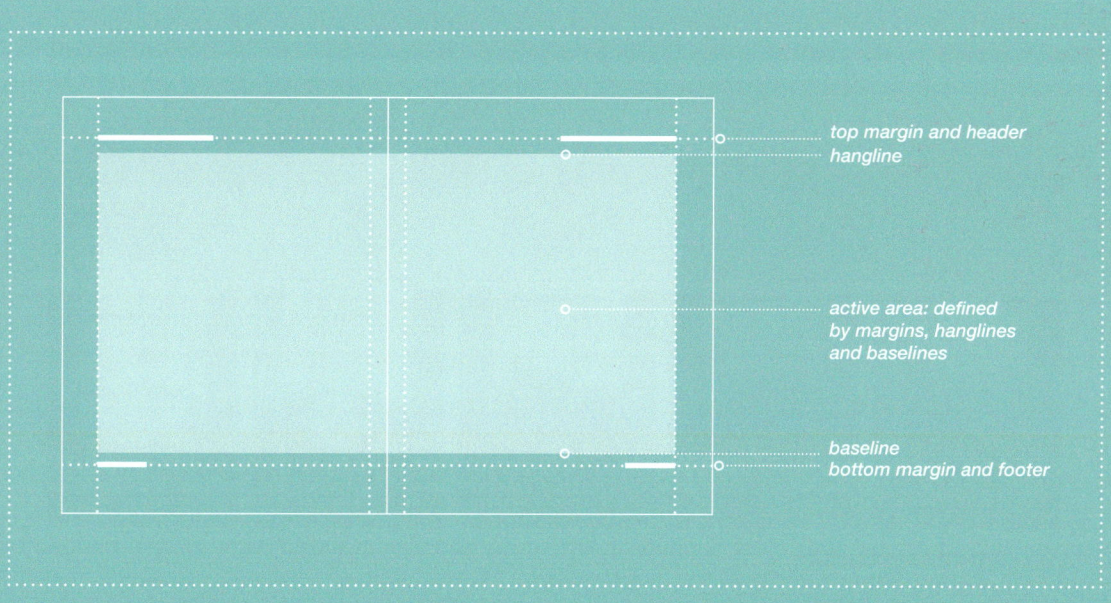

Page margins with header and footer material define the active area of a page.

Designing the Active Area

[17] The active area of a layout—or live area as it is often called—is basically the area of the layout that is available to place visual material. Designing the active area is an important step in the visual organization of a portfolio. It allows page after page of different graphic material to read as if it all belongs cohesively together.

The active area is defined by the margins established in the layouts and includes the folio matter—header and footer material—as well as the hanglines and baselines.

Margins

The margins that are established in the document have an incredible importance in the visual structure of the entire portfolio. They make the difference between a well-designed piece and an ill-conceived attempt at layout design. A well-designed set of margins clearly defines the active area and is consistently used page after page. These margins allow enough white space on the page to firmly root the visual material to the page. A poorly designed set of margins either has too much white space around the visual material or not enough white space. Too much white space makes the images feel compressed as if the white space has too much visual power over the images—it becomes difficult to visually enter the material. Too little white space makes the images feel as if they are sliding off the page and can make the images so uncomfortable on the page that it is again difficult to visually enter them. However, as always, there are opportunities to break these rules.

Luckily, there are a few very simple rules to follow that will make the design of the page margins simple and successful. Just remember that ultimately setting up the margins is purposefully designing the active area.

Constructing the Persuasive Portfolio: the only primer you'll ever need

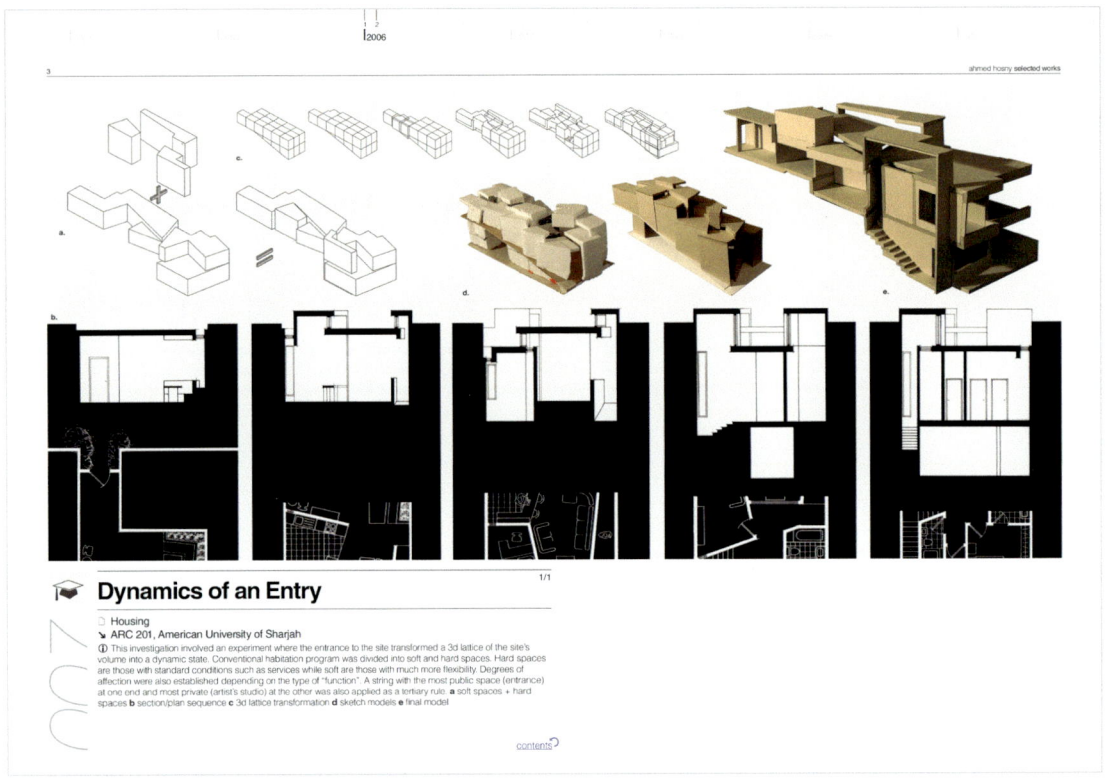

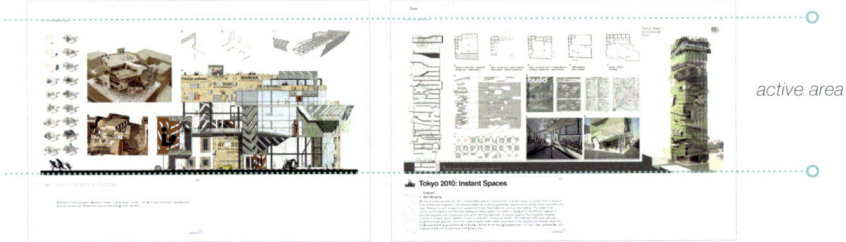

active area

The active area is defined by strong top and bottom horizontal margins. In this case, the designer has used the top margin for a timeline that organizes all projects across time. The bottom margin is used exclusively for text descriptions. Portfolio design by Ahmed Hosny.

Designing Portfolio Systems—Systems of Visual Structure

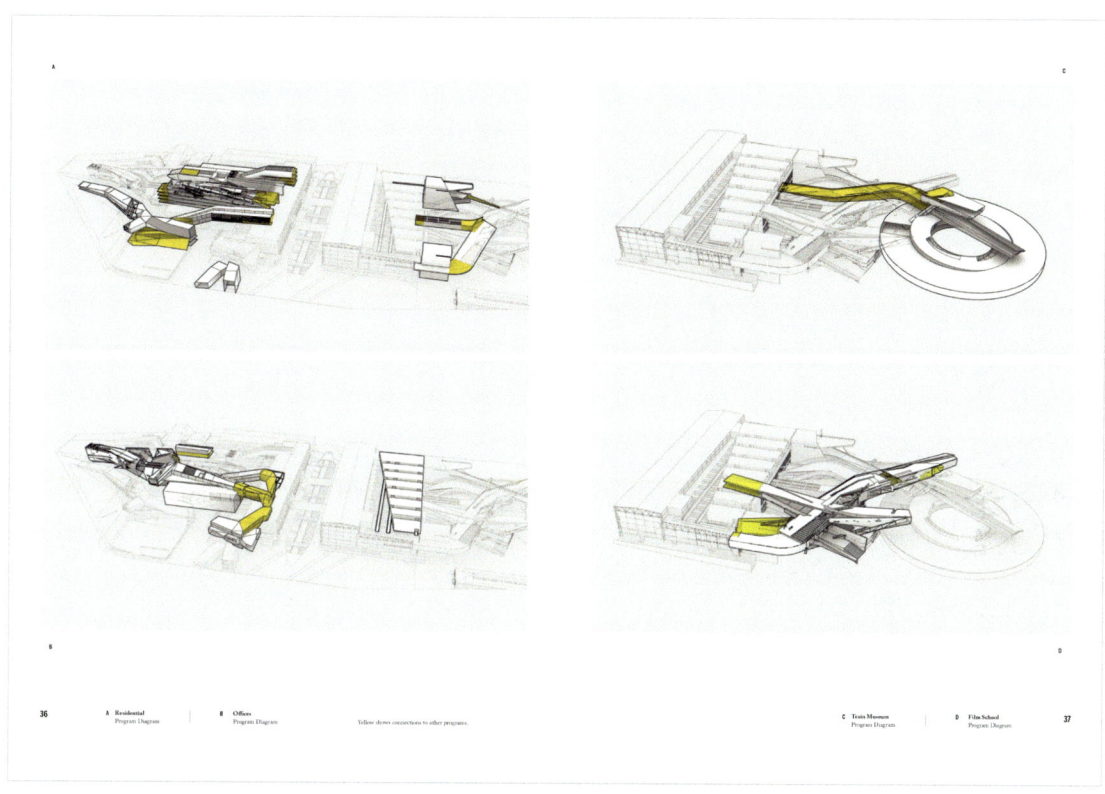

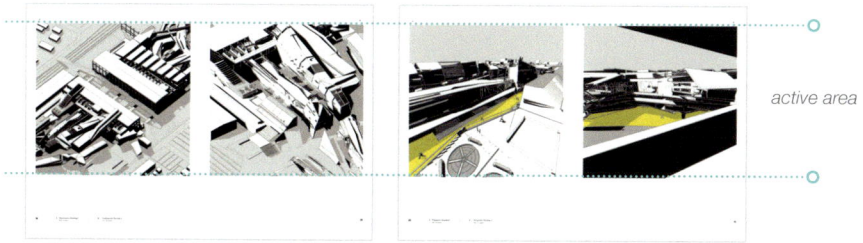

active area

The active area is defined by strong top and bottom horizontal margins.
Portfolio design by Ryan Tyler Martinez.

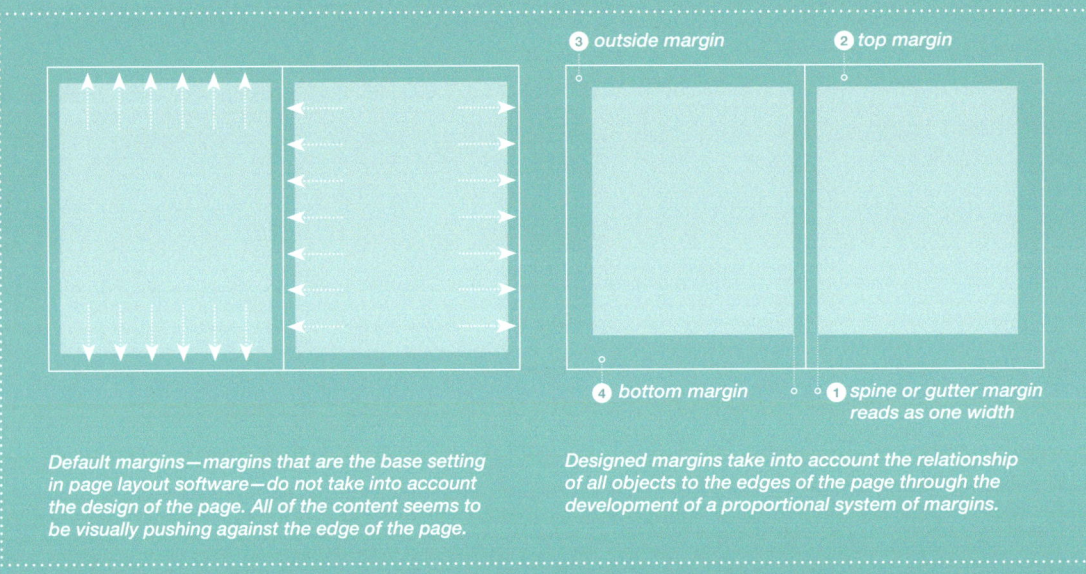

Default margins—margins that are the base setting in page layout software—do not take into account the design of the page. All of the content seems to be visually pushing against the edge of the page.

Designed margins take into account the relationship of all objects to the edges of the page through the development of a proportional system of margins.

Design your page margins; do not rely on the default settings.

The following margin guidelines move from the smallest margin to largest.

1. Spine Margin: The smallest margin should be at the spine. There does need to be a margin here because otherwise images will visually fall into the gutter. This margin is also called the inside margin.

2. Top Margin: The top margin should be larger than the spine and should allow for some visual room at the top of the page. Using 1/4" or less for any page margin is too small—it creates an uncomfortably small relationship between an image and the page edge.

3. Outside Margin: The outside margin should be the same or larger than the top margin. The outside margin has the same "proximity to edge" issues as the top margin and has the added issue in print format of being the location for the hands holding the book which could obscure any content located too close to the edge.

4. Bottom Margin: The bottom margin should be the largest margin of all of the layout margins. The bottom of the layout page has to respond to issues of optical weight and the visual gravity of the page. Just as objects in three-dimensional space have a relationship to gravity, so too do visual objects on a page. Simply put, if the bottom margin is at the same distance as the outside margin, objects will appear to fall off the bottom of the page. By increasing the bottom margin slightly, it gives adequate white space to balance the visual tendency for graphic material to slide uncomfortably down to the bottom of the page.

There are always exceptions to any rules defined by the designer in the portfolio structure and there are certainly times when the rules that define the active area should be broken.

Designing Portfolio Systems—Systems of Visual Structure

When to Break the Rules

Optical Edge and Margins

One way to break the rules relative to margins and the active area of a layout is by passing a graphic beyond the optical edge of a margin. Small pieces of drawings, titles or, in some cases, punctuation can extend into the page margin as long as the primary visual material stays within the optical edge. Determining what can extend beyond the optical edge depends largely on the visual weight of the piece considered for extension. Extending a visually heavy graphic beyond the optical edge will effectively shorten the margin. So only extend those items beyond the optical edge that are visually lighter than other objects on the page. This will visually maintain the proper margins while allowing for some flexibility right at the optical edge.

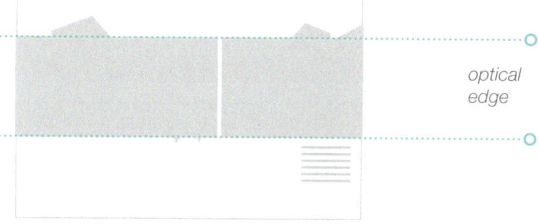

Breaking the horizontal image margins by using the optical edge along with left and right bleeds creates a great deal of dynamism within the white space and makes it very easy to visually enter the images. Portfolio design by Callie Eitzen.

Bleeds

Bleeds are another way to effectively break the rules that define the active area of a layout. A bleed is an image that essentially bleeds over the edge of the page, extending past margins and covering the entire page. There are several types of bleeds:

1. Full bleed: A full bleed is where the image bleeds over all four edges of a layout, obliterating any margins that have been established.

2. Partial bleed: A partial bleed obliterates the margin in one to three of the edges of a layout. So at least one edge still maintains the proper, established margin.

Sometimes content just does not work with all the visual rules that have been established for the portfolio. The bottom line is this: if the layout looks strange to the point that it is visually distracting to the content, change the layout.

There is some content that needs to rely on optical correctness so that it simply "looks" correct. In these cases, rely on the designer's eye to correct the visual distractions. Just be careful not to stray too far away from the system. An entirely new visual distraction could be developed!

Don't forget the intrinsic value of consistent graphic indicators: the table of contents, header and footer material, page numbers, section divider spreads, typeface use consistency, and project introduction pages. These pieces of visual structure are vitally important to support the overall visual structure established in the portfolio and help maintain persistent structure throughout. It is imperative that these graphic indicators remain absolutely consistent throughout the entire portfolio.

Keeping the graphic indicators consistent will allow for the occasional breaking of the structural rules without completely disorientating the reviewer.

Designing Portfolio Systems—Systems of Visual Structure

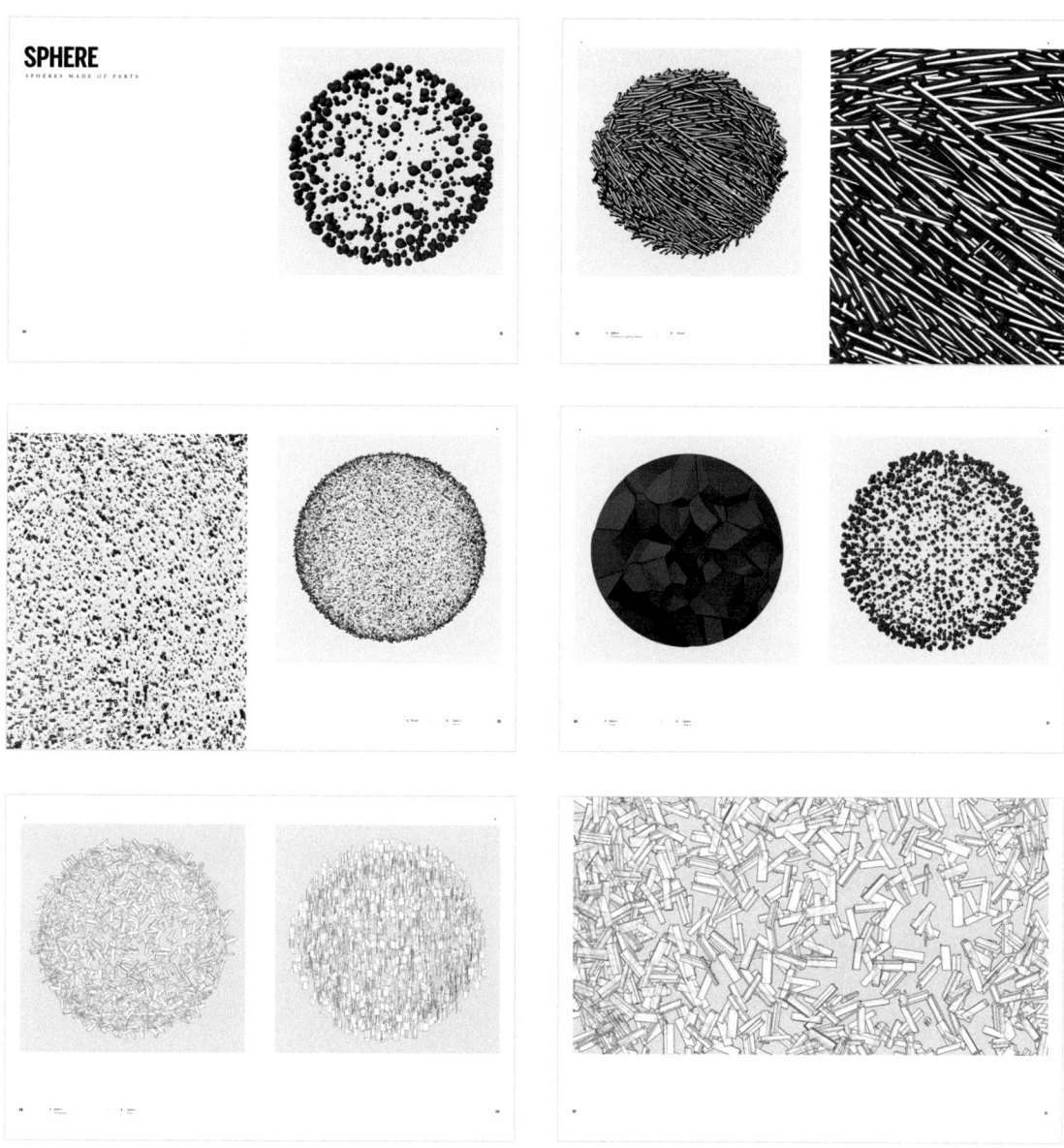

Bleeds working in a variety of directions are used to expand the visual space of the page. Portfolio design by Ryan Tyler Martinez.

following page: *A full bleed image is used just as it is in the author's portfolio, to establish a visual break in the portfolio and allow a moment of pause to view the depth of the image. Portfolio design by See Jia Ho.*

Visual Relationships between Objects on a Page

There are important visual relationships between objects on a page that can adjust the reading of the content. These relationships are defined by each object's proximity to the next. Each object on the page has a margin around it that determines its specific adjacency to the next object. Objects that have smaller margins are often read as pairs or sets of objects and therefore will be read as a unit. Adjusting these margins to reflect the relationships between objects on a page will help organize the visual content.

Visually Entering the Content

One of the primary goals of including material in a portfolio is to have someone actually understand what the designer has been working on, how they think through things and what they think is important. How the visual information is arranged on the page affects a person's ability to visually enter the content on a spread. What does that mean exactly? There are really two ways a person can view a portfolio spread:

1. They can see the pattern that is present through the grid and adjacencies that you employ OR

2. They can visually enter an image and immediately comprehend the intent of the content.

Obviously, it is better to have a portfolio reviewer understand the content rather than just view it at a surface level, only seeing the pattern of the arrangement of images. Ultimately, the actual design work should remain in the mind of the reviewer—an image or series of images that they will relate back to the author. It would be a shame if all they remembered were the patterns of image alignments and not the work itself.

So, part of the challenge in the design of a portfolio is to make appropriate visual arrangements and alignments so that the content is understood. There are many strategies to achieve this and it is usually a combination of them all that works best.

Visual Stickiness: The Power of the Primary Image

Visual stickiness is the idea of an image or series of images that is so visually powerful that it only takes one glance for that particular image to be remembered. It is a good strategy when setting up a portfolio to have the idea of visual stickiness in mind. The best scenario outcome is for the reviewer of the portfolio to be able to remember specific content long after reviewing the work. Consider designing project layouts so that there is an obvious primary image that can stand as visual representation for the entire project; this image should be large and visually powerful relative to other content for that project.

Adjacency Relationships between Content: Packs and Pairings of Visual Information

Visual content that is placed in a purposeful adjacent relationship will be read together. It is important to know that slight spacing adjustments between visual content can vary the reading and understanding of graphic material widely. In portfolio design, this simple ordering principle can be used in a powerful way. However, it is important to understand the ramifications of these adjacency decisions.

Visual content located in close adjacency will be understood as a grouping of information and can be read with the same content definition.

Content Pairs
Content pairs operate in sets of two. The adjacency relationship must allow the two elements to visually attach to one another and separate from the remainder of the content on the page. Content pairs can have either a vertical or horizontal relationship.

Content Sets
Content sets operate similarly to content pairs but with a greater amount of content elements in play. The adjacency relationships between all elements in a content set must be similar such that the entire set reads as a whole. Content sets can have solely vertical relationships, solely horizontal relationships or a combination of vertical and horizontal relationships.

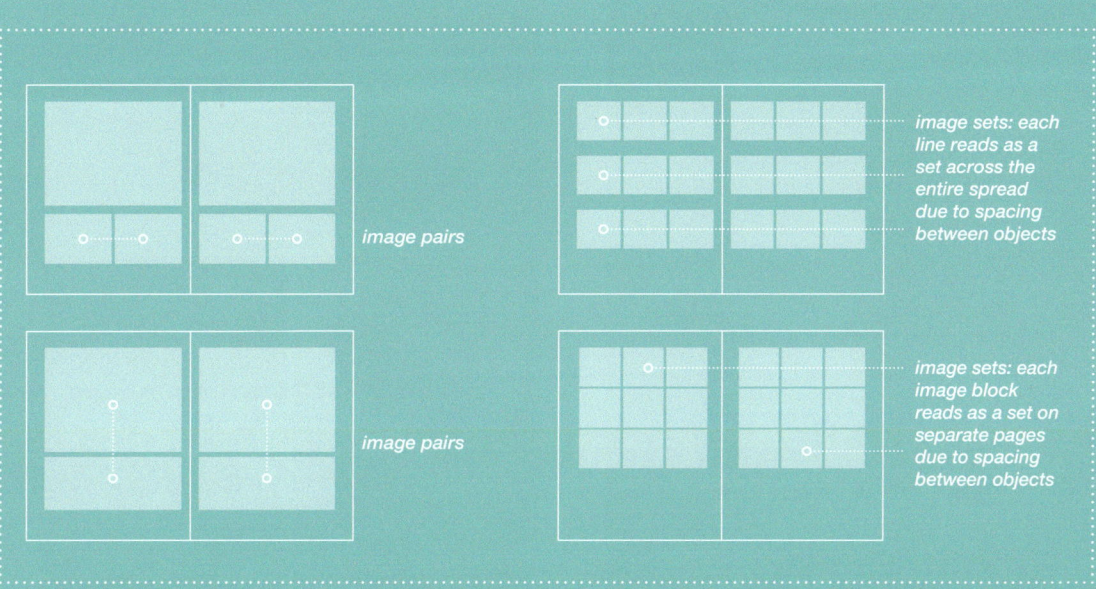

Image pairs and sets should be used to group like items together so they will be read and considered whole.

Content Series
A content series typically shows content elements in relation to one another. In this type of visual set, the content needs to be visually similar such that the reader can determine the differences between each piece of content in the series.

Chronology Content
Chronology content displays content in the order in which it was generated. While chronology content is relative to time in the sense of order, the chronology is not tied to specific periods of time.

Timeline Content
Timeline content is similar to chronology content. However, timeline content is tied to specific intervals of time.

Video and Film Content
Video or film content provides specific challenges in a print portfolio. However, it can be quite effective to display film stills in an adjacent relationship. There is no way to show all of the film stills so selections need to be made based on the visual importance of the individual film stills. The film stills should read continuously—just as film stills and films are understood—with no visual gaps between the images. It is an effective technique to shift each row of content so that the stills do not line up in a vertical fashion—this aids in the horizontal reading of the stills. Also, letting the images bleed off the page both right and left implies movement—this also aids in the visual understanding of the stills in a cinematic relationship.

Constructing the Persuasive Portfolio: the only primer you'll ever need

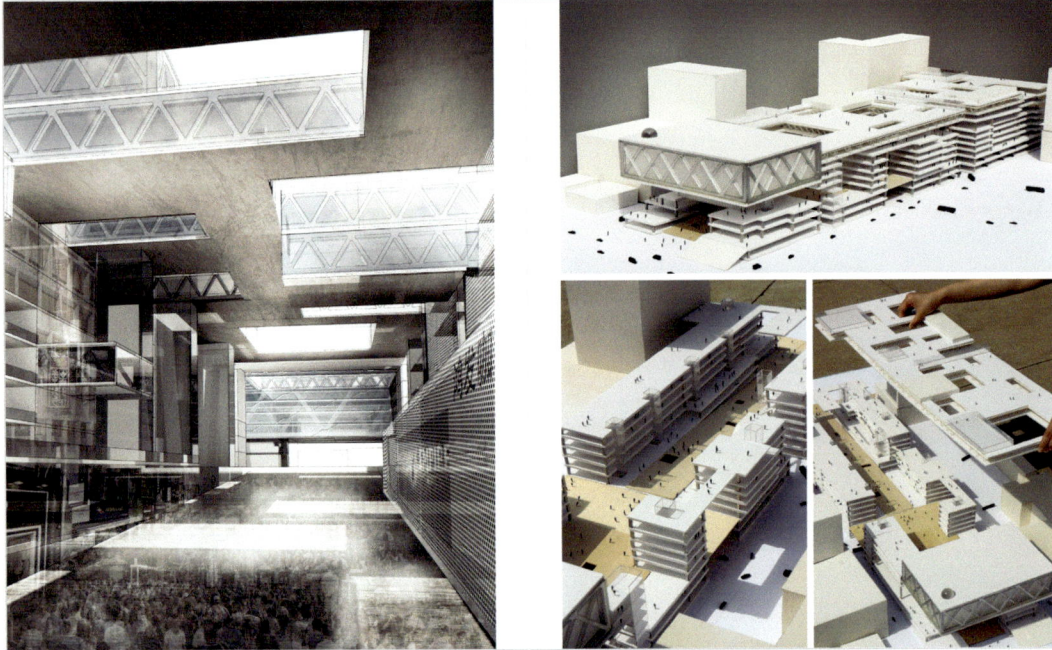

Image pairing is used to emphasize the floor plate relationships. Portfolio design by Oliver Vranesh.

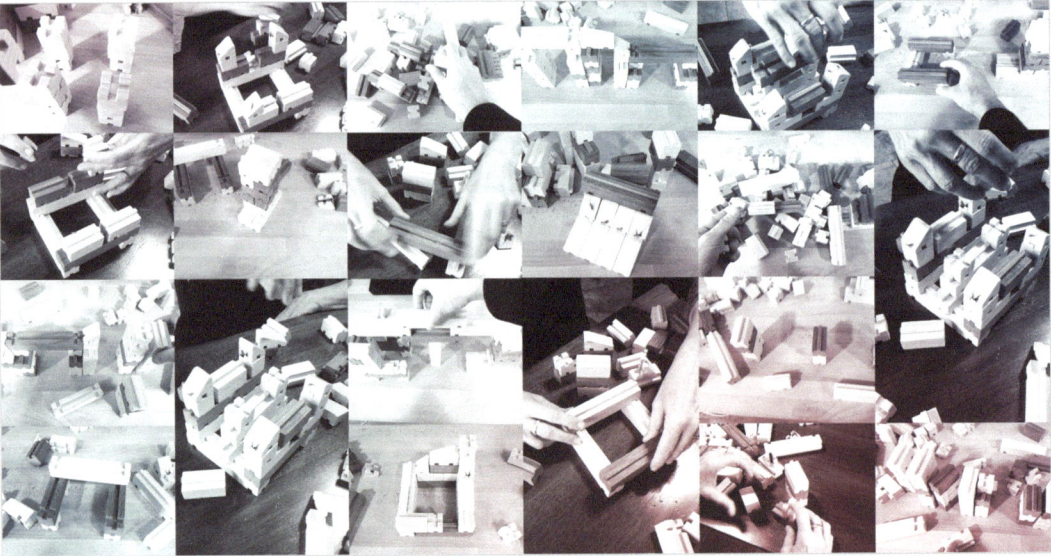

A large image set describes the assembly method. Portfolio design by Casey Tucker.

Designing Portfolio Systems—Systems of Visual Structure

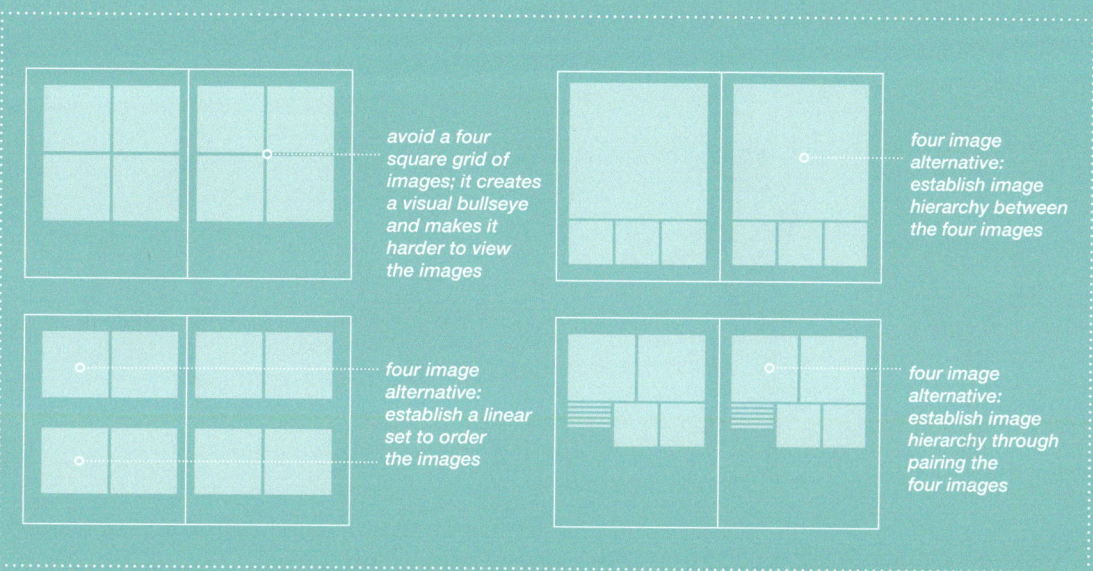

Arranging images in a four square grid creates a bullseye in the middle of the margin intersection and distracts from the viewing of the actual images. Try an alternate layout instead.

Four Square Grids
Four square grids are a common alignment system that should be avoided. When content is arranged in a four square grid, the most powerful visual element is the white space void at the intersection of the grid. If the eye goes automatically to the center point of the grid, then the content is visually missed.

Rule of Thirds
The rule of thirds is a basic compositional technique typically used to organize elements in a photographic composition. The idea is that major elements are placed on an equal nine-square grid at the intersection of the horizontal and vertical grid lines. The rule of thirds also works for page layout.

A Note on Caption and Title Adjacencies
Captions and titles need special care when they are arranged on the page. The adjacency relationship to the content they define is critical. If captions are visually too far from their respective content, two things happen. First, the caption reads as a separate visual element on the page, further cluttering the legibility of the content on the page. Second, the role of the caption—to specifically define visual content—is lost.

Title adjacencies work in a similar fashion. Without proper adjacency to the content they title, extra visual elements clutter the page and the contents are not defined—a confusing visual situation at best.

Constructing the Persuasive Portfolio: the only primer you'll ever need

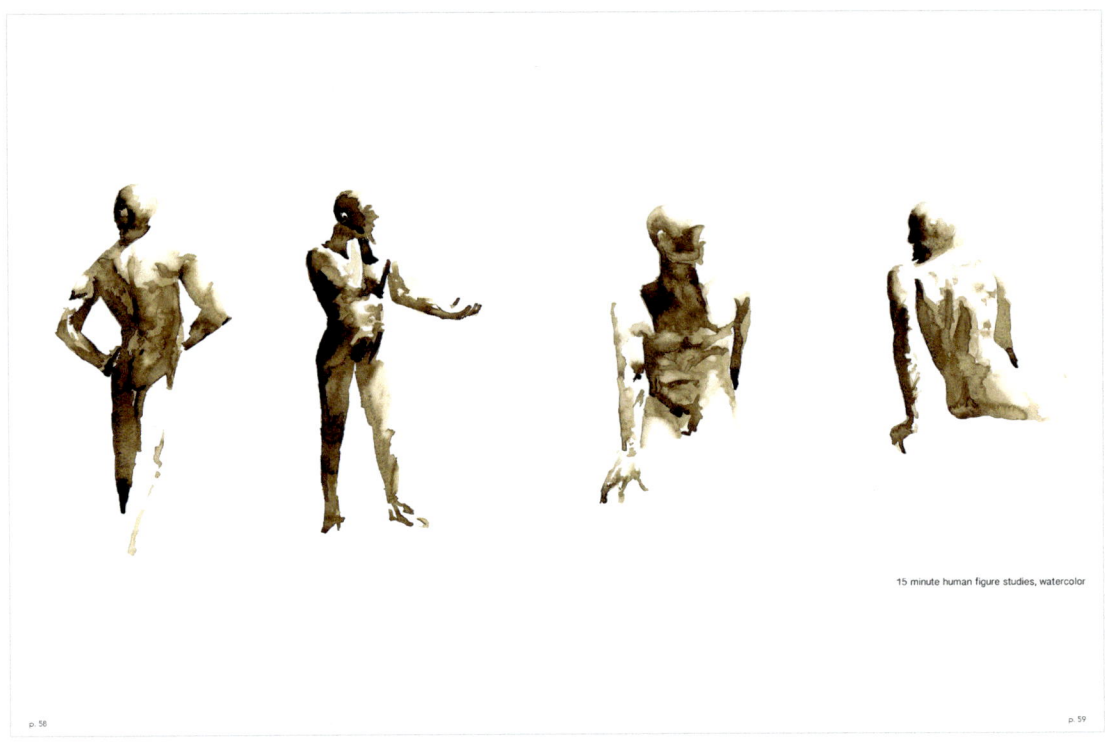

Irregular white space around the figures allows the eye to roam the page. Portfolio design by Christopher G. Beck.

White Space on Page

The design of white space on a page can be tricky. Fight the urge to fill up every bit of a page with imagery; it is one of the biggest mistakes made in portfolio design. There are instances where image series or sets on a spread make sense but there are specific adjacency rules to which to adhere.

Sufficient white space allows directionality for the eye to move around on the page. Directionality on the page is a good thing; it tells the reviewer where to visually move their eyes next. A successful page layout uses white space to give some visual breathing room so the eye can enter content and retreat from content. All of this happens subconsciously, but without the necessary white space the eye begins to read the pattern again instead of the content.

As discussed in the adjacency section, remember multiple images on a page will often be read as a set, particularly if all the images are the same size with the same margins between them. This adjacency relationship is not necessarily a bad thing, but just make sure to make it a purposeful decision.

Varied White Space versus Equal White Space
If the content on a spread has equal white space on the page—equal on all sides of the images—then the content appears very static and it becomes difficult for the eye to move around the page and actually "enter" or "see" the content of the visual material. Varied white space provides a dynamic layout that encourages the eye to move quickly in some areas and linger in others. Be aware that neither varied nor equal is necessarily better, they are just different and it is important to understand the difference.

Overlapping Content

As a general rule, overlapping content can be visually distracting and should be approached with caution. For starters, overlapping an image with another image tends to look like something that was included in a scrapbook made for a family member in elementary school. That's not exactly the impression to be given with a professional portfolio, is it? Avoid overlapping images entirely.

It is fine to overlap an image with text but this should be used with discretionary caution. There are many instances where text by necessity has to overlap an image—it could be caption text, title text, etc. Be careful when there is so much text over an image that either the text becomes illegible or the image becomes illegible. Long sections of text over an image are problematic because usually an image has a variety of color values and part of the text may read clearly, while another portion of the text may blend in with the color in the image and disappear. One solution to this is to put a solid block of color on a layer between the image and the text. This solid block of color needs to have some transparency applied to it so that it is not entirely opaque. Done in this manner, the image can be seen through the transparent film while the text can still be read clearly. Experiment with this at each application; the image, text and transparent film are all separate variables for each instance.

It is possible to have images or drawings physically impose on one another but not visually overlap. This scenario is more readily applied when you are working with drawings or images that have a white background so that the actual overlap disappears into the white of the page and is not read as an overlap at all.

When Content Jumps the Gutter

When working on a double page spread that will be printed, consider the content that either falls into the gutter or jumps the gutter. The gutter of a book is the margin area that is pinched by the binding at the center of the spread. Since layouts are digitally designed as if they are always flat and open, the situation in the gutter is often overlooked. If planning a printed portfolio with a spiral binding, the gutter will actually be a split gap between the pages. This type of binding will lay flat but the image will be physically split apart. If the printed portfolio has a soft or hard case binding, the pages won't be physically separated as in the spiral binding but there will be a gutter area at the binding that will swallow visual material if it isn't carefully placed.

The gutter obviously doesn't exist in digital portfolios since there isn't the physicality of two pages bound together in a spread; no need to worry there. If, however, the portfolio has been designed to work both in print and digital formats—and that would be the smart way to do it—pay attention to the content in the gutter.

The bottom line on this issue is that nothing important should be close to the gutter.

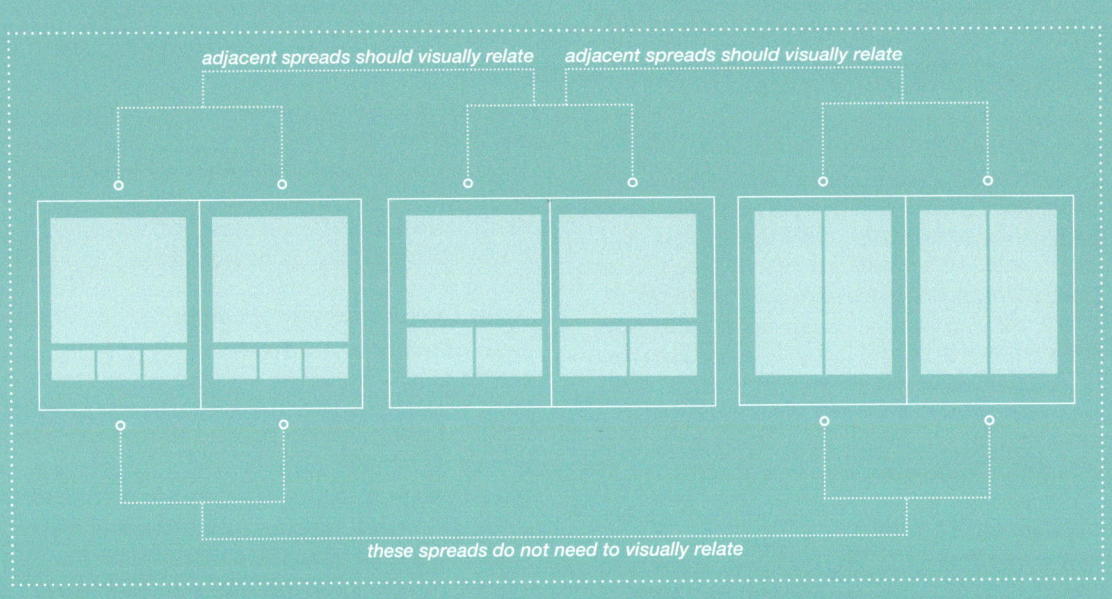

Pace design option one—visually relate adjacent spreads.

Visual Pace

19

Pace was previously discussed in the visual storyboard section but it bears mentioning again in relation to structural grids and adjacencies. Be careful not to get in a layout rut and use the exact same alignment grid on every single spread. It is tricky because the layouts need to be similar enough so they are read as a set but different enough so they don't get monotonous. The only time this is a significant problem is if the exact same layout is used page after page. Once this happens, the reviewer begins to recognize the pattern of the layout design and is no longer able to see the content of the images.

One way to do this is to try to think of each layout as a design project in of itself. Each layout has to relate to the previous spread and the forthcoming spread. Another strategy is to simply insert visual breaks between repetitive spreads to alter the visual relationship between adjacent spreads. Inserting a full-page bleed is one of the most effective ways to create this visual break. Visual variety as the reviewer moves through the portfolio is necessary to keep them engaged in the visual content.

Designing Portfolio Systems—Systems of Visual Structure

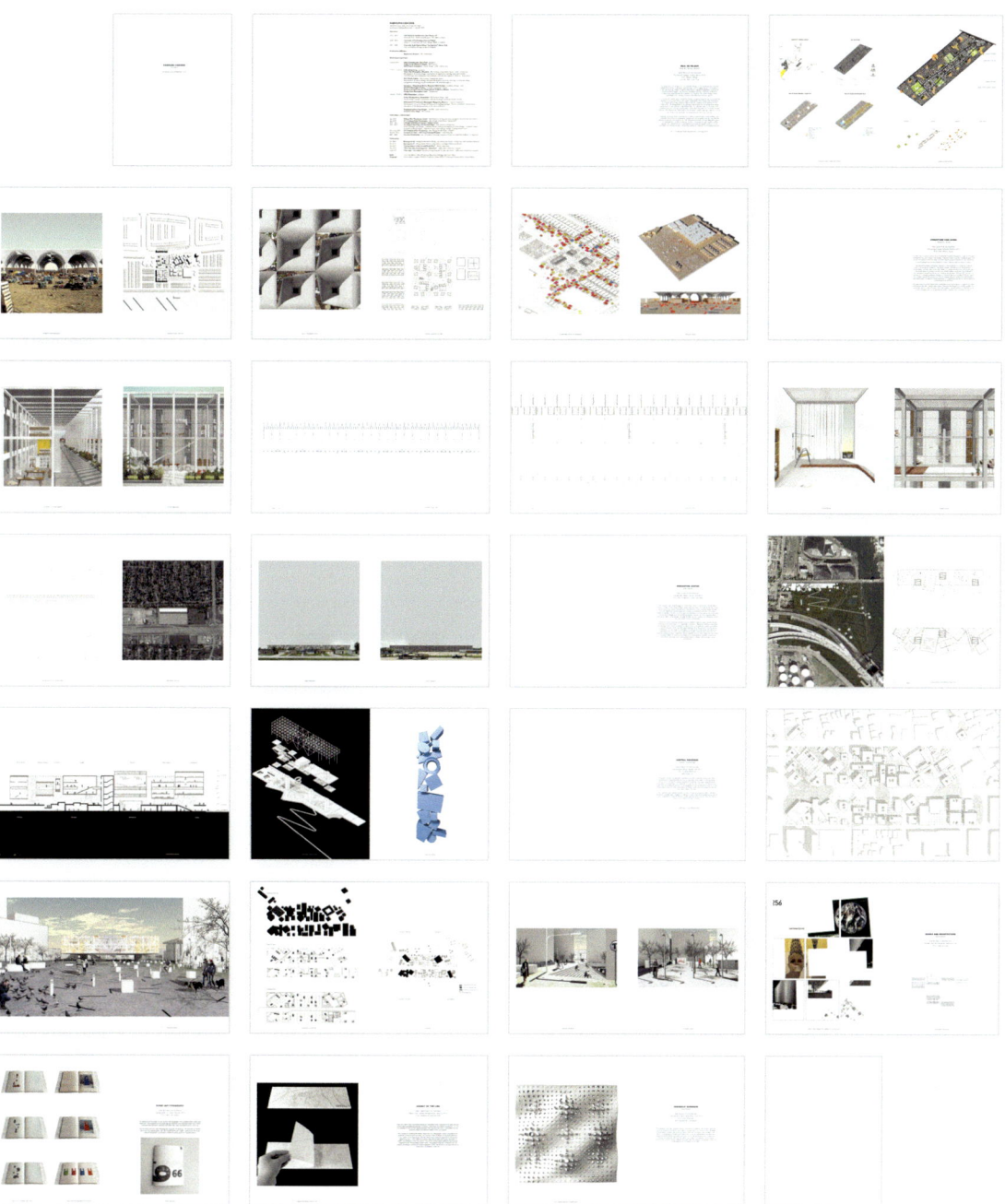

Pace design option two—break the rhythm of similar layouts with images that are partial or full bleed images. Portfolio design by Karolina Czeczek.

Designing the

94 Representation Strategies: Graphic Design Basics
Visual Order and Visual Hierarchy
Typography
Graphic Punctuation
Graphics: How Far Is Too Far

120 Project Narrative Visual Representation
Determining Holes in the Project Narrative
Representing Work: Does Additional Material Need to Be Produced?
How Many Projects Should Be Included?
Visual and Verbal Representation of Design Thinking
Architectural Symbols and Conventions for Presentation Drawings

Graphic Layout

144　Text in Your Portfolio: What it Says and How it Looks
What it Says: The Value of Words
How it Looks: The Graphic Presence of Text in a Portfolio
Content and Visual Goals of Text in a Portfolio
Architecture Specific Text Issues

156　Editing and Reviewing Your Work
Visual Review Process
Editing Checklists

Designing the

Design Actions

 Establish visual order and visual hierarchy. page 94

 Get a handle on graphic rules of typography and implement them. page 108

 Learn correct graphic punctuation and put what you've learned to good use. page 115

 Don't screw it all up with goofy graphics. page 116

There are quite a few ideas that can be borrowed from the profession of graphic design to use as guidelines for our purposes in portfolio design. This section covers graphic issues of primary importance. For additional information, there are many good texts on graphic design available. Keep in mind, however, that graphic design and architecture are two very different professions. Graphic design should be viewed through an architectural lens to stay relevant to issues of visual communication in architecture. Not all graphic design principles apply to visual communication in the realm of architecture.

Visual Order and Visual Hierarchy

Visual order and visual hierarchy are two design principles that are very closely related; yet these two principles achieve different goals for a design layout. For the purposes of this discussion, relate both of these ideas to the specific design of page layouts and spreads.

Visual Order

Visual order describes the visual cohesiveness of objects ordered together on a page. In general, the visual goal is

Graphic Layout

Representation Strategies: Graphic Design Basics

for a two-page spread to read as a cohesive ordered set of information. There could be an instance where visual discordance works for visual emphasis, but this situation should be the exception to the rule of cohesive order. There are several principles to discuss relative to visual order; keep in mind the goal of visual cohesion and order on your designed portfolio spread with each one.

Visual Hierarchy

Visual hierarchy and visual order are very closely related. Properly applied strategies of visual hierarchy actually strengthen the visual order and vice versa. Remember, to create visual hierarchy, objects on the page must recede visually in order for something else to come forward. Incidentally, this is also an apt description of principles of visual order.

To simplify: Visual order helps with the legibility of your graphics. Visual hierarchy is one of the primary tools used to establish visual order.

Many different components of the design portfolio are discussed in this publication. Principles of visual hierarchy are embedded in the majority of these discussions. In fact, the entire section on Project Narrative Visual Representation and all of the organizational strategies found throughout this book are describing the complexity of systems that lead to visual order through visual hierarchy. Pay attention to typeface relationship and hierarchy, image adjacency and hierarchy, relationship of the content to the page, a variety of levels of reading of a portfolio, and the list goes on. Suffice it to say, all things related to graphic layout have visual hierarchy as an underpinning.

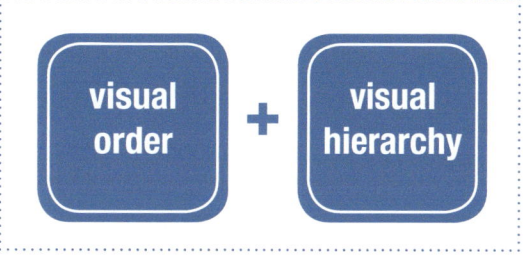

Visual order and visual hierarchy work together and act as ordering systems for the content in your portfolio.

Constructing the Persuasive Portfolio: the only primer you'll ever need

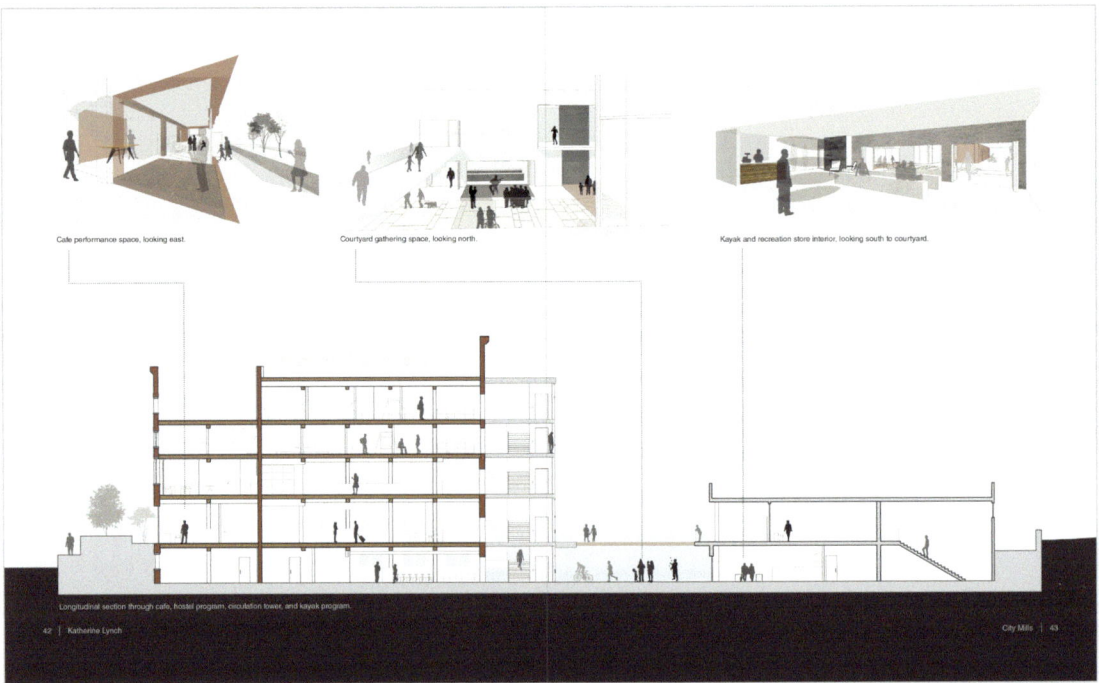

Primary image—longitudinal section—is supported by secondary explanatory images. Portfolio design by Katherine Lynch.

Location of Primary Images

Primary images—those images that have been identified as most important to the message being delivered—need to be carefully sized and placed on the designed spread. Do not be afraid to make the primary image(s) significantly larger than other images on the page. In fact, they can be the only image on the page! If all of the images are the same size, the eye won't understand where to focus on the page and the ability to clearly, visually deliver your ideas will be lost.

Images versus Text

On each and every layout, determine what element(s) should be the most visually prominent. This decision depends on what component of the content narrative is most important to deliver. A clear understanding of what type of content best conveys that goal is needed.

Keep in mind that images and text will often visually compete with one another, particularly if an appropriate visual hierarchy hasn't been determined. A typical strategy is to say that on project introduction pages, there is a specific balance between text—project title information—and the main introduction image. On project content pages, the images have hierarchical precedent over the visual presence of the text.

Designing the Graphic Layout—Representation Strategies: Graphic Design Basics

Single primary images allow the reviewer to focus on exactly what is being visually described in each selected image. Portfolio design by Israel B. Sanchez.

Constructing the Persuasive Portfolio: the only primer you'll ever need

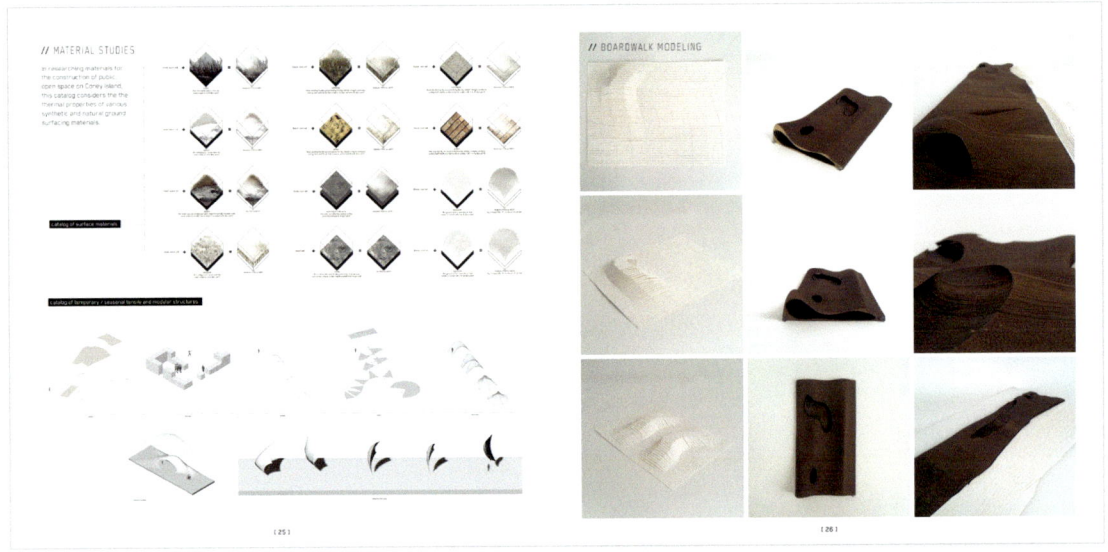

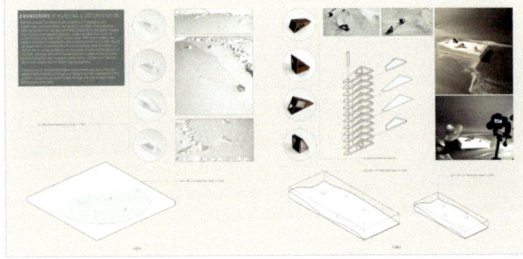

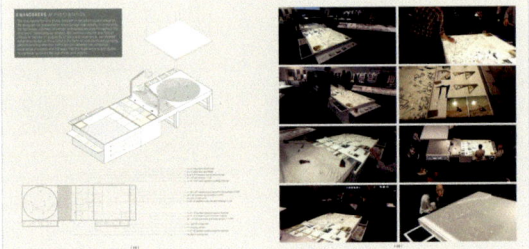

White Space and Adjacencies

White space gets a lot of discussion as a design tool. In this application—the understanding of visual order on a designed spread—white space can be used to help understand which elements on a page belong to one another. Considering all of the elements that need to be combined on a page to convey meaning, it is important to be able to group the relevant information together. These groups are visual packs that together deliver a message about your project. The adjacency relationship between these elements relies on white space to be able to recognize the appropriate separations and adjacencies.

Designing the Graphic Layout—Representation Strategies: Graphic Design Basics

The use of designed white space to gather and pack images together adds visual organization to the design layout for a variety of project types. Portfolio design by Callie Eitzen.

opposite: *Uniform margins between sets of images separate visual information into similar content sets. These sets can then be understood together. As you can see, white space doesn't actually have to be white. Portfolio design by Devin Dobrowolski.*

Constructing the Persuasive Portfolio: the only primer you'll ever need

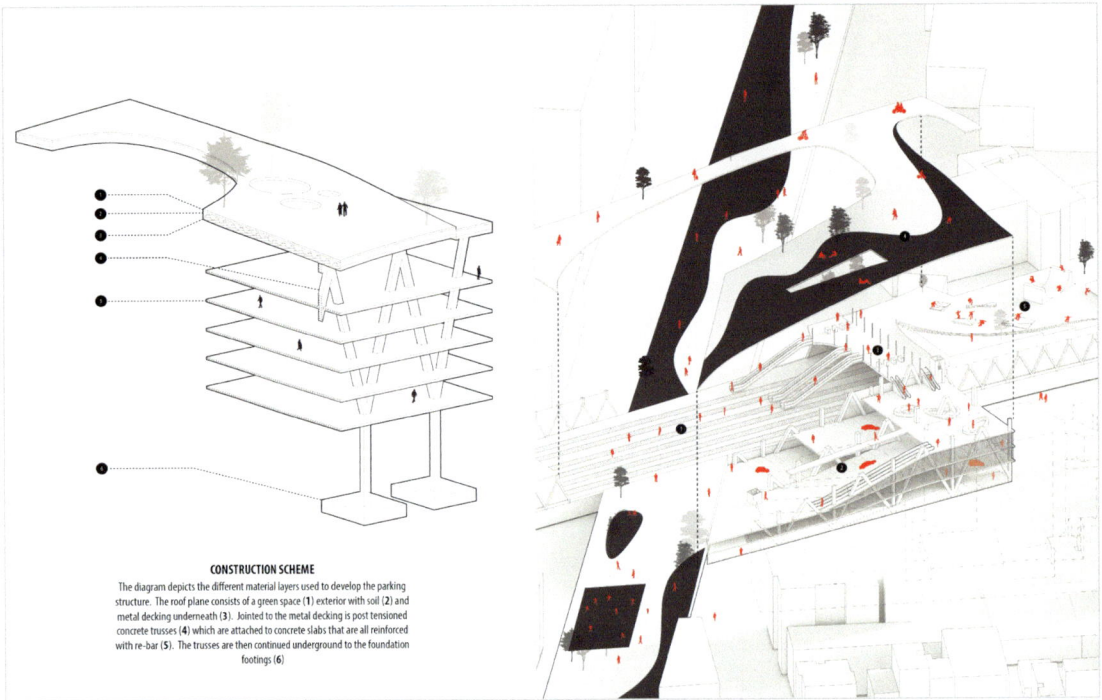

Visual weight is focused on the right-hand side of the spread. Portfolio design by Ibrahim W. Salman.

Visual Weight

There are a few different ways to look at the issue of visual weight as it relates to the designed page. One is a consideration of the western reader's relationship to the physicality of a printed book and the other is a consideration of the perceived relationship between the reviewer and gravity.

Relationship to Printed Book
The way a person flips through a physical book generates guidelines related to visual weight on the page. This phenomenon is only applicable to the design of a physical book that will be printed. When a reader flips through a book, the tendency is to hold the book spine in the left hand and flip through the book with the right hand. This action displays the majority of the right-hand pages of a book. It stands to reason that to catch someone's eye and get them to actually take some time to look through a portfolio, graphic material of visual importance should be located on the right-hand side of the page layout.

Relationship to Gravity
Our relationship to the three-dimensional world translates to our relationship to the two-dimensional world primarily through our understanding of gravity.

For the purposes of this discussion, let's think about gravity as a force that attracts us to any other physical body of mass—the force that attracts the body to the center of the earth. This is a principle we readily

Designing the Graphic Layout—Representation Strategies: Graphic Design Basics

understand. Considering the visual representation of the idea of gravity, think of the image of small objects clustering around a larger object—this automatically sets up a visual hierarchy and thus order. Or consider the visual weight on the page relative to the two-dimensional expression of gravity with the visual weight located at the bottom of the page.

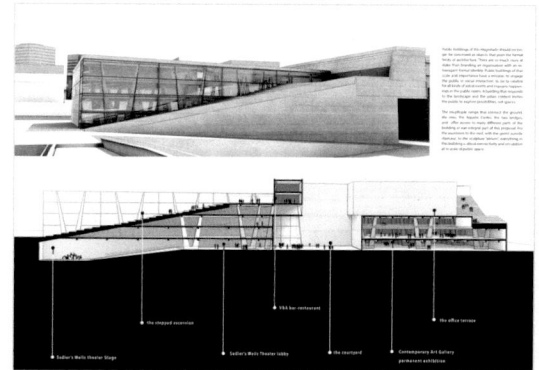

Visual weight located at the bottom of the page. Portfolio design by Fani Christina Papadopoulou.

Constructing the Persuasive Portfolio: the only primer you'll ever need

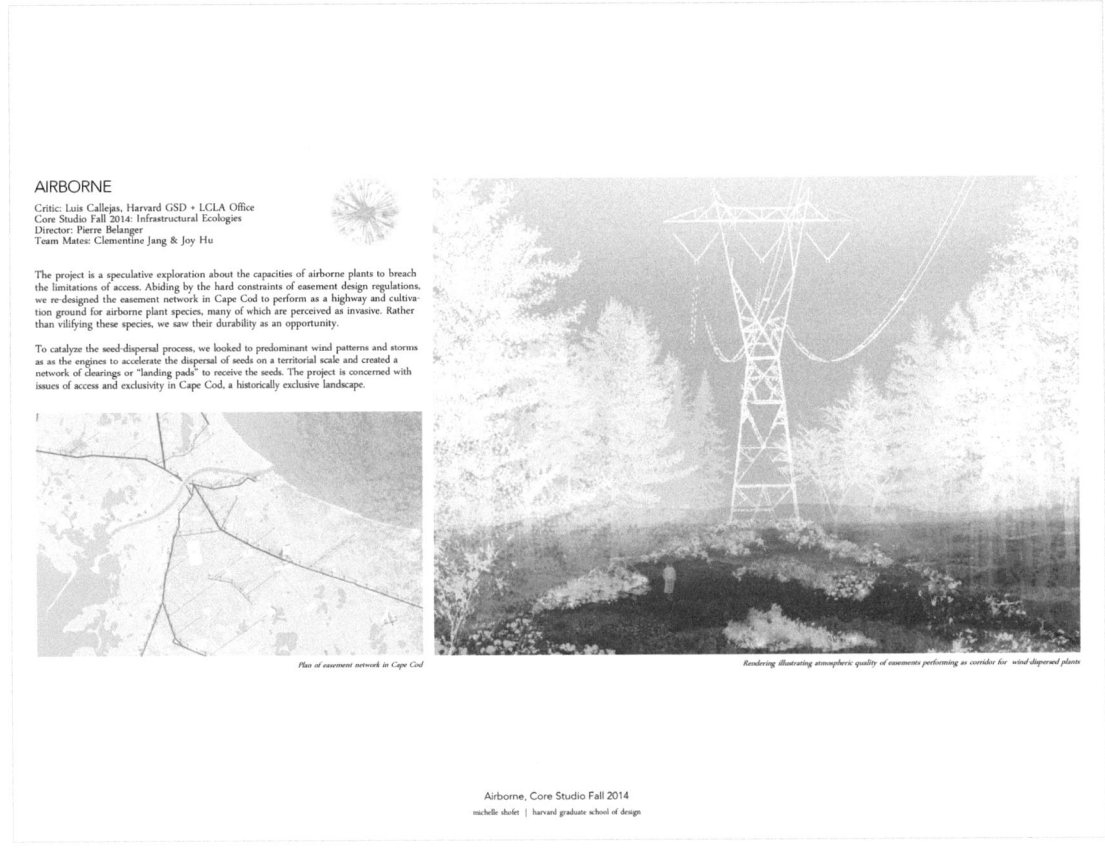

Airborne, Core Studio Fall 2014
michelle shofet | harvard graduate school of design

Use of Color

Color can also play a significant role in the application of visual hierarchy. Consider the use of color for visual hierarchy in two ways.

First, think of color used in a color family to help an entire spread order itself visually. In this case, a color family on a designed spread can visually coalesce the material on the page. You can also think of color in a singular application that will draw the eye and either pull something forward or help it recede.

Color can be used as a visual organizer within a project or throughout the entire portfolio. It can be applied to certain text selections to visually emphasize key words or can be applied in a graphic way for things like section cuts and elements in other drawings to make an entire body of work appear cohesive.

Consider the application of color throughout the entire portfolio as an additional way-finding system to make it easier for the reviewer to understand what section of the book they are in. All of these applications of color should reinforce established ordering principles of the work within the portfolio.

Color versus Black and White

Application of a monotone black and white color family can be just as effective as the application of a more colorful variety. The impact occurs when there is a

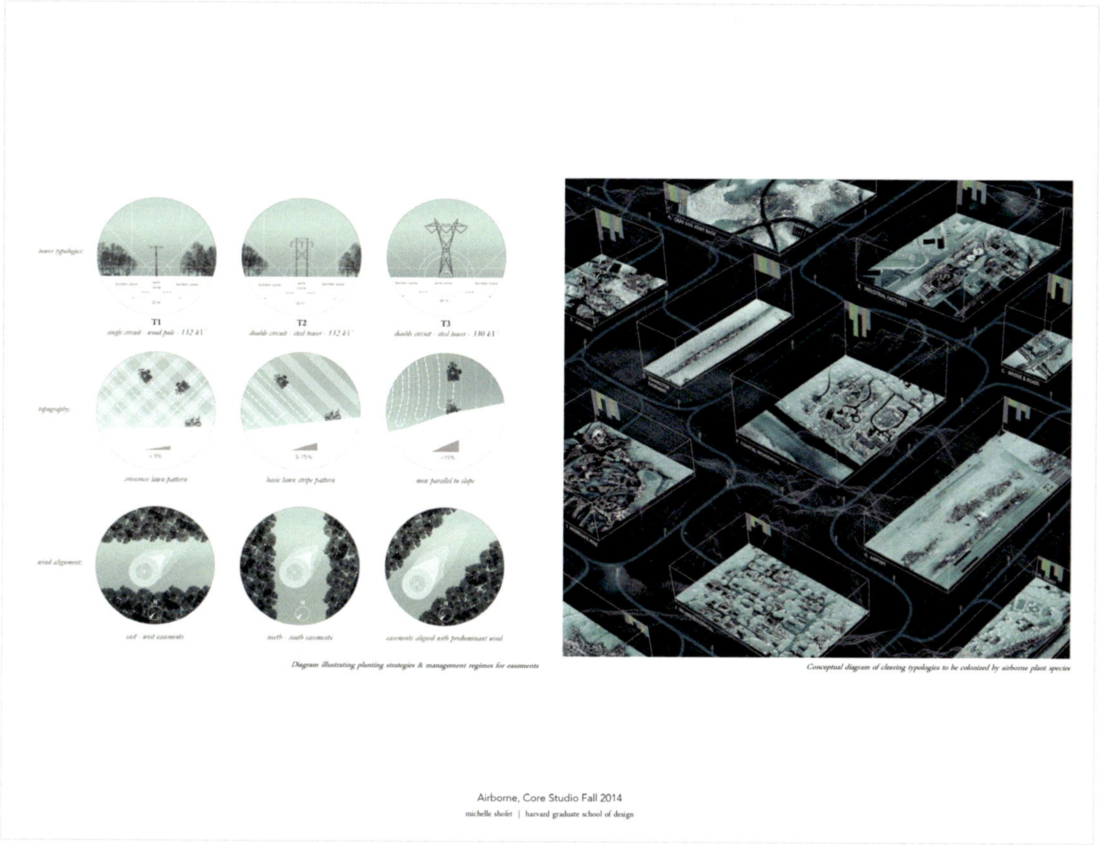

Designing the Graphic Layout—Representation Strategies: Graphic Design Basics

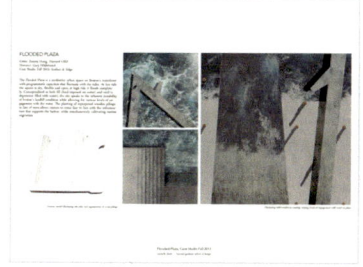

above and opposite: *Beautiful use of color families visually unite the various images and spreads for a cohesive approach to the project artifacts. Portfolio design by Michelle Shofet.*

Constructing the Persuasive Portfolio: the only primer you'll ever need

The Langford revitilzation project focused on crossing phenomenally transparent spaces, pedestrian paths, and light in order to attract more activity and "wake Langford up."

Bright shades of green with deep russet and gray make for a powerful color combination without being distracting to the legibility of the work. Portfolio design by Ethan Miller.

moment of change from an existing system. Don't just think, "I need to add red!" Often a subtle color change can have a striking impact.

Also, when analyzing the use of color on a designed spread, keep in mind that the color family of all of the content on a spread should be balanced. For instance, if there are three model images of a chipboard model and one image of a white museum board model, there may be color match issues. In this case it might work to convert the images of the chipboard model, which are very yellow in nature, to black and white to better balance with the other model image, which is predominantly white.

When designing for print layout that has facing pages, consider the layout of the entire spread as one designed unit. Each single page can be considered separate from the other visually but there must be a higher visual order that relates both pages of a spread together.

Designing the Graphic Layout—Representation Strategies: Graphic Design Basics

Subtle application of bold color visually ties the spreads together. This portfolio has particularly clear use of headers and margins to define the active area. Portfolio design by Chris Kay.

Constructing the Persuasive Portfolio: the only primer you'll ever need

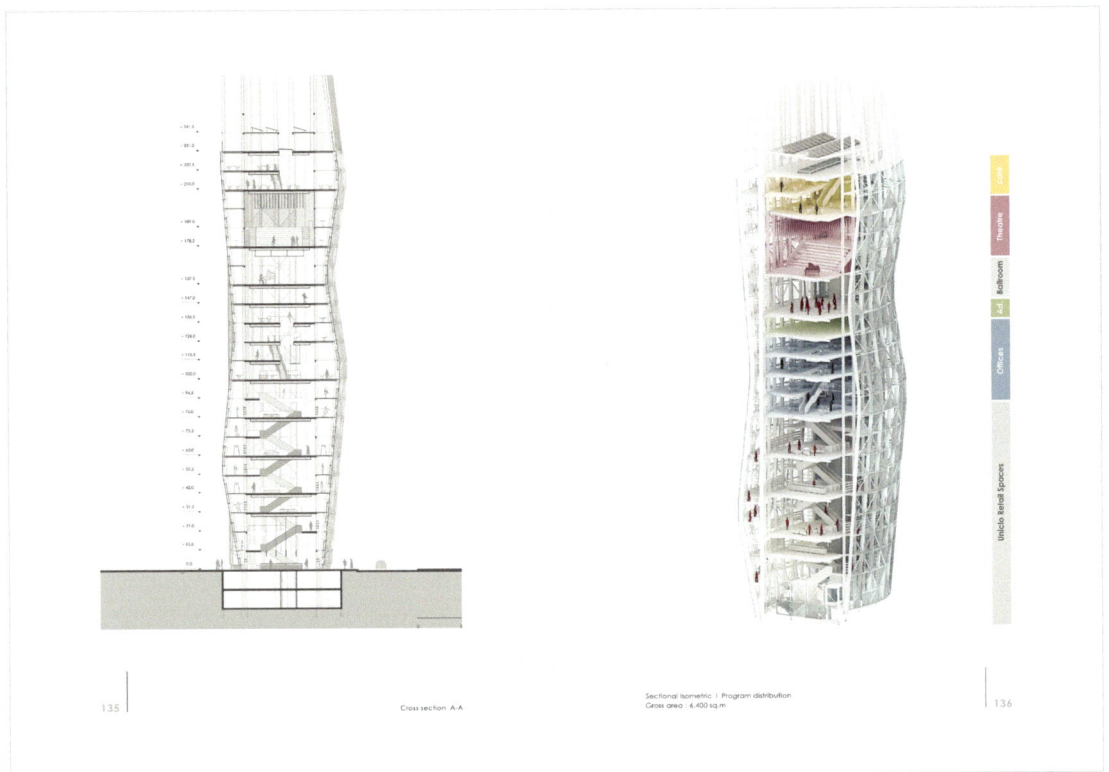

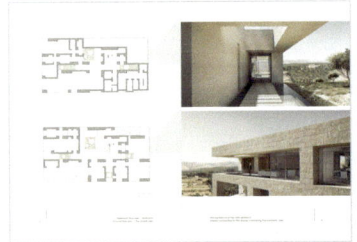 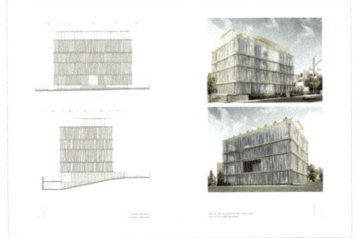 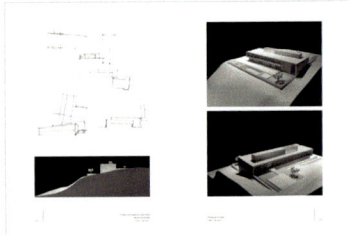

Balance is achieved throughout the portfolio with a single column grid layout. Portfolio design by Rasem Kamal.

opposite: *Balance is achieved through juxtaposition of one large centrally located image and a pair of smaller remote images. Portfolio design by Thomas Johnston.*

Balance versus Symmetry

Balance versus symmetry is a bit of a complex discussion since there are applications of each that are in fact very successful. Because of this, it is hard to make a firm recommendation. Understanding the difference is perhaps the best way to begin.

Symmetry is the easier of the two concepts to discuss. A symmetrical layout is one that has an organization of content that is exactly reflected across a central axis. In layout design the content isn't exactly the same, but the shape of the content is exactly the same.

Pros: A completely symmetrical layout can provide legibility of instant order because it is so easy to read the order. Symmetry is one of the clearest forms of order.

Cons: A purely symmetrical layout can stagnate the viewer's ability to visually enter the content because since the balance of white space is exactly the same, the eye has fewer opportunities to roam around the page.

However, a symmetrical layout with just two large elements tends to be quite successful.

A balanced layout relies on the equal distribution of visual weight without the use of symmetry. This design principle depends on the careful arrangement of different elements to successfully move the eye around the page.

Pros: A balanced layout generates varied white space. This varied white space encourages fluid eye movement around the content. More elements are understood with this visual movement.

Cons: A balanced layout can be difficult to achieve when working with strict grids. Over time with experience your ability to utilize optical balance to determine if something appears balanced will improve.

Typography

When putting together a portfolio, the first thing that comes to mind is a direct focus on the projects that should be included in the portfolio. What needs to be photographed? What needs to be scanned? What needs to be redrawn? How many models need to be repaired? Was the model ever completed? As with all design projects, there are a great number of variables that contribute to the successful design of the portfolio. In this section, typography will be discussed exclusively.

What exactly is the art of typography and why can't typefaces that are just cool be used? First and most importantly, there are graphic conventions that pertain to the use of typography in a visual structure—in this case, the portfolio—that are radically different than typeface conventions previously learned as they relate to writing conventions for something like an English class. It is a completely different scenario when typefaces are used to support the visual structure of a graphic layout. The visual structure of a portfolio relies heavily on the hierarchical framework created through the thoughtful and appropriate use of typography. Think of the typography choices as the visual framework for each spread. By establishing an appropriate visual typeface hierarchy the reviewer can be directed to specific content. Sounds important, doesn't it?

It is easy to identify a portfolio that has been visually destroyed through the use of poor typographic practices. It is also easy to identify a portfolio that has been visually strengthened through fantastic use of typographic practices. The problem is how to convert initial ideas and beginning abilities into something spectacular.

So, what does all of that mean? Some typographic issues are easier to understand than others. There are also some areas for visual choice and, as always, there are just some things that should never be done.

Graphic Rules for Typography: Things You Never Learned in English Composition

When it comes to the written word, there are quite a few differences between rules and guidelines learned in high school or college English courses and rules and guidelines that are part of the profession of design. In particular, there are many graphic design basic guidelines that should be learned and used as part of your portfolio design. Some of these guidelines may run against visual guidelines previously learned. Keep in mind that the visual guidelines learned up to this point have had more to do with a teacher's ability to read and grade an assignment than rules of graphic legibility. So don't fret if something here is different than what you've previously learned; you are in new professional territory now and there are new things to learn!

Typeface Selection

The primary guideline to follow when selecting a typeface for a portfolio is to remember to keep it simple. The typeface should in no way overpower the images and drawings that are the primary focus of the portfolio. Also limit typeface selection to no more than two different typefaces in the entire portfolio. The primary typeface can be used for titles. The secondary typeface can be used for all the other categories: subtitle, body text, caption, drawing or diagram label, and header / footer. However, keep in mind appropriate typeface hierarchy is required and can be achieved while using one typeface. See the section on Typeface Range below.

Establish a visual hierarchy within the typeface selection that establishes the appropriate visual focus on each typeface while keeping in mind the typeface should always support the visual image and should never overpower your content graphics. Follow this list as a guideline of typeface hierarchy from most visually prominent to least visually prominent:

1. Title
2. Subtitle
3. Body text
4. Caption
5. Drawing or diagram label
6. Header or footer including page numbers

helvetica neue ultralight
helvetica neue thin
helvetica neue light
helvetica neue regular
helvetica neue medium
helvetica neue bold
helvetica neue condensed bold
helvetica neue condensed black

It is important to select a typeface with a wide visual range so there are plenty of hierarchical options.

Aa — serif, typeface is georgia 60pt

Aa — slab serif, typeface is rockwell 60pt

Aa — sans serif, typeface is tahoma 60pt

Make purposeful selections based on the visual legibility of the typeface in the specific design of your portfolio.

Typeface Range

When choosing a typeface, select one that has a broad visual range. That means it has built into its style at least three ranges of weight—usually a light, medium and bold. A weight range like this will afford enough variance to establish an appropriate hierarchy of typefaces within your graphic spread.

If a typeface doesn't have enough hierarchical range, the amount of black can be reduced creating a lighter body of text in gray. This automatically establishes a hierarchical relationship between the black text and the gray text.

Serif versus Sans Serif

There are different schools of thought when it comes to the selection of serif or sans serif typefaces for practical typeface legibility. First, the difference needs to be defined. Individual characters in a serif typeface have serifs associated with them; a serif is a small line attached to the end of a stroke in a letter. So typefaces that have this additional line are called serif typefaces and typefaces without this additional line are called sans serif typefaces.

Determining which style to select depends entirely on the legibility of the typeface at the actual size it will be presented in the portfolio. Some argue that serif typefaces make it easier for the eye to read the shape of words and therefore are more legible than sans serif typefaces. Others argue that sans serif typefaces are visually cleaner than serif typefaces and are therefore easier to read.

Determine typeface selection by testing different typefaces in your portfolio to determine which is best. Select the typeface that is the least visually distracting on the page while still being legible.

The human eye uses the visual reference of typographic ascenders and descenders found in lowercase letters to help identify words by the actual shape of the word while simultaneously reading the word letter by letter. When you put a paragraph of text in all uppercase letters, you are denying the reader the ability to recognize the shape of the word and it becomes much more difficult to read the body of text.

THE HUMAN EYE USES THE VISUAL REFERENCE OF TYPOGRAPHIC ASCENDERS AND DESCENDERS TO HELP IDENTIFY WORDS BY THE ACTUAL SHAPE OF THE WORD WHILE SIMULTANEOUSLY READING THE WORD LETTER BY LETTER. WHEN YOU PUT A PARAGRAPH IN ALL UPPERCASE LETTERS, YOU ARE DENYING THE READER THE ABILITY TO RECOGNIZE THE SHAPE OF THE WORD AND IT BECOMES MUCH MORE DIFFICULT TO READ THE BODY OF TEXT.

It is easier to read large portions of text if it is lowercase because the eye can recognize the shape of words because of the ascenders and descenders.

Uppercase versus Lowercase

Using all uppercase letters rather than lowercase in a body of text is not a great idea. The human eye uses the visual reference of typographic ascenders and descenders found in lowercase letters to help identify words by the actual shape of the word while simultaneously reading the word letter by letter. Ascenders extend above the mean line and descenders extend below the baseline. When a paragraph of text is in all uppercase letters, the reviewer does not have the ability to recognize the shape of the word and it becomes much more difficult to read the body of text.

X-Height Variations

X-height is essentially the line that establishes the mean line for each specific typeface. As its name suggests, it is the height of the lowercase x. The x-height is important because the x-height of a letter is what actually conveys the visual weight of the typeface. Therefore when selecting a typeface be mindful and understand that even typefaces that are the same size will have a different visual weight.

Understand that typeface weight is not just driven by its size; x-height variation is a large contributor as well. For legibility purposes avoid a typeface that works against your intentions of typeface hierarchy on a graphic layout.

Underlining, Bold and Italics

These guidelines are simple. Use bold and italics to extend the visual range of typeface selections. However, avoid underlining like the plague. Underlining creates a hard line within the visual space of a paragraph and is distracting. See what I mean?

Designing the Graphic Layout—Representation Strategies: Graphic Design Basics

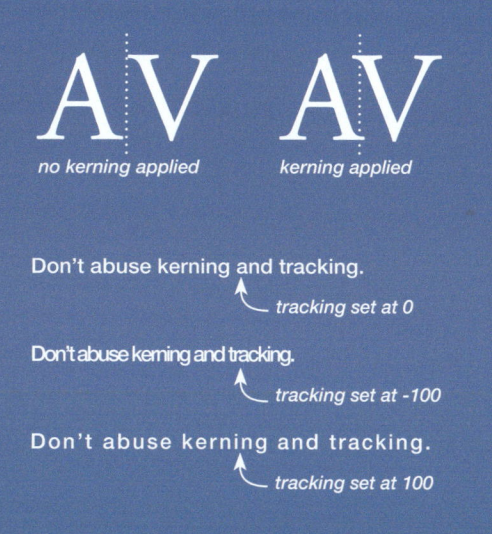

Visual rivers are irregular spaces that show up in text when you insist upon continuing to double space after each sentence. Graphic rules for visual text are very different than clarity rules you learned so your English teacher didn't go cross-eyed reading your term paper. There are double spaces after the sentences in this paragraph. Squint your eyes and the rivers will appear very clearly.

Visual rivers are irregular spaces that show up in text when you insist upon continuing to double space after each sentence. Graphic rules for visual text are very different than clarity rules you learned so your English teacher didn't go cross-eyed reading your term paper. There are double spaces after the sentences in this paragraph. Squint your eyes and the rivers will appear very clearly.
— river

Remove all double spaces in your text to prevent visual rivers from appearing in the text block.

AV — no kerning applied   AV — kerning applied

Don't abuse kerning and tracking.
— tracking set at 0

Don't abuse kerning and tracking.
— tracking set at -100

Don't abuse kerning and tracking.
— tracking set at 100

Only using kerning and tracking to adjust for legibility issues in your text.

Rivers Caused by Double Spacing in the Text

Throughout an academic career, starting with 8th grade English class, it was often taught to put a double space between two sentences. That was great for the legibility of an English composition paper but when it comes to a graphic layout using a large body of text, these double spaces cause another visual problem and that problem is called rivers. Bottom line: only use a single space after a sentence. There are no double spaces in graphic layouts of text. . . period. Rivers can also be caused when setting a body of text to a justified width.

Kerning and Tracking

The only information needed regarding kerning and tracking is what they are, when to use them and when not to use them. It's pretty simple.

Kerning is manually adjusting the space between a pair of letters in a word. It is used primarily by graphic designers to correct irregular spaces created through the adjacencies between some specific letters.

Tracking is manually adjusting the overall space between letters in a larger piece of text and not just between two letters, as is the case with kerning.

But here's what really needs to be understood. Adjusting kerning and tracking relies on a series of subtle moves and should not be noticeable to the eye when looking at a piece of text. Using either kerning or tracking to force fit a piece of text into a space allotment by either spacing it out to make it longer or condensing it to make it smaller means the tools are being used incorrectly. If more text is needed to fill a space, write more text. If less text is needed in a visual space, edit it.

Lorem ipsum dolor sit amet, consectetur adipiscing elit. Duis eu bibendum dolor, nec tempor risus. Phasellus aliquam id neque at convallis. Praesent sodales justo eget elit porttitor, vel faucibus nunc tristique. Integer at pretium nunc. Ut eleifend, urna fringilla volutpat luctus, diam dolor egestas est, sed porttitor arcu odio vel elit. Aenean pretium vitae libero quis lobortis. Curabitur eget eros in lectus convallis consequat vestibulum.

automatic leading

Lorem ipsum dolor sit amet, consectetur adipiscing elit. Duis eu bibendum dolor, nec tempor risus. Phasellus aliquam id neque at convallis. Praesent sodales justo eget elit porttitor, vel faucibus nunc tristique. Integer at pretium nunc. Ut eleifend, urna fringilla volutpat luctus, diam dolor egestas est, sed porttitor arcu odio vel elit. Aenean pretium vitae libero quis lobortis. Curabitur eget eros in lectus convallis consequat vestibulum.

leading set lower than automatic, used to visually condense body of text

Lorem ipsum dolor sit amet, consectetur adipiscing elit. Duis eu bibendum dolor, nec tempor risus. Phasellus aliquam id neque at convallis. Praesent sodales justo eget elit porttitor, vel faucibus nunc tristique. Integer at pretium nunc. Ut eleifend, urna fringilla volutpat luctus, diam dolor egestas est, sed porttitor arcu odio vel elit. Aenean pretium vitae libero quis lobortis. Curabitur eget eros in lectus convallis consequat vestibulum.

leading set higher than automatic, used to visually expand body of text

Only using leading settings to adjust for legibility issues in your text.

Leading

The term leading references a time when actual pieces of lead were used to create spaces between lines of metal type. As imaginable, leading is the art of adjusting the spacing between full lines of text. Adjusting the leading can be extremely helpful in managing the visual weight of a piece of text. Just be careful of overuse; it is very similar to overuse issues for kerning and tracking. Leading is generally measured baseline to baseline.

There are more visual reasons to adjust the leading than either kerning or tracking. Lean on leading to make visual space adjustments for pieces of text.

Measure

Measure is defined simply as the number of characters (including spaces) in a line of text. Measure matters because it affects legibility. We have all seen paragraphs of text that seem awkwardly narrow in width and we have all seen text that seems awkwardly wide. Both extremes make it very difficult to read through the multiple lines of text in a paragraph. If the width of the paragraph is too narrow, reading line to line becomes jumpy because the eye is forced to return to the next line multiple times within a sentence. If the paragraph is too wide, the eye physically gets lost as it returns to the next line. Luckily, there's a clear rule of thumb. For single column bodies of text, use between 45 and 75 characters per line; something around 65 is usually about right. For multi-column bodies of text, 40 to 50 characters per line is ideal.

Text Alignment

Before knowing which text alignment style to select, it is important to know the options and the pros and cons of each choice.

Lorem ipsum dolor sit amet, consectetur adipiscing elit. Duis eu bibendum dolor, nec tempor risus. Phasellus aliquam id neque at convallis. Praesent sodales justo eget elit porttitor, vel faucibus nunc tristique. Integer at pretium nunc. Ut eleifend, urna fringilla volutpat luctus, diam dolor egestas est, sed porttitor arcu odio vel elit. Aenean pretium vitae libero quis lobortis. Curabitur eget eros in lectus convallis consequat vestibulum.

rag right

Lorem ipsum dolor sit amet, consectetur adipiscing elit. Duis eu bibendum dolor, nec tempor risus. Phasellus aliquam id neque at convallis. Praesent sodales justo eget elit porttitor, vel faucibus nunc tristique. Integer at pretium nunc. Ut eleifend, urna fringilla volutpat luctus, diam dolor egestas est, sed porttitor arcu odio vel elit. Aenean pretium vitae libero quis lobortis. Curabitur eget eros in lectus convallis consequat vestibulum.

rag left

Lorem ipsum dolor sit amet, consectetur adipiscing elit. Duis eu bibendum dolor, nec tempor risus. Phasellus aliquam id neque at convallis. Praesent sodales justo eget elit porttitor, vel faucibus nunc tristique. Integer at pretium nunc. Ut eleifend, urna fringilla volutpat luctus, diam dolor egestas est, sed porttitor arcu odio vel elit. Aenean pretium vitae libero quis lobortis. Curabitur eget eros in lectus convallis consequat vestibulum.

justified, watch out for rivers

Make purposeful selections regarding the paragraph alignment of your text blocks. Don't automatically default to justified just because it has clear right and left edges. Justified text has its own set of problems that have to be resolved.

Rag Right: A paragraph of text set to rag right means that it is aligned to the left and is not aligned on the right leaving the text edge uneven—thus the label rag.

Pros: Rag right is the most typically used text alignment style and is easily legible because the left edge aligns at the same edge with each line.

Cons: Rag right can be visually problematic when the rag edge is either overrun with hyphenated word breaks or is very dramatically uneven. Both of these things need to be visually managed when working with a rag right text alignment style.

Rag Left: A paragraph of text set to rag left means that it is aligned to the right and is not aligned on the left leaving the text edge uneven—thus the label rag.

Pros: Rag left provides a straight hard right edge that can emphasize a prominent right-hand edge in a layout.

Cons: Rag left can be tricky particularly for a large block of text. When reading, the eye registers back to the left edge of text to start reading the next line of text. When using rag left, this "start" location jumps around and can make it more difficult to read the text.

When using either rag right or rag left, it is considered best form to set the paragraph style in Adobe InDesign to "no hyphen." This is because when using rag right or rag left, there is an automatic setting to break multi-syllabic words at the end of the line with a hyphen. When there are multiple hyphen breaks at the edge of a paragraph, it is visually distracting and leans toward visual illegibility.

Justified: A paragraph of text that is justified is aligned on both the right and the left edges of the text.

In hac habitasse platea dictumst. Duis ipsum tellus, convallis eget imperdiet iaculis, elementum ut mauris. Donec ultrices, tellus id porta ornare, nisi metus fermentum nunc, non porta diam massa sed magna. Cras elementum laoreet magna, in ultricies quam rutrum scelerisque. Aenean rutrum neque metus, et dictum arcu condimentum a. Sed diam dui, gravida in condimentum et, tincidunt varius velit. Pellentesque felis leo, pretium sed tristique eu, pellentesque vitae orci. In feugiat scelerisque turpis, vel congue mi fringilla vitae. Nam vestibulum leo sit amet sapien aliquet lobortis. Maecenas porttitor sagittis diam, in viverra eros egestas in pellentesque cursus.

Sed ut porttitor ante. Curabitur rhoncus eget eros in

↳ *orphan*

↱ *widow*
lectus convallis consequat vestibulum.

In hac habitasse platea dictumst. Duis ipsum tellus, convallis eget imperdiet iaculis, elementum ut mauris. Donec ultrices, tellus id porta ornare, nisi metus fermentum nunc, non porta diam massa sed magna. Cras elementum laoreet magna, in ultricies quam rutrum scelerisque. Aenean rutrum neque metus, et dictum arcu condimentum a. Pellentesque felis leo, pretium sed tristique eu, pellentesque vitae orci. In feugiat scelerisque turpis, vel congue mi fringilla vitae. Nam vestibulum leo sit amet sapien aliquet lobortis. Maecenas porttitor sagittis diam, in viverra eros egestas in. Pellentesque cursus pellentesque leo, non cursus dolor dictum sollicitudin.

Correct all instances of orphans and widows in your text. There must be at least two lines of text at the top or bottom of a column of text.

Pros: Justified text provides both a strong right and left edge which makes it very easy to visually reinforce your layout grid.

Cons: Be careful when using justified text. This alignment style sets the tracking of the paragraph line by line so that it has a sharp edge on both the right and left sides of the paragraph. All of the characters and words on each line are spaced differently to accommodate the line width on each line with a completely different set of characters. This forced alignment and automatic tracking creates large gaps, called rivers, in the body of the text and can be visually distracting.

Centered: A paragraph of text that is centered means just what it says; each line of text is centered about a central axis.

Pros: Centered text can lend a sense of center balance to a page.

Cons: Centered text should not be used for paragraphs of text. It is visually illegible for large arrangements of text and does not give any edge to align to any images or drawings in your portfolio. The left edge is particularly problematic since it shifts back and forth to accommodate the center.

Orphans, Widows and Runts

An orphan is a single line of text left by itself at the bottom of a column of text. A widow is a single line of text left alone at the top of a column of text. A runt is a single word on a line by itself at the end of a paragraph.

Neither orphans, widows nor runts are acceptable and diminish the legibility of a body of text. Fix them!

In hac habitasse platea dictumst. Duis ipsum tellus, convallis eget imperdiet iaculis, elementum ut mauris. Donec ultrices, tellus id porta ornare, nisi metus fermentum nunc, non porta diam massa sed magna. Cras elementum laoreet magna, in ultricies quam rutrum scelerisque. Aenean rutrum neque metus, et dictum arcu condimentum a. Pellentesque felis leo, pretium sed tristique eu, pellentesque vitae orci. In feugiat scelerisque turpis, vel congue mi fringilla vitae. Nam vestibulum leo sit amet sapien aliquet lobortis. Maecenas porttitor sagittis diam, in viverra eros egestas in. Pellentesque cursus pellentesque leo, non cursus dolor dictum sollicitudin. Sed ut porttitor ante. Curabitur rhoncus vestibulum.

 runt

Correct all instances of runts in your text. Never leave a single word on a line by itself.

visually clean paragraph beginning
In hac habitasse platea dictumst. Duis ipsum tellus, convallis eget imperdiet iaculis, elementum ut mauris. Donec ultrices, tellus id porta ornare, nisi metus fermentum nunc, non porta diam massa sed magna.

Cras elementum laoreet magna, in ultricies quam rutrum scelerisque. Aenean rutrum neque metus, et dictum arcu condimentum a.

visually distracting paragraph beginning
   In hac habitasse platea dictumst. Duis ipsum tellus, convallis eget imperdiet iaculis, elementum ut mauris. Donec ultrices, tellus id porta ornare, nisi metus fermentum nunc, non porta diam sed magna.

   Cras elementum laoreet magna, in ultricies quam rutrum scelerisque. Aenean rutrum neque metus, et dictum arcu condimentum a.

Err on the side of visual cleanliness and avoid indented paragraphs; they unnecessarily clutter the page.

Graphic Punctuation

There are a handful of punctuation rules and styles that every designer should be aware of. These are often different from things you've been taught in the past but are commonly known to all graphic designers. These particular rules regarding punctuation and style have graphic consequences and should be applied to improve the visual order of the designed page.

Dashes

There are actually three different types of dashes and all have very specific applications. Learn the differences between a hyphen, an en dash and an em dash.

Hyphen
A hyphen is the smallest of the dashes and is only used in compound word construction: self-evident.

En Dash
An en dash is of medium length and is only used when describing a range in time or numbers: 1999–2001 or pages 34–45.

Em Dash
An em dash is the longest of the dashes and is used in sentence structure to set apart a phrase: Bananas, apples and chicken—these are some of the things needed from the store.

Of the three dashes, the em dash is most flexible. A hyphen is only for compound word construction; an en dash is only for number ranges. Basically an em dash is a piece of punctuation that is used for any other application. Do not use hyphens or en dashes for anything other than what they are intended.

There are no spaces either before or after the hyphen, en dash or em dash.

Ellipsis

An ellipsis is a piece of punctuation used to indicate a portion of the text has been removed. It is also permissible to use an ellipsis to indicate a pause or moment of thought in a written statement. Graphically do not use the automatically generated ellipsis from your word processing program. A proper ellipsis is formed like this: word dot space dot space dot space. . .

Lists and Bullets

Using bullets in lists can often create an overpowering visual line of large dots on your page. Use much smaller dots than the standard offered in word processing software. Or generate a list through the use of changes in leading (the space between the lines of text).

Hyphen Settings for Paragraphs

In Adobe InDesign you have the ability to decide when to turn hyphen settings on or off for a body of text. When using rag right or rag left, turn off the hyphen settings so the risk of having multiple end-of-line hyphens appearing is removed. Turn hyphen settings on with justified text so the aggressive spacing adjustments needed to maintain justified text can be monitored.

Paragraph Indentation

Starting a new paragraph in the text is an important strategy to set apart different parts of a verbal argument. When beginning a new paragraph, use a single line of separation between paragraphs. Do not indent the beginning of the paragraph. Paragraph indention creates an additional and blocky rag edge to the body of text. This irregular white space is visually distracting to the order being established on the page.

Graphics: How Far Is Too Far?

Be aware that one of the things that can completely get away from you is the appearance that the entire portfolio has been overdesigned. This will become evident through the overuse of prominent graphic elements that don't have anything to do with the actual design work. Architecture students, in particular, have a difficult task. Enough knowledge of basic graphic design is needed to make the portfolio clear and legible—the goals of this publication—but too much of a good thing will ruin a portfolio.

Be comfortable in your ability to determine how far is too far with the graphics. The goal is to stand out but be taken seriously. The graphics in your portfolio should perform the necessary tasks without taking visual emphasis off the contents.

Ultimately the content material should be the visual standout rather than an overworked graphic convention. In other words, don't make it too graphic-y.

The best way to manage this is to review a typical content page and be honest if the portfolio graphics are more powerful than the content graphics. If so, reduce the portfolio graphics and work to improve the visual impact of the content.

Designed Simplicity

Also be very careful about packing a gazillion visual elements on one spread. This will be the initial urge! A page chock-full of content tends to read as one large visual set and it becomes very difficult to visually enter the content.

A page with a highly ordered grid that fills the page edge to edge will simply read as a series of boxes. All that will remain with the viewer is a mental image of a large group of rectangles in a grid. A page filled edge to edge with content that has no order also doesn't permit the viewer to visually enter the content. In this case, not even the overpowering grid is memorable.

Designing the Graphic Layout—Representation Strategies: Graphic Design Basics

Emory at Oxford Arts School
Oxford, GA
Jude LeBlanc

Living and Learning Community
Atlanta, GA
Michael Gamble

New Zealand School of Music
Wellington, NZ
Nick Roberts

Designed simplicity is achieved through single image use, clear typographic hierarchy, subtle use of color and rag right paragraphs. Portfolio design by Pavan Iyer.

Constructing the Persuasive Portfolio: the only primer you'll ever need

flexible program divisions

The new design of the courtyard divides the space into various areas of activity. The main walkway acts as an artery for circulation flanked on either side with spaces to relax, read, or a place to chat and eat lunch. The courtyard and north entrance can be closed off from the rest of the school after hours to host community events. The wood paneled wall and the steel overhang in the middle of the walkway create a new lateral axis of symmetry to the lower, depressed area, providing a potential stage area for these events.

(above) north-south section elevation through the courtyard during school hours
(right) diagram defining school-time circulation and resting areas

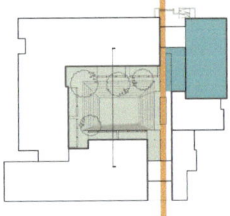

Simple typographic hierarchy is used to establish order on this well-balanced spread. Portfolio design by Nico Forlenza.

(above) *east-west section elevation showing how the walkway and depressed space can double as a stage*

(right) *diagram defining the areas of the school which can be used for community activities after school*

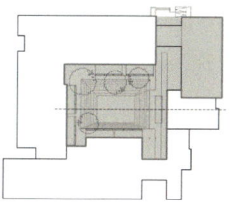

Designing the

Design Actions

 Determine the project narrative for each project being considered for inclusion. — page 122

 Decide if you have representational artifacts to match all of the ideas from the project narrative. — page 123

 Decide which projects should be included in your portfolio. — page 123

 Determine the appropriate order for each project narrative. — page 124

 Apply hierarchical relationships to support the project narrative. — page 126

 Understand best practices for typical architectural symbols and conventions and apply them. — page 128

 Use labeling systems appropriately. — page 131

 Make sure your presentation drawings are legible at the scale of the portfolio. — page 139

Correct issues with image quality in your portfolio. — page 143

Project narrative has already been defined and discussed, put in context relative to the visual narrative and content narrative, but let's have a refresher. First and foremost, the project narrative in a portfolio relates to each individual project. This is the specific visual and written project representation material required to convey the thinking behind the work.

It is important to convey this thinking; don't leave anything in your head and assume it will be obvious to the reviewer. To do this, make a list of all the ideas to be conveyed and make sure all of these ideas can be represented visually with support from the text in the portfolio.

Also keep in mind that the project narrative does not need to be represented as it was defined in the academic studio; the portfolio is an opportunity to define your own specific narrative about each project.

When beginning the artifact collection for a portfolio, usually the first thing done is simply to start dropping images into the design layout to see what happens. As crazy as it may seem from someone who is writing an entire book on portfolio design, this is not actually that bad of an idea! Sometimes, just seeing what material is available, and putting it in the new context of a portfolio, will trigger some significant ideas about how to visually display a project. After all, as designers, we know

Graphic Layout

Project Narrative
Visual Representation

that all the planning in the world can't actually solve a design problem; one has to act and react and then do something again to move through the design process. However, putting energy and forethought into what to do will make better use of your efforts and will ultimately result in a better portfolio. A little bit of work on the front end will make better use of time on the back end.

Three Levels of Visual Reading of a Portfolio

Another important thing to remember with portfolio design is that there is not always an opportunity to be present to tell the reviewers what is important for them to understand about a project. Therefore the portfolio has to do all of the communication work. Do not rely on large paragraphs of descriptive text to convey all of the ideas; the text rarely gets thoroughly read during a portfolio review. In fact, it is best to understand the reviewing of a portfolio through the three levels of visual reading of a portfolio. Below are the descriptions of the three levels of visual reading for a portfolio.

1. High-level browsing: this is a quick flip through of the portfolio. The reviewer discovers a brief understanding of project range, design skill and ability to diagram ideas and projects.

2. Mid-level browsing: this is a slower perusal of a portfolio and is actually sitting down with a portfolio and turning page to page. This time the reviewer is likely going back through the portfolio after a high-level browse has landed the portfolio in a "look at this again" pile. This time the reviewer is taking in full project spreads and is reading snippets of easily accessible text. For instance, the reviewer is reading project statistics and well-placed diagram and image captions. The reviewer is also taking a little bit of time to understand the correlation between ideas and the visual representation of those ideas.

3. In-depth review: this is the full on, take your time and really understand everything review and frankly this does not happen very often. In this type of portfolio review, every bit of text is read and the reviewer is attempting to stitch together the entire design argument through written text and representative imagery.

A good strategy to use when trying to figure out how to convey an idea is to make it your priority to convey each idea through visual means and then support it through the appropriate use of text. Visual communication is supported by verbal communication and definitely not the other way around. If there is a point that is only being made in the text, consider this a direct indicator that there is a drawing or image or diagram, a piece of visual communication, missing.

Determining Holes in the Project Narrative

For each and every project under consideration for inclusion in the portfolio, make a list of the types of artifacts that should exist for that project. This is a list of artifacts that just covers the basics: site plan, plans, elevations, sections, descriptive diagrams, etc.

For each and every project under consideration for inclusion in the portfolio, make a basic list of artifacts that are missing for that project. On this list, include things such as: "I never finished that exploded axonometric," or "What was that model my professor was always telling me to think about?" Make this a robust and complete list. This list is not a task list of things to be produced, but this list should contain any ideas of things never completed while working on the project.

The next thing to tackle is a list of all of the project ideas that need to be conveyed. This list should include everything attempted for each design problem. This also needs to be a complete and robust list. Do not leave any ideas off this list.

Now it's time to make some decisions. It is always better to communicate a few ideas and communicate them well than to throw everything at the project and hope something sticks. In the case of a portfolio, the reviewer spends a relatively short amount of time with the work in the portfolio and it is critical that the thinking behind the work has been clearly conveyed. It is not enough to show just drawing skills or model-building skills or even computer rendering skills. There is an assumption if a person has graduated from an accredited school of architecture, they will have these skills.

Representing Work: Does Additional Material Need to Be Produced?

At this juncture, it is likely that additional material of some sort (drawings, models, diagrams) will need to be produced to flesh out the visual argument being made. It is a critical step in the clarity of your portfolio to be realistic with yourself about what needs to be done. Reality in this case is referring to a couple of different things. First, be honest whether the material on hand actually represents what needs to be conveyed. It can be painful to realize that a project that was toiled over for 10 weeks still needs additional attention. Second, be honest about what is actually possible to accomplish within the time available. If there are only a few hours to dedicate to producing something new, be focused and accomplish something of utmost hierarchical value.

Remember, project work in a portfolio is not just a representation of what was accomplished during studio (or similar situation). Project work in a portfolio has a new life of its own. The portfolio is a new presentation of the work and therefore can and should have a new layer of attention placed on its representation. Don't think that the only items that can be included are the items that were previously accomplished. The portfolio offers new opportunities to think through and produce what is needed for a project in this new presentation format.

It is imperative that the portfolio demonstrates abilities to think through and solve complex problems. We've already established that the design of the portfolio is a rather complex design problem. Be aware that the evaluation of the portfolio is based on the clarity and conveyance of ideas through the portfolio design as well as on the work presented within the portfolio.

The next exercise is a hierarchy exercise to determine what are the most important ideas to convey. Start by describing in a concise manner the main ideas about a project, then from this description create a list that identifies the single most important idea to convey along with three or so secondary ideas that are also important to explain.

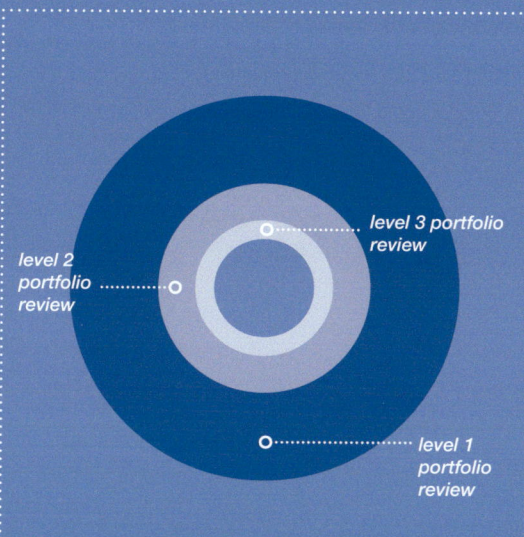

It is more likely that your portfolio will get a high level review (level 1) than a detailed review (level 3). Make sure your ideas are legible through a quick review of your portfolio.

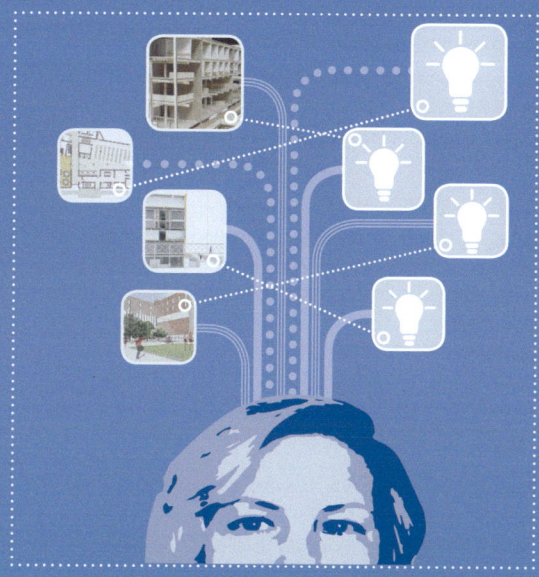

Make sure to match project artifacts to ideas you want to convey in your portfolio.

Cross-reference this list with the list of design artifacts created earlier in the process and literally assign artifacts to ideas. Determine which drawings, images or diagrams do the best job of visually describing these ideas. Be honest. It is quite possible that additional material will need to be generated or a section drawing has to be improved or a model re-photographed. In fact, it is not only possible. . . it is very likely.

How Many Projects Should Be Included?

A frequent question from designers working on their portfolio is: "How many projects should I include in my portfolio?" There isn't a standard formula for this and it will vary from case to case but there are some guidelines to follow to help make this decision. First and foremost, do not include any project in the portfolio that could not stand alone if it was the only project available to review! There is no way to control what someone focuses on in his or her review of a portfolio. They could only have the time to look at one project: it could be the best project or it could be the worst project.

When it comes time to determine what to include in your portfolio, remember: every project must be able to stand on its own. If it can't do that, then either rework it so it is stronger or don't include it at all!

Some applications will have a limit on the number of pages that can be included. In this case, obviously, only include the absolute strongest work.

Visual and Verbal Representation of Design Thinking

One of the single most difficult objectives to achieve with a portfolio is a true and powerful visual and verbal representation of design thinking and not just a display of project artifacts.

With portfolio design it is easy to try to trot out all of the artifacts produced while directly working on a project and place those images in a relatively visually pleasing arrangement in the portfolio. This method of portfolio production is just that. . . a production portfolio. It only demonstrates that artifacts were made, that there is a skill set—could be analog, could be digital—but it is missing a radically important skill and, frankly, a more elusive skill to demonstrate: the skill of design thinking.

Imagine the role of the portfolio reviewer—there are about 10 portfolios a day to review and the objective is to find the best designer in the bunch. Every single one of the 10 applicants has graduated from an accredited school of architecture and every single one of the 10 applicants has very similar demonstrable skills—they can all build models, they can all digitally model, and they can all produce a set of drawings. These are hard skills that are expected upon graduation, there's nothing special about it at all. But think more clearly about who you are claiming to be—a designer! By the very nature of the discipline, a designer requires a robust and curious mind! A designer means something very different than a model-builder or a draftsman. A designer creates; a designer works to reveal something previously unknown. How does one display the nature of what makes a designer an actual designer through the design of a portfolio? How is a unique brand of design thinking demonstrated? There are multiple ways to accomplish this. The important thing is to actually do it and to make sure the reviewer is pointed to exactly what they should see and understand.

Remember this, the portfolio designer alone has control over what the reviewer sees and understands about their work—use this fact to your advantage. Don't just include the material that is on hand. New material might need to be produced in order to explain the beauty of your design ideas.

Order of the Project Narrative

It is important to rethink the order in which each project is presented in the portfolio. It is natural to organize the project narrative based on the order in which the material was produced. Often when presenting work in a jury setting, the work is ordered and presented something like this: "Well, first I did this, and then I did this and that lead to this and so, yeah. . . that's what I did." Is that really the grand plan to use for presenting your work?

Think about this instead: go back to the lists generated earlier about project artifacts—existing and missing—and project ideas. From these lists, decide what visual material best represents the most important ideas to be conveyed. This is how the visual presentation should be started, with the most important image that conveys the most information about the project. It could be a powerful rendering of a significant space of the project, it could be a model image, it could be a detailed and annotated site plan or detailed and annotated diagram that explains everything about the project.

The order of project presentation does not have to be precedent, site analysis, process material, site plan, plan, section, elevation, renderings and model images. Instead, strive to visually tell a story of the design nature of the project through the order of the images within the project narrative. It is important to have a better design story to tell than: "This is the order in which I produced the work."

Remember, the portfolio designer has control of what the reviewer understands about the work—absolute and complete control.

Project Text

This section is just for the basics about project text; for detailed information on this subject see the chapter titled, Text in Your Portfolio: What it Says and How it Looks.

For each project presented in the portfolio, a basic set of text information should be included. At a minimum,

The primary initial image sets the tone for the upcoming project without overwhelming the reviewer with exhaustive site analysis material. Portfolio design by Ethan Miller.

this basic set of text information should include: project title, project location, project size, basic introductory descriptive text, credits for team projects, captions for all visual material and appropriate labels and titles for all diagrams and drawings.

It is incredibly important to think of all of the text in the portfolio in a supporting role to the visual information. Every single important point to be made regarding a project must be represented first through visual imagery then with the text used to reinforce the visual imagery. With this in mind, captions take on a very important role. For example, for an image of a project in model format, don't use the caption, "Model View." Isn't it obvious it's a model view? Say something that very specifically directs the reviewer to a definitive area of importance in the image. Point them to why the image was included in the project narrative. A caption such as, "View from south showing spatial connection between entrance sequence and outdoor classroom," is much more effective to successfully convey design ideas.

It is a missed opportunity to leave these directed captions out of the portfolio. It is not difficult to complete and does not take a great amount of time to do. If the effort has been made to figure out what visual material to include and why it is important to the conveyance of the project narrative, these captions should be very simple to generate. The captions have an enormous amount of value relative to the difficulty of generating them; they do the best job of directing reviewer attention to exactly what it is they should see and understand.

As mentioned time and time again, the portfolio designer has sole control of what the reviewer understands about the work—absolute and complete control.

Hierarchical Priority for Portfolio Images

Primary Images and Support Images: Support to the Design Argument
A hierarchy that needs to be established within project imagery is a decision about which images are more important to the design argument. Once this determination is made, automatic decisions about both the placement of each image and the relative size of each image becomes easier. For instance, images that are most important to the design argument should lead the visual presentation and should be large relative to other objects on the page. This is a very simple but powerful strategy. It seems obvious, doesn't it?

Once the primary images have been identified, it is time to determine which images should act as support images. Primary images are the images that best convey the objectives and are generally larger on the page. Support images are images that need other images to be meaningful or images that are purposefully subordinate to a primary image. It is important to understand this relationship between images, to identify the relationships early and to let this information influence the design layouts.

Size of Images and Visual Legibility
A secondary way to think through image hierarchy is to make determinations about which images will be acceptably legible at a smaller size and which images really need to be larger to allow the viewer "inside" the image. Use a ranking system as follows:

1. Image needs to be a full page to be legible.

2. Image needs to be a half page to be legible.

3. Image is legible as a thumbnail.

Designing the Graphic Layout—Project Narrative Visual Representation

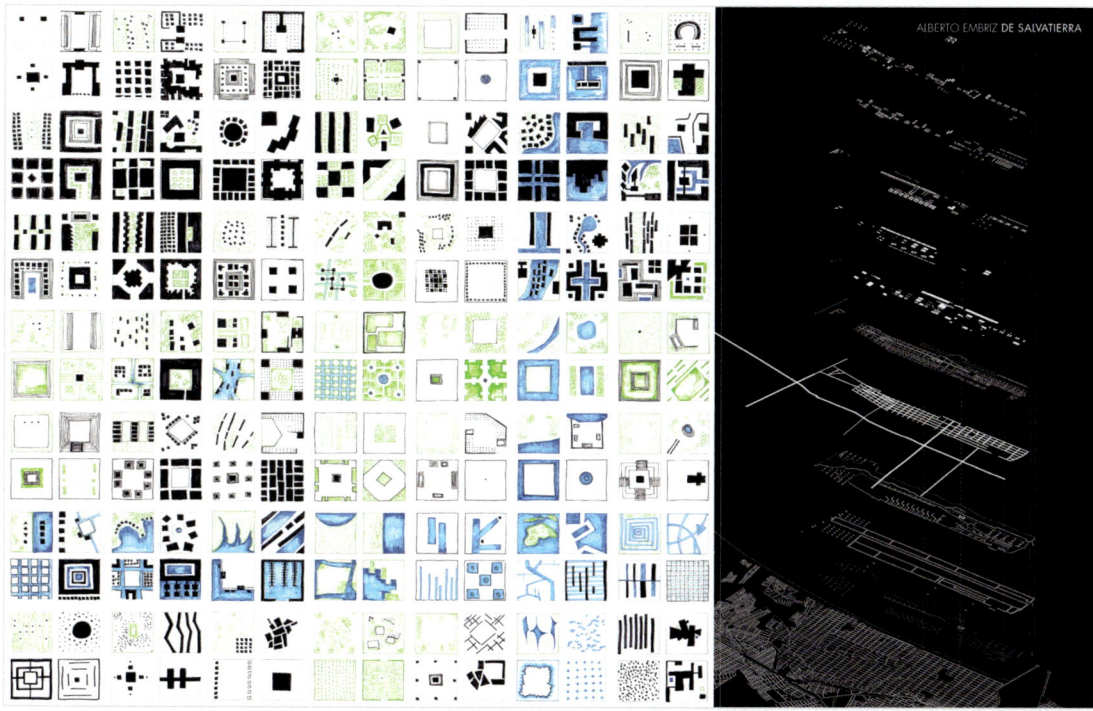

This simple system can help focus on which images need additional design attention. Keep in mind that an undercooked rendering can look great when it is 3" x 4" and absolutely horrible and unresolved at 9" x 12". It all has to do with the design resolution of the proposed image. In this example, resolution does not refer to image resolution—as in pixels and digital image size—but, rather, it is referring to design resolution—how much of the design is resolved in the image. So a rendered image with only schematic design resolution will actually look more powerful if presented at a smaller scale and perhaps in a series of multiple views.

Sketch studies have more visual impact shown at a small scale together. Portfolio design by Alberto Embriz de Salvatierra.

opposite: *Axonometric diagrams at small scale support the understanding of the primary image. Portfolio design by Brian Kerr.*

Constructing the Persuasive Portfolio: the only primer you'll ever need

Graphic options for north arrows are endless. Select one that best fits the graphic sensibility of your work and stick with it.

Architectural Symbols and Conventions for Presentation Drawings

It is easy in the haste to complete a portfolio to forget the basics when it comes to architectural symbols and drawing conventions. Remember these basics and include them with all architectural drawings. They make the difference between a portfolio that merely includes drawings and models to a portfolio that has explanatory representations of architectural designs—it's actually a very significant difference.

There are some cases where it could be argued that each project in a portfolio was produced at a different time in one's design education and therefore much different graphic styles were employed relative to how each project is represented. For example, there may be a mix of hand-drawn projects and digital projects. There is no way to make all of the architectural symbols match unless every project is redrawn in a similar way, and that actually doesn't make much sense. The rule of thumb is to match symbols and conventions where appropriate. Make sure they are included everywhere because inclusion is not only appropriate, it's mandatory.

Symbols and Conventions

North Arrow
Every project that is drawn in plan needs a north arrow associated with the site plan and the ground floor plan. There are several styles of acceptable north arrows; chose the one that is most in line with the graphic sensibilities being employed and use this same north arrow style for all locations in the portfolio as appropriate.

Graphic Scale
When projects are produced for presentation and discussion, they are usually represented at an architectural scale: 1/4" = 1', 1cm = 0.5m, etc. When the scale of these drawings is reduced and they are placed in a portfolio, these architectural scales are no longer correct and it actually doesn't make sense to try to figure out what they are at the reduced scale. Something like 5/64" = 1' isn't an architectural scale and therefore isn't measurable. Thus it becomes necessary to use a graphic scale—also called a bar scale—with the drawings in the portfolio. The easiest way to get the graphic scale correct is to draw it correctly with the drawings at the scale that generated the drawings and then downscale both the drawing and the graphic scale at the same time. Since the graphic scale travels with the drawing as it is reproduced at any scale, it always maintains a scalar relationship to the drawing and can be used as a mini-measuring device to determine dimensions on a scaled drawing as needed.

Again, there are a variety of ways to draw a graphic scale. Choose the one that is most in line with the graphic sensibilities employed and use this same graphic scale style for all locations in the portfolio.

Section Cut Lines and Appropriate Section Labels
Plans need section cut lines to mark where the drawing sections are cut. There should be a section cut line drawn in plan for every section presented with a project.

Designing the Graphic Layout—Project Narrative Visual Representation

Bar scales are important to include for the scalar understanding of a project but don't need to be intrusive to the graphic layout. Portfolio design by Scott Wooten.

Constructing the Persuasive Portfolio: the only primer you'll ever need

Diagram call-outs are legible but not distracting to the graphic nature of the drawings. Also, a very clean graphic scale is included for scalar legibility of the section drawing. Portfolio design by Natacha Schnider.

However, only use section cut lines for the sections actually included in the portfolio. Ideally, the section cut lines should be repeated on every plan level shown.

There are a variety of ways to draw section cut lines on plan drawings, and it is very important to not allow the section cut line to become visually distracting to the plan drawings. There are subtle yet legible ways to draw these cut lines; do not let the cut lines pull your eye in any way. If the cut lines go all the way through your plan, they need to be a very light, dashed line in a dash that is different than any other dashed line type on the drawing set. However, if possible, it is better if the cut lines do not go all the way through the plan drawing; they run the risk of conflating with the actual lines in the drawing. The style of the direction indicator at the edge of the section cut line is also very visually important. A kludgey arrow used as a direction indicator will always draw the eye to the arrow—it seems visually out of place. Use a more elegant direction indicator that is in line with the graphic style of the remainder of the drawings in the portfolio. A simple rectangular bar perpendicular to the section cut line works well.

Visually Stack the Plan Drawings
It is important when describing an architectural project with multiple plan drawings to stack the drawings appropriately. The most correct way to stack plans is to have the bottom level at the bottom of the stack and move up through the floors in sequential order above this bottom level. When the plan drawings are stacked properly, the reviewer can visually collapse the plans on top of one another and have a three-dimensional understanding of the building.

It is not always possible to include plan drawings stacked vertically. If this is the case, do not despair. Make logical choices keeping the idea about visually collapsing the drawings in mind.

Labeling Systems

Drawing and Diagram Titles
All drawings and diagrams included in the portfolio need titles. These titles reinforce the objective of the drawing, and are another way to direct the reviewer to exactly what they should see.

Drawing and diagram titles as well as program labels and diagram call-outs can and should point the reviewer to exactly what should be known about a project. For example, notice the difference between the diagram label, "program diagram," and the diagram label, "program diagram of inside / outside connections." See the difference? The first diagram title just lists the obvious. The latter diagram title tells the reviewer what to look for in the diagram.

Plan Program Labels
There are several distinct schools of thought on how to label the programmatic elements of a set of plan drawings. Each camp feels very strongly about it, so much so that they will say it's the only way to do it. The real truth is that there are a couple of effective ways to note program on a plan and there are pros and cons associated with each method. Determine what makes the most sense to what you are trying to accomplish. Either one—if done correctly—can be effective and beautiful.

Option One: Include the program labels directly on plan

Pros: Including the program labels directly on the plan makes it simple to quickly understand the programmatic relationships because the reviewer is simultaneously reading the drawing plan and the written program.

Cons: Including the program labels directly on the plan can be quite distracting to the legibility of the actual plan. It's a graphic problem of visual hierarchy.

Solution: To make this method work, it is imperative to do a series of visual studies to determine the appropriate visual hierarchy between the legibility of the plan and the legibility of the program labels. First and foremost, the plan must be legible. The program labels must be visually secondary. This can be achieved through increasing the visual strength of the line work or poché and reducing the visual strength of the program labels. To increase the visual strength of the line work or poché, darken or make more prominent those areas that have been cut in the plan. Then reduce the visual strength of the program labels; select a sans serif typeface, reduce the size and change it to a gray tone instead of pure black.

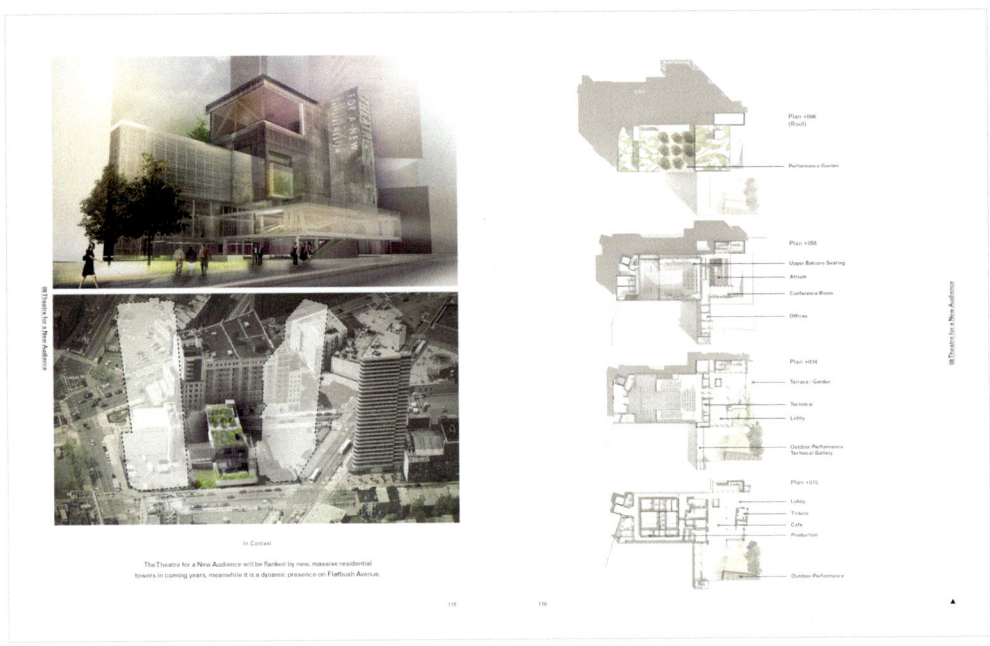
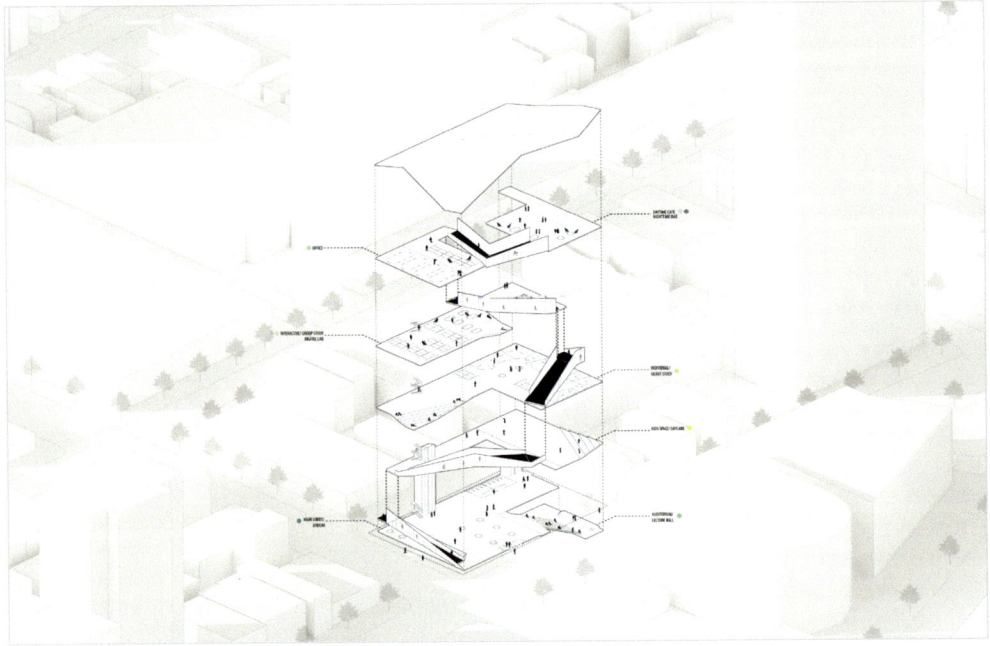

Designing the Graphic Layout—Project Narrative Visual Representation

Option Two: List program labels in a key located adjacent to the plan

Pros: Listing the program labels in a key located adjacent to the plan visually opens the plan drawing because the only additional elements on the plan are small letters or numbers. There is less visual clutter of program labels to distract from the legibility of the plan.

Cons: Listing the program labels in a key located adjacent to the plan forces reviewers to constantly move their eyes between the plan and the key. This can reduce their immediate understanding of the plan.

Solution: It is imperative to the success of this plan labeling method that the program key is located in a place immediately adjacent to the drawing it is referencing. The numbers or letters located in the plan need to be arranged in an orderly fashion and should be in a sans serif typeface and should not visually distract from the plan legibility. There should be no visual information that comes between the drawing and the key; they must be immediately adjacent.

Secondary Diagram Labels and Call-Outs
Don't omit secondary diagram labels and call-outs. The reviewer doesn't always know what seems obvious to the designer. Use the secondary labels and call-outs as a supporting method to be very clear about what is being conveyed.

above: *Program labels are included directly on the plan drawings. Portfolio design by Jeffrey Collins.*

opposite top: *Program labels are used as call-outs on the plan drawings. Also note the plans are properly stacked so that the lowest floor is at the bottom of the vertical stack of plans. The reviewer can visually reassemble the plans when ordered correctly. Portfolio design by Phillip Denny.*

opposite bottom: *Diagram call-outs are used to identify program elements without disturbing the visual legibility of the diagram. Portfolio design by Ibrahim W. Salman.*

Constructing the Persuasive Portfolio: the only primer you'll ever need

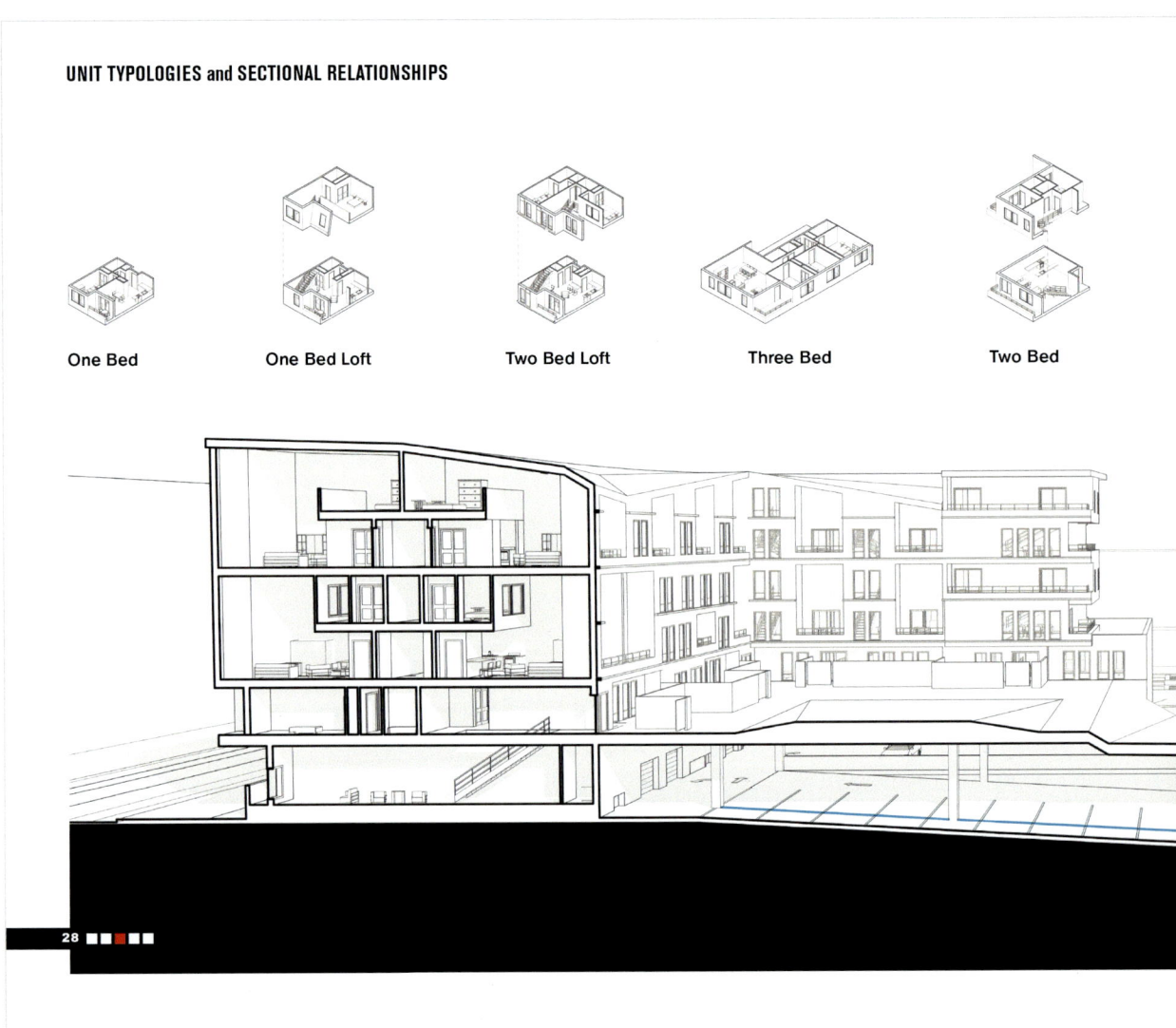

Small axonometric diagrams do an excellent job providing supplementary information for the overall understanding of the section drawing. Portfolio design by Joseph Pucci.

Designing the Graphic Layout—Project Narrative Visual Representation

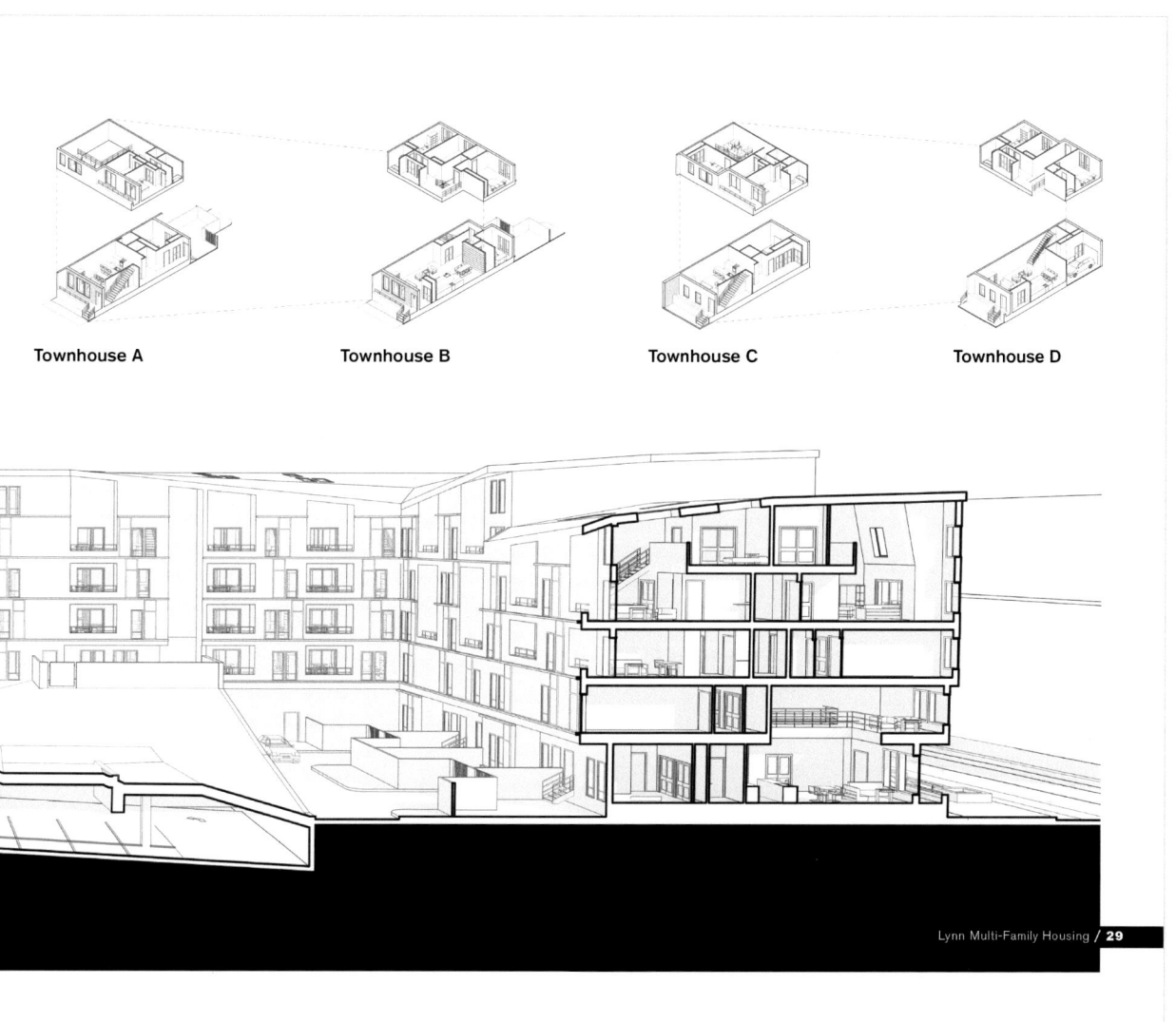

Townhouse A　　　　Townhouse B　　　　Townhouse C　　　　Townhouse D

Lynn Multi-Family Housing / **29**

Constructing the Persuasive Portfolio: the only primer you'll ever need

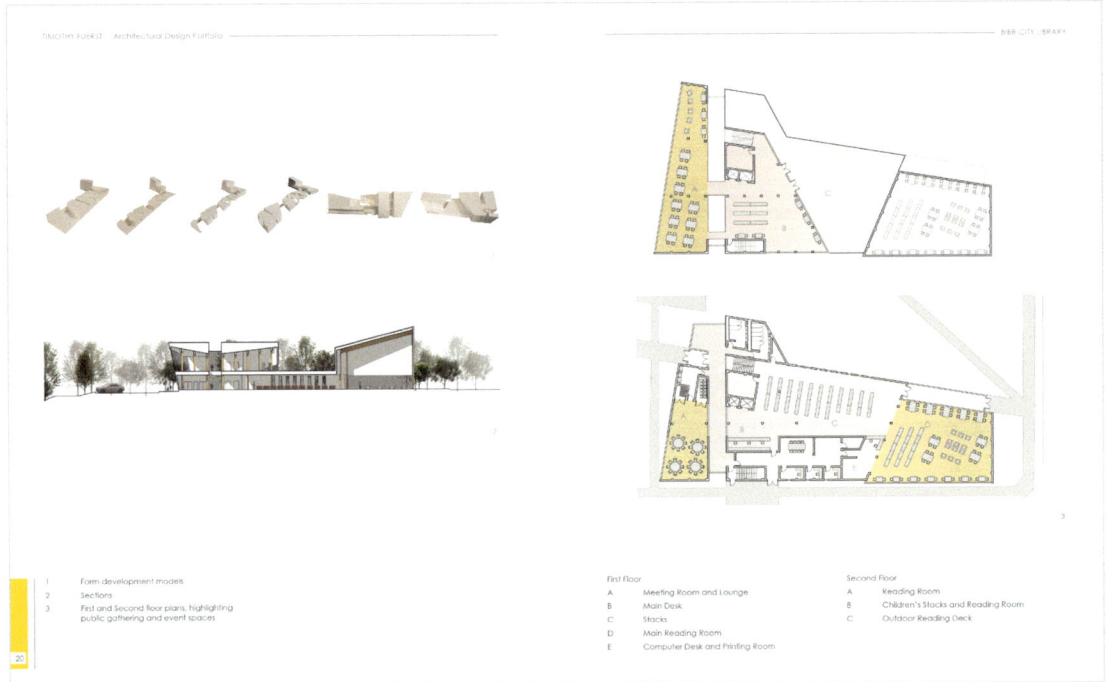

A program key is used to label spatial elements in the plan. Portfolio design by Timothy Fuerst.

Diagram call-outs are used to identify program elements by tying the plan with the three-dimensional model. Portfolio design by Israel B. Sanchez.

Designing the Graphic Layout—Project Narrative Visual Representation

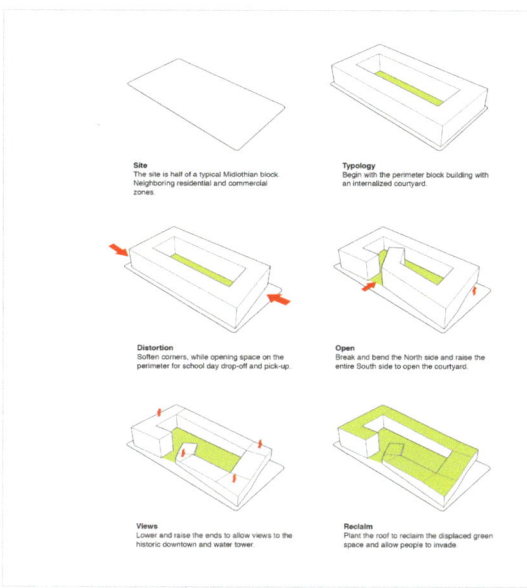

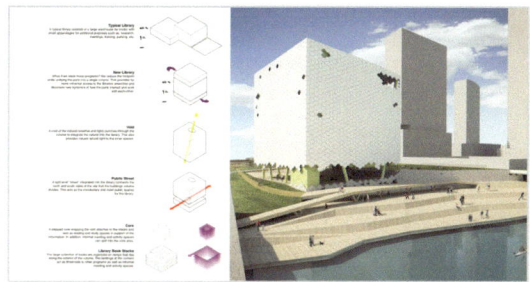
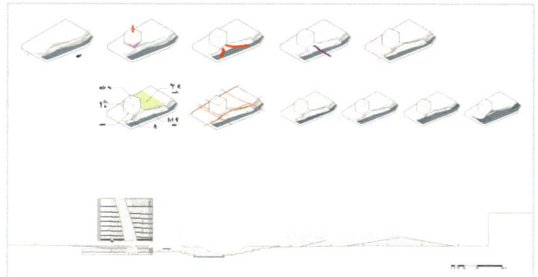

Visual and verbal descriptive diagrams are utilized throughout this portfolio to easily explain conceptual underpinnings of the projects. Portfolio design by Casey Tucker.

Constructing the Persuasive Portfolio: the only primer you'll ever need

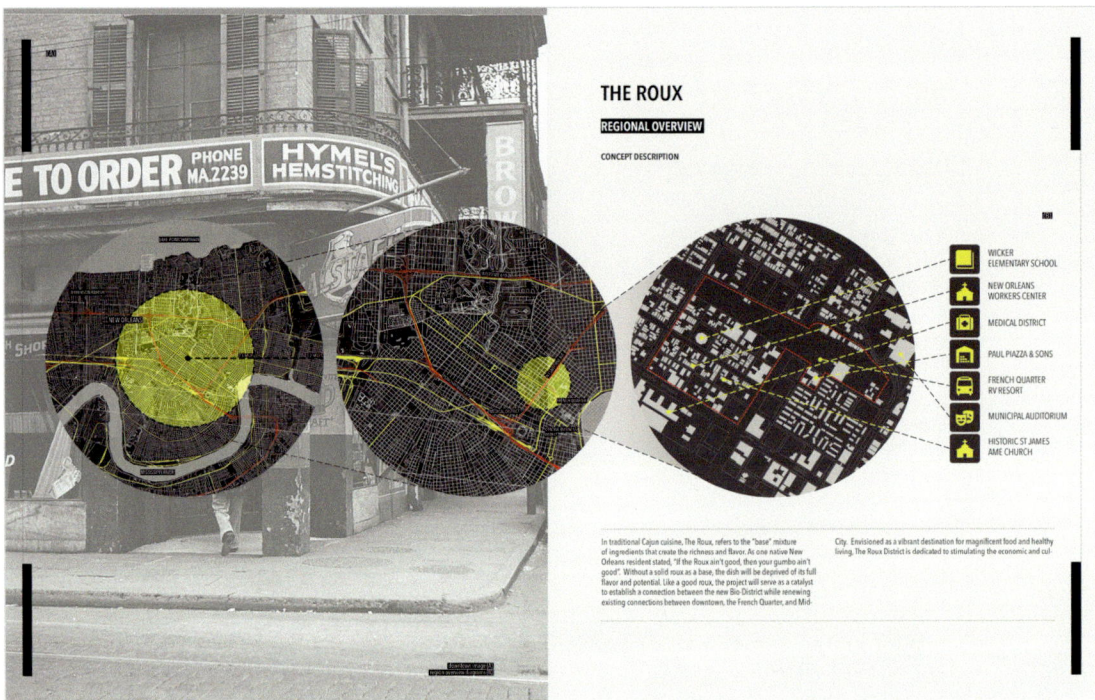

Diagram call-outs and graphic icons are used to explain the urban condition. Note the three scales of diagram expansion. Portfolio design by Xavier Encerrado.

Diagram call-outs and graphic icons are used to explain the programmatic relationships in the three-dimensional diagrams. Portfolio design by Angela Ng.

Visual Legibility of Presentation Drawings: Or How to Make Drawings Legible at Such a Small Scale

There is a difference in style and legibility between presentation drawings and construction drawings. Programs such as AutoCAD and Revit are designed for the construction industry and by default cater to the legibility conventions for that purpose. For work shown in a portfolio, there is a different purpose—that of design legibility. Design legibility in line drawings demands a different set of legibility conventions and requires adjustments to be made to the drawings to ensure clear understanding of spatial conditions described in the two-dimensional drawings. Make sure to use the software tool that is appropriate for the job at hand: for construction drawings, use software designed for the construction industry—AutoCAD, Revit and the like—for presentation drawings, use software designed for line work flexibility—Adobe Illustrator and similar.

Another issue with architectural drawings in a portfolio is the scale of the drawing. If the original presentation intention was for the drawing to be reviewed at 1/4" = 1' or 1cm = 0.5m, there was a set of legibility conventions followed for presenting at that scale. Now that the drawings have been reduced significantly to fit in the portfolio, some changes need to made to the drawings to maintain spatial clarity. Below is a list of operations that need to be addressed primarily for orthographic drawings—plan, section, elevation—but look through all paraline or perspective drawings for issues as well.

All of these operations have to be addressed at the actual scale that each drawing appears in the portfolio. It isn't helpful to make these adjustments first and then scale the drawing down in the portfolio to see how it looks. Work back and forth between Adobe Illustrator and Adobe InDesign to get the adjustments correct for the new portfolio scale of the drawings.

Line Weight

One of the most important things to get correct for the legibility of drawings in the portfolio is the line weight. The rules are commonly known, but below is a quick refresher. And remember in this case, the line weights being referenced are at the scale of the portfolio. Review the drawings at the scale they are displayed in the portfolio to be able to make these line weight adjustments. Adhere to no more than five line weights:

1. Line weight 01 is the darkest and should be used to indicate the planes that have been cut through.

2. Line weight 02 is slightly lighter than 01 and indicates those edges closest to the planes that were cut.

3. Line weight 03 is slightly lighter than 02 and indicates those edges beyond those drawn with line weight 02.

4. Line weight 04 is slightly lighter than 03 and indicates those edges beyond those drawn with line weight 03.

5. Line weight 05 is reserved for construction lines and should be the absolute lightest line.

Using this simple system can alleviate headaches when it comes to figuring out what line weight to use. There is no use trying to develop line weight hierarchy beyond the three described above that are depicting edges that are receding in space—line weights 02, 03 and 04. Anything more than those types leads to a drawing that actually begins to lose spatial depth legibility.

Contour Lines in Plan

Traditionally on the ground floor plan of a project, the site or context plan that is indicative of how the project connects to its context is included. This work often includes contour lines. Make certain that the contour lines are an appropriately scaled line. The contour lines should act as support information to the remainder of the context and should be visually lighter than the other line work in the context.

Poché

At the greatly reduced scale of drawings in a portfolio, it is a good idea to add poché, if it isn't already there, to the planes that are cut through in plan and section. If a lot of work has gone into getting the line weights correct at the portfolio scale, the drawing might be legible, but take an honest look at the drawings, squint your eyes, and see if the drawing is really clear or if that's just wishful thinking to avoid more work. The poché can be black or a gray tone or even a color, but it really needs to be there. This step coupled with the proper line weights will greatly increase the legibility of all drawings.

Hatch
Hatching is the use of a series of lines in a pattern to create the illusion of a solid tone and is a style setting that comes from AutoCAD and should not be used in a presentation drawing. Hatch does not scale well and creates strange moiré patterns when reduced. Also it forces multiple vector software calculations thus creating an incredibly heavy Illustrator file. If a solid tone is needed in the drawings—for poché, or to describe floor plates and program zones—draw a solid tone in Illustrator. There will be more options than in AutoCAD and the tone can be adjusted through opacity or the tonal intensity of the color selection to create a range and variety of easily customized colors.

Verify when printing continuous tone in drawings that it actually remains a continuous tone. Different printers will handle a continuous tone in a variety of ways. Sometimes, solid tones do print in a moiré pattern. However, solid, continuous tones print much better than a tone created through a hatch pattern. The hatch pattern always, most definitely, prints poorly. Avoid hatch patterns for solid tones altogether.

Compound Line Edits
There are several instances where compound lines are needed in a plan to represent different types of situations. Examples of these compound lines are instances such as the multiple lines at a window cut in plan or section where two lines are shown for the glass cut with lines for the sill or wall edge beyond. These compound lines make sense when they are shown at the scale they were drawn. However, when they are greatly reduced in scale to be included in a portfolio, the compound lines compress and instead of reading like a series of very thin lines, they read as one thick line. These compound lines essentially inverse the line weight relationship between the wall and the window. Because of this inversion, when reducing a plan or section for a portfolio, remove some of the multiple lines at window locations so that they read visually thinner.

Another place that has compound line issues when greatly reducing a drawing in scale is at a run of stairs in plan. Sometimes it is necessary to go in to the drawing and remove every other stair line so that it doesn't read as a solid block at the smaller scale. The same thing happens with the stair lines as with the window example: the lines visually compress at the smaller scale and read as a thicker line.

Arrows
Arrows in drawings are tricky. They can be very visually distracting elements in drawings because they are a completely different shape than anything else found in the drawing. Reduce their visual impact through a variety of adjustments. After all, the plan should be spatially legible and great big bulky arrows are not going to support your legibility objectives. Follow these guidelines to adjust the weight of the arrows in your presentation drawings:

1. Make sure the arrow head is appropriate for the drawing. Stay away from cartoon-like, soft-edged arrows in orthographic drawings. Also avoid arrow heads that are pure, geometric triangles; these are equally distracting because they have a geometric structure that competes with the geometric structures found in the drawings. Instead, look for arrows that have pointed edges not soft edges and have elongated triangle-shaped heads.

2. Make sure the stroke of the arrow is not too thick. There should be a perfect balance between the stroke of the arrow and the head of the arrow. If either one is not in the correct proportional relationship, the arrow will be too visually prominent simply because it looks strange to the eye and will be visually distracting when reading the drawings.

3. Make sure the arrow is in proper proportion with the overall drawing. Too large or too small in relation to the scale of the drawing will also be visually distracting.

4. And finally, the arrow should be reduced in tone so it does not read as strongly as the actual line and poché of the drawing.

Designing the Graphic Layout—Project Narrative Visual Representation

Level 4 Floor Plan

401 Classroom   402 Office   403 Storage   404 Auditorium   405 Audiovisual Closet   406 Catering   407 Conference Room

Floor plan with presentation plan edits: door swings are removed to reduce visual clutter, compound line edits are made at stairs and windows, contour lines are the proper line weight, poché is added for spatial clarity, solid tone is used with no hatch pattern. Level 4 Floor Plan of Carnegie Mellon University—Gates Center for Computer Science and Hillman Center for Future Generation Technologies, courtesy of Mack Scogin Merrill Elam Architects.

Constructing the Persuasive Portfolio: the only primer you'll ever need

Floor plate clarity is described with the use of solid tone in the plan. Portfolio design by Katherine Lynch.

Door Swings

Door swings can be an important element in plan drawings. They convey how one enters or exits a space and display understanding of egress constraints. However, they are not a real line that exists in physical space but, rather, they are an indication of the movement of the door.

Solid-line door swings in a plan drawing can be the single most distracting element in a plan—they completely block the legibility of the flow of space and they are a prominent curved element in the drawing that stands out strongly. If nothing else gets corrected, fix this. Luckily, there are several effective ways to make this correction. The challenge is maintaining the eye's ability to move through the plan and visually connect all of the spatial conditions. Every time the eye hits a solid door swing, it stops and has to jump to the next space effectively destroying any spatial continuity trying to be achieved. Make the door swings transparent enough that the eye can pass through them. Here are the options:

1. Remove the door swings completely. However, leave the actual doors open.

2. Change the door swing line to a very thin line.

3. Change the door swing line to a very thin dashed or dotted line.

4. Change the door swing line to a reduced opacity so it is not solid black.

5. Change the door swing line to a combination of any of the above.

Floor Plate Clarity in Plan: Marking Spaces that Are Open to Below

It is a standard practice to mark spaces in plan that do not have a floor plate so they are essentially open to the plan level below. However, there is often confusion about the use of a pair of diagonal lines that cross at the center of the space. These lines should only be used at chase locations—spaces that are not physically accessible in plan. These chases are typically vertical mechanical spaces and are not intended to be occupied. Do not use these diagonal crossed lines for architectural spaces that do not have a floor plate. If there is a large "X" on the plan over these spaces, it becomes impossible to read that the space visually continues across a plan. Instead, place the words "open to below" in the plan using a small, legible typeface with a slight gray tone so it does not compete with the line work of the drawing.

If the floor plan has openings in the floor plate that contribute to the spatial design, then it is a good idea to place tone on the plan drawing to make clear what is solid floor plate and what is open to below. In this case, the lack of tone at the open location makes it clear that certain areas are in fact open to below and it is not absolutely necessary to mark these spaces as "open to below" in the plan.

Image Quality

Ensure that all of the images included in the portfolio are of the highest quality. Now this doesn't mean the "highest quality possible"; they must be at an acceptable level of image resolution. Basically that means if it is obvious something is off in the image, it is not good enough to use. Period.

Image Resolution and Pixelation
Images that are over-scaled in relation to their resolution will appear pixelated. Do not include any images with distinct, visible pixelation in the portfolio.

Image Focus
All photographic images in the portfolio need to be properly focused. Any images that are blurred must be removed. However, it is permissible to use an image that has a very deep focal point; this will make portions of the foreground blurred. Use this technique when trying to identify something deep in the spatial range of an image. Be careful that the foregrounded blur isn't distracting.

Image Hot Spots
Hot spots on the backdrop have already been discussed but hot spots can also become a problem on the model itself—particularly on a white model. When photographing models using studio lighting, make sure no hot spots—blown out white areas—appear in the image. Usually this can be corrected by diffusing the light source or redirecting it so it is not directed parallel to a surface face of the model.

Line Work
Verify that all line work in the drawings is legible when printed at the correct scale in the portfolio. Drawings that have been digitally scanned are notoriously difficult to successfully adjust in Photoshop. Be very careful that lines are not lost as you are trying to remove the tone in the background of the drawing. For vector drawings that are directly placed in your digital portfolio files, line work legibility is still an issue. Do plenty of test prints to determine the lightest line that will still print. For most commercial printing services, the minimum line weight is usually a .25pt line or a .50pt line.

Rich Black Issue
Rich black is technically a color formula used in printing to achieve a more intense, deep black. There are several acceptable formulas for rich black; a common formula is 40% cyan, 40% magenta, 40% yellow and 100% black.

Why does this matter? There is a particular instance in portfolio design where rich black becomes a significant problem. A model image with a 100% black background (this is a Photoshop file) placed within a bounding box in InDesign with a black fill produces a printed file with a visible difference in the blacks. The black in the Photoshop file appears much darker than the black in the InDesign bounding box. There are two ways to correct this. The first is to make the black in the InDesign bounding box match a rich black formula. The second way is to simply increase the canvas size in Photoshop. This creates the entire black background in one program—Photoshop—and eliminates the need for rich black correction altogether. The Photoshop correction is more reliable than the rich black InDesign correction and is seen as the best practice for correcting this issue.

Designing the

Design Actions

 Improve your word selection throughout the portfolio. — page 146

 Review and implement writing tips. — page 146

 Understand and implement the content and visual goals of text in your portfolio. — page 148

 Get straight how you are approaching architecture specific text issues in your portfolio. — page 150

One of the most common questions about portfolio design is focused on the text that should be included in the portfolio. Usually this question comes near the end of the portfolio design and goes like this. . . "So, how much text should I include for each project?" or, "Do I really need to put captions in?"

These questions should raise a red flag in terms of missed opportunities in the conveyance of information through the portfolio design. Yes, it is true that text could be left to one of the last tasks completed; however, it is completely wrong thinking to do this.

In other sections we've discussed the need to use image and word to convey meaning in a portfolio. Taking that statement at face value as true, it stands to reason that by leaving the text work to the end, half of the design work of the portfolio is being purposely avoided. Now, that doesn't make any sense, does it?

While it is not difficult to understand why the development of text might be left until the end, it's still a mistake. The text descriptions should be developed alongside the imagery in the portfolio. Remembering

Graphic Layout

Text in Your Portfolio: What it Says and How it Looks

from the project narrative development discussion, it is totally and completely within the designer's power to control what the reviewer sees and understands about the work. Text should always be used to convey exactly what the reviewer needs to understand about any given visual artifact. And remember when a project is presented in a portfolio, there is no obligation to state what the topic of discussion was within the studio. This is a moment of reflection to decide what the project was really about for you personally or even to decide what you now want the project to focus on.

Obviously, these decisions are incredibly important and should be made at the beginning of the portfolio design exercise and not at the end. Think about it this way: leaving the text until the end—and this includes descriptive text, diagram labels, captions and titles—completely limits what can be said about the work. Resolve the message at the beginning of the process so that it can be delivered to the reviewer about each project, then spend energy making sure that message gets delivered.

There are several different types of text that need to be included for each project. At least the following should be accommodated:

Project Title / Subtitle

Project Statistics: this could be project location, size, type, credits, etc.

Descriptive Text

Captions

Drawing and Diagram Titles

Drawing and Diagram Labels

With all of these different types of text, don't forget the outline of the three levels of reading of a portfolio described in the introductory section of Project Narrative Visual Representation. Keeping these rules in mind will help guide the type of text appropriate for each category.

What it Says: The Value of Words

We've already discussed the importance of text in a portfolio to direct the audience to exactly what they should understand about the projects through the project artifacts. It is incredibly critical to realize the importance of the precise selection of words. This importance has to do with ultimate clarity in what is being conveyed and this requires a very specific selection and collection of words. The more concise and precise the word selection, the clearer the message will be. Don't leave text out and assume the intent is obvious through drawings and images. This is a mistake! The value of the word selection begins with the table of contents and extends through all project text in the entire portfolio.

Project Title

Assign project titles based on what the audience should know about your specific design approach to the project rather than what the professor originally named it on the problem assignment.

Project Descriptive Text

Spend energy here focusing on no more than one primary idea along with several secondary ideas that are important to convey about the project. Make sure to order them starting with the most important point, keeping in mind not everyone is going to read all of the descriptive text. If the suggestion to include project statistics—location, size, brief project description, date of completion, role, etc.—is employed, it is not necessary to repeat any of this information in the descriptive text and energy can be focused on design ideas.

Captions, and Drawing and Diagram Titles and Labels

Captions, and drawing and diagram titles and labels should all be treated similarly when thinking of the value of the selection of words. The amount of text is limited for each of these types of portfolio text and means that each word has an incredible amount of value in conveying direct meaning. Again, write these text types to direct the audience to exactly what they should see in the project imagery. These ideas should completely support the ideas proposed in the project descriptive text.

Writing Tips

Writing style says a lot about what the designer thinks about his or her work. Lazy writing implies only laziness. Keep these writing tips in mind while working through the text in the portfolio:

1. Write first, edit second.

2. Write when in a good mood. It is important to avoid writing when exhausted.

3. Avoid the first person. Don't say, "I did this, then this, then this, etc."

4. Write about the work, not about yourself.

5. It's easier to catch errors in print.

6. There should be absolutely no spelling errors.

7. There should be absolutely no punctuation errors.

8. There should be absolutely no grammar errors.

9. Keep it simple.

10. Keep it concise.

11. Consider the writing to be a design project and approach it accordingly.

How it Looks: The Graphic Presence of Text in a Portfolio

While there should be consideration for what the text in the portfolio says, there also needs to be consideration for the graphic styling of text in the portfolio. Be very careful with typeface selection. It is expected that a professional, legible typeface will be utilized. There is a certain balance and visual correctness that comes with properly placed text. Getting this right can be the difference between a beautiful and convincing visual argument and a completely unprofessional effort.

Okay, so how is this done? It depends on several factors that are different for each designer but there is a set of guidelines to follow and at the very least these guidelines will make the decisions purposeful instead of happenstance. These are the ideas to keep in mind when working through typeface decisions:

1. Choose serif or sans serif based on legibility factors—see the typeface section on this issue.

2. Choose a typeface that has a broad hierarchical range—look for something with, at a minimum, bold, medium and light weights. It is a bonus if there is an extended range beyond this. A trick to extend the hierarchical range of a typeface is to remember that it isn't necessary to always use 100% black for text. Extend the typeface range by including gray as well as black text.

3. Make justification decisions carefully and based on the legibility of the text.

4. Establish a typeface hierarchy system and use it.

Typeface Hierarchy System

Establish a visual hierarchy within the typeface selection that establishes the appropriate focus for each typeface, keeping in mind that the typeface supports the visual image and should never overpower the content graphics. Follow this list as a guideline of typeface hierarchy; they are organized from most visually prominent to least visually prominent:

1. Titles

2. Subtitles

3. Body text

4. Captions

5. Drawing or diagram labels as well as drawing or diagram titles

6. Header or footer including page numbers

Keep in mind that the typeface hierarchy is not just which piece of text is bigger or bolder. Visual hierarchy has to do with the determination of what holds the most visual prominence on the page. And this visual prominence can be achieved in a variety of ways—color, style, weight, etc.

Flexibility Within the Relationships of the Typeface Hierarchy System

There is some flexibility within the above system but don't stray too far from this system or there won't be a framework to work within. If it is decided to develop a different typeface hierarchy system than is listed here, there are some hierarchical relationships that should stay correct. This might get a little confusing but let's try to work through some of the relationships to maintain.

The title needs to be the most important visual piece of text on a project introduction page. It acts as a signal that a new project is starting and directs the reviewer to the correct subject matter—basically what should be known about the project that is coming up. However, this doesn't mean that the title is necessarily biggest or boldest or in an outlandish typeface.

The relationship between the title and the subtitle has a lot of flexibility. We've already established that the title needs to be the most visually prominent on the project introduction page. The subtitle is delivering a secondary piece of information about the project that is important enough not to get buried in the body text so it definitely needs visual legibility. However, it is not so important that it should be as visually prominent as the title. It does need to be smaller than the title and different than the body text.

The relationship between body text and caption is an important one to get correct. The body text should be more visually prominent—in this instance it really is a case of it being larger. The body text needs to read as a block of text that is the most important visual block of text on the page—it contains the synopsis of the design strategies. The caption style must be smaller than the body text, and the difference needs to be great enough that there is no visual confusion between the body text and the caption text.

The caption text and the diagram label text can be the same style if necessary. However, there should be a slight adjustment to the hierarchy for drawing and diagram titles. These might be the same size as the caption text and diagram label text but perhaps in a bold or italic. As mentioned before, do not underline—it is visually distracting.

Typeface to Layout: Balance of Graphic Hierarchy between Image and Text

Not only should the hierarchical relationship within the text pieces of the portfolio be considered, but the hierarchical relationship between the images on the page and the visual presence of the text also needs to be considered. All of the text elements—title, subtitle, body text, caption, drawing or diagram labels, drawing or diagram titles, and header and footer text—take up visual space on the page and need to be managed so the visual narrative that is being told through the imagery remains the primary focus.

Adjacency relationships are important when trying to balance the graphic hierarchy between image and text on a page layout. There are several basic adjacency rules to keep in mind:

1. Descriptive text or body text can float on a page and fill a visual hole. It can act as an objective physical item to counterbalance image placement.

2. Captions must be adjacent to the image they reference. Never let a caption float too far away from its object without a clear visual reference.

3. The same rule governs drawing or diagram titles and labels: do not let these text types stray too far physically from the thing they are titling or labeling.

Content and Visual Goals of Text in a Portfolio

Each text component in the portfolio has different content and visual goals relative to the legibility of the project it is associated with as well as the legibility of the systems within the entire portfolio. Let's discuss each text type separately to understand the similarities and the differences.

Titles

Content Goal: The content goal of each project title is to direct the viewer to the primary objective of the project.

Visual Goal: The visual goal of the project title is to announce the beginning of a new project section within the portfolio.

Subtitles

Content Goal: The content goal of the subtitle is to support the content goal of the title with additional information. This information could be a variety of things and really should be thought of as "What's the second most important thing to announce about a project?"

Visual Goal: The visual goal of the subtitle is to create a typeface buffer between the title and the remainder of the page. The subtitle also visually acts as a support for the title.

Body Text

Content Goal: The content goal of the body text is to convey, as clearly and concisely as possible, the main objectives of the project. This text should be written from your point of view and should not just be a repeat of the assigned problem statement. The body text allows the opportunity to direct the reviewer to the ideas the project is specifically about. It is not necessary to mention every little piece of information that was required to be addressed when the project was first tackled. Once a project becomes part of a portfolio, it can take on a life of its own. Therefore, it is now permissible to design the project narrative to convey exactly what you personally deem significant. Take advantage of this and refocus the project description if needed.

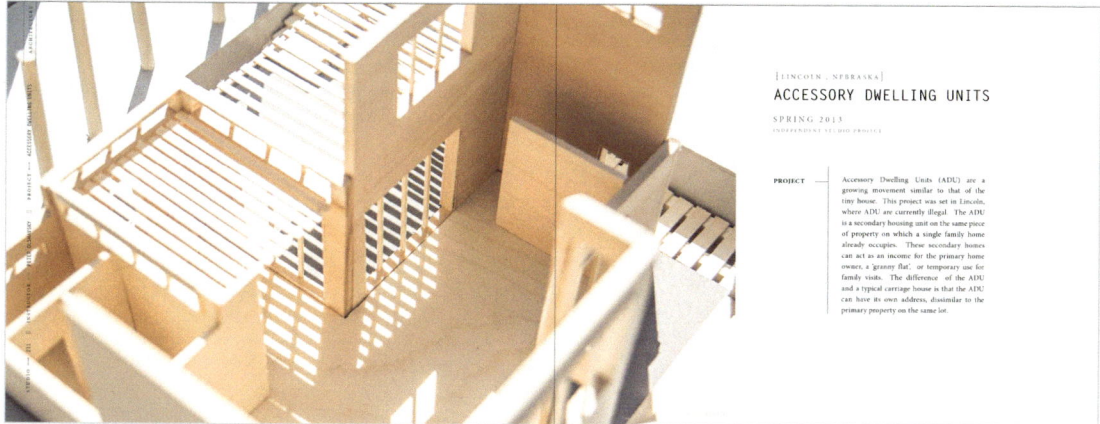

Project introduction page with exemplary illustration of typeface hierarchy. Portfolio design by Liz Szatko.

Visual Goal: The body text takes on a bit of an unusual visual role on the page. Its presence announces that there is substance to a project. It may not always get read but without it a project appears to have no thought behind it. This text also can provide a series of substantive physical edges to use in aligning other visual material.

Captions

Content Goal: The caption acts as the single most powerful focusing device for each specific image. Take advantage of it. The caption, if written correctly, tells the reviewer exactly what to focus on in an image, drawing or diagram and can reinforce or support the conveyance of the project narrative.

Visual Goal: The visual goal of a caption is similar to the visual goal of a subtitle; it lends visual credence to the image it is supporting.

Drawing or Diagram Titles

Content Goal: The drawing or diagram titles announce the purpose of the drawing or diagram. They tell the reviewer the value of the study. Don't assume, even if the drawing or diagram is a normative one, that the reviewer will understand the significance of its inclusion. This is yet another opportunity to let the text support the project narrative.

Visual Goal: The visual goal of the drawing or diagram titles has to do with a fine-grained text resolution on the page. Placing a small collection of words in grounding locations gives the eye a place to start and then visually enter the drawing.

Drawing or Diagram Labels

Content Goal: Drawing or diagram labels provide the sub-level layer of information that is required to understand some of the nuances of a design project. They are each a little different in content so should be discussed separately.

Drawing labels refer to items such as program labels in a plan drawing. It is imperative that some indication is given in the plan drawings of at least significant programmatic elements, particularly as they relate to the project narrative. It is not always necessary to label all programmatic elements. This will need to be determined on a case-by-case basis and is related to not only the information to be conveyed but also the physical space available on the layout to do it.

Diagram labels are a little peculiar in that they often convey a different amount of information than something like a program label on a plan drawing. Diagram labels can very concisely convey project operations or concise project objectives and should be worded very carefully. A significant amount of power is available in the words of diagram labels—take the time to construct them purposefully.

Visual Goal: Visually, both types of labels do similar things as the drawing or diagram titles; they provide visually grounded locations to help the eye move in and around a drawing or diagram.

Header or Footer Including Page Numbers

Content Goal: The content goal of headers or footers is simple. These pieces of text act as orienting devices. The page numbers tell the reviewer where they are in a given portfolio and help navigate through different project sections. The header and footer information reinforces what section of the portfolio the reviewer is in and in this way can reinforce the conveyance of the overall content narrative of the portfolio. The header or footer also often includes the designer's name. This is a promotional strategy and acts as a constant reinforcement through the visual proximity of the work and the designer's name in hopes that an association between the quality of the work and the designer who produced it will be established.

Visual Goal: The visual goal of the header and footer is to define the active area of the page along with appropriate margin settings.

Architecture Specific Text Issues

There are certain text issues that are specific to presenting architectural work. Below is a list to help generate ideas about these issues.

1. When writing dimensions choose a style and remain consistent. Square feet can be abbreviated as Sq. Ft., sq ft, SF or sqft. Meters can be abbreviated as MTRS or m.

2. Ground Floor and First Floor are not actually interchangeable everywhere. Generally in the United Kingdom, Ground Floor is the level entered on and then one level up is the First Floor. Just about everywhere else, Ground Floor and the First Floor are the same. Make sure to be consistent in the labeling throughout all of the projects.

3. Writing level versus floor: just choose one and be consistent when labeling.

4. If labeling plans with a separate key, keep in mind that numbering systems often correspond to their respective floor. For example, the numbering for program labels in a basement should begin with 00, 01, 02, 03, etc. First floor program labels should begin with 10, 11, 12, 13, etc. Second floor program labels should use 20, 21, 22, 23, etc., and so forth as one moves up through the building.

5. It is important in collaborative situations—these occur frequently in the pursuit of architecture—to make sure that all members of a team are included at some point in the project presentation. While it is acceptable to include work produced by other team members to present the comprehensive project, it is imperative that each portion you specifically produced is properly identified. It is a highly desirable skill to be able to collaborate. Show it off!

36

Portfolio exhibits effective use of footer as way-finding system. Also displays compelling use of diagram labels and call-outs. Portfolio design by Ashley R. Claussen.

Designing the Graphic Layout—Text in Your Portfolio: What it Says and How it Looks

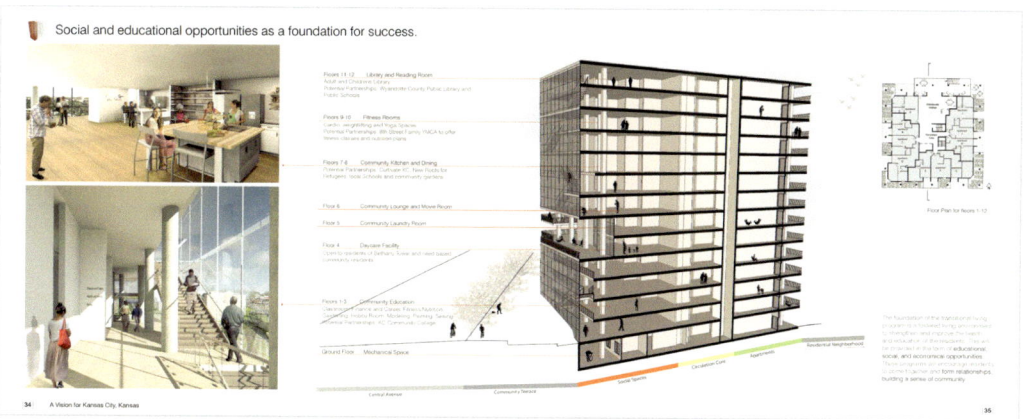

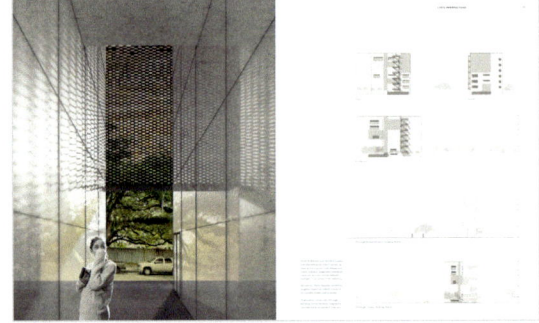

Portfolio layouts demonstrate clear understanding of principles of typeface and image hierarchy. Portfolio design by Thomas Johnston.

Designing the Graphic Layout—Text in Your Portfolio: What it Says and How it Looks

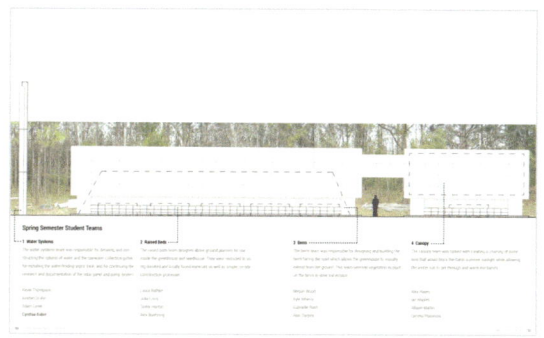
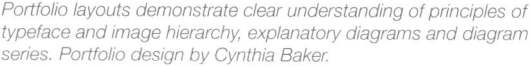

Portfolio layouts demonstrate clear understanding of principles of typeface and image hierarchy, explanatory diagrams and diagram series. Portfolio design by Cynthia Baker.

Constructing the Persuasive Portfolio: the only primer you'll ever need

How adaptive reuse can respond to community needs.

Existing Bethany Tower Conditions

1. Existing Building

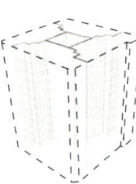
2. Existing Structure

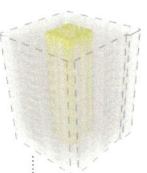
3. Circulation Core

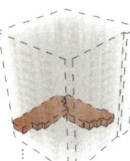
4. Existing Social Spaces

3. Circulation Core: the existing circulation core does not invite social interaction. It is closed off from any views and natural daylight. The proposal connects social spaces to the circulation core and opens views out to the community, as well as inviting social interaction.

4. Existing Social Spaces: the existing community spaces are located on the ground and mezzanine levels, closing off views. Some spaces have no windows and limited natural light. Within the proposal, the social spaces move to the north side, connecting with the activity of Central Avenue.

|30| A Vision for Kansas City, Kansas

An excellent example of typeface hierarchy used to support the graphic layout. Portfolio design by Ashley R. Claussen.

Proposed Design Moves

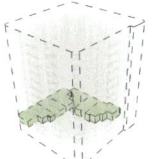
5. Transform to Apartments

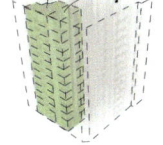
6. Relocate Apartments

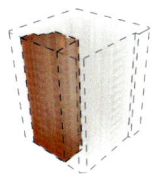
7. Create Social Spaces

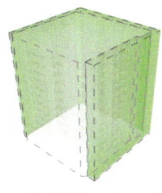
8. Add Greenhouse Envelope

9. Structure Addition

5. Renovate existing social spaces to apartments.
6. Change select apartments to two bedroom, relocating residents and increasing occupancy.
7. Renovate north apartments to social spaces to respond to active life of Central Avenue.
8. Greenhouse envelope provides private greenhouses to all residents on balcony.
9. Structure addition to provide additional balcony space to exterior and support for greenhouse addition.
10. Final view of Proposal

Designing the

Design Actions

(37) *Perform a thorough visual review of your portfolio.* page 158

(38) *Review your portfolio page by page against the graphics editing checklist.* page 158

(39) *Review your portfolio page by page against the copy editing checklist.* page 159

Graphic Layout

Editing and Reviewing Your Work

One of the single most important things you can do and the absolute last thing you'll want to do is review and edit your design work. Reviewing and editing your work happens at the end of the process when you would really just prefer to be done with the portfolio altogether. However, it should be noted that a properly edited portfolio is a direct sign of professionalism and is a step that you cannot afford to skip. The best way to move through this tedious task is to work within a specific system of review.

There are really two different types of editing reviews for your portfolio. The first is a visual review and has to do with the nature of the graphic representation of your portfolio as a whole. The second type of editing review is a copy editing review. It is designed to catch all of the specific text, grammar, style, etc. issues.

Visual Review Process

For any type of review process, it is best to work from a printed version of your portfolio—even when designing a digital portfolio. Once the portfolio is printed, red-line the entire document and work back and forth through the printed pages to ensure consistency in editing. Then work through the editing checklists taking one item at a time and go page by page making sure to mark off the edits as they are corrected. Just as you need to work through graphic edits and copy edits, it is important to work on your editing at a variety of scales. Pinning up your portfolio in its entirety will help you see the design of the portfolio holistically. This is the best way to begin your graphic review.

Editing Checklists

Below are two checklists that can be used as a beginning guide to perform the editing checks on your portfolio. Add items to the list as you think of them! Take one item at a time and work through the entire portfolio marking that one item. Then move to the next item on the list and so on.

Graphics Editing Checklist

Similar graphics are consistent throughout.

Color implementation is verified as same color throughout as appropriate.

Each page is uncluttered visually.

Proper typeface hierarchy has been established and maintained throughout.

Headers are the correct typeface and size throughout.

Footers are the correct typeface and size throughout.

Titles are the correct typeface and size throughout.

Subtitles are the correct typeface and size throughout.

Body text is the correct typeface and size throughout.

Captions are the correct typeface and size throughout.

Diagram labels are the correct typeface and size throughout.

Delete any dummy text that has not been used.

Page margins are the same throughout.

Avoid word breaks and therefore hyphens at the end of each line.

Check that there are no widows in the text.

Check that there are no orphans in the text.

Check that there are no runts in the text.

Bullets are not too large visually—reduce them in scale if necessary.

Images that are supposed to be aligned are indeed aligned.

Margins between images are correct, consistent and equal throughout.

All images are in focus.

All images are high enough in resolution—no pixelation.

All scanned drawings have clean edges—no erroneous lines at the drawing edges.

All spreads have color consistency between elements on the spread.

All images have proper lighting with no hot spots.

All digital images have been properly edited; all dust, dirt and junk have been digitally removed.

Images and diagrams are the proper scale relative to the page.

Captions and labels are the correct and consistent distance from the images.

Arrow heads are not graphically distracting.

Bar scales are included where needed.

Section cut lines are included where needed.

North arrows are included where needed.

Drawings have proper line weights.

Compound line edits have been addressed in drawings.

Door swing style has been addressed in drawings.

Copy Editing Checklist

Table of Contents is properly formatted to match hierarchy established in portfolio.

Table of Contents has correct page numbers.

Table of Contents has correct heads that match project sections and / or project titles exactly.

Page numbers on all pages are correct.

Headers on all pages are correct.

Footers on all pages are correct.

All typos have been eliminated.

Spelling is correct. Run spell check.

Spelling is consistent.

Punctuation is correct.

Punctuation is consistent.

Capitalizations are correct.

Capitalizations are consistent.

Check for subject and verb agreement.

Tense doesn't change mid sentence.

Tense is consistent throughout portfolio.

Captions are correct to the image or drawing they are referencing.

Abbreviations are correct and you've spelled out the abbreviation the first time it is used so that the abbreviated reference is understood.

Long sentences are divided for clarity.

Phrases are listed in a parallel manner.

Formatting and punctuation of lists is clear and consistent throughout.

Use consistent terminology. Make sure you're using the same name for the same thing each time.

Correct spelling and capitalization of product names, particularly software.

Numbers follow correct guidelines—spell out numbers one through nine. Use numerals for 10 through infinity.

Hyphens are used correctly. A hyphen is used in word construction: self-evident.

En dashes are used correctly. An en dash is used when describing a range in time or numbers: 1999–2010.

Em dashes are used correctly. An em dash is used in sentence structure to set apart a phrase: Bananas, apples and chicken—these are some of the things I have to get at the store.

Adjust type so there are no more than three lines in a row that end with a hyphenated word.

All double spaces are removed from text.

Remove paragraph indentions throughout.

Page numbers are odd on the right-hand side of the spread and even on the left-hand side of the spread.

Either roman numerals are used on front matter for pagination or page numbers have been removed from these pages.

No headers or footers are found on section divider spreads or on other pages that don't require them.

Choose Sq. Ft., sq ft, SF or sqft (or MTRS or m) style and stay consistent throughout.

Determining P

Portfolio Format

162 **The Printed Portfolio**
  Print Portfolio Types
  Portfolio Dimensions and Orientation
  Deciding on a Production Method
  Printing Options
  Binding the Portfolio
  Material Choices

172 **The Digital Portfolio**
  Determining Digital Portfolio Goals
  Digital Portfolio Types
  Issues Presenting Architectural Work Digitally
  Basic Web Guidelines

Determining P

Design Actions

- ㊵ *Understand different print portfolio types and determine which ones need to be produced from your designed portfolio system.* page 164

- ㊶ *Review and implement portfolio dimensions and orientation guidelines.* page 165

- ㊷ *Decide on a printing method.* page 166

- ㊸ *Decide on a binding type.* page 166

- ㊹ *Decide on cover material and design.* page 170

- ㊺ *Decide on paper type.* page 171

Portfolio Format

The Printed Portfolio

Determining appropriate portfolio format seems like it is the most important task of all the portfolio design tasks. Well, the truth of the matter is… it is and it isn't. The best way to manage the issue of portfolio format is to think of it more as portfolio flexibility. This flexibility extends to the design of the portfolio, the content of the portfolio and ultimately the output of the portfolio.

Think back and reference the previous discussion about the necessary flexibility of the portfolio format. The best plan is to design one system that is flexible enough for a variety of formats. In the case of an architectural portfolio, it is much easier to design for print and convert to digital than the other way around. As architects, we design in systems. The flexible portfolio is the ultimate designed system.

There are several different types of typical portfolio formats to be aware of, each with specifically different goals. Flexibility of the portfolio system should be able to accommodate any of the types listed here. Even though there are many different nuanced types of formats, there are two main categories: print portfolio or digital portfolio.

Tactile Qualities of the Printed Portfolio

One of the best things about a printed portfolio is the physical nature of the book and its relationship to the human body. A printed portfolio has a tactile quality that can be used to advantage if appropriate design decisions are made regarding materials and production methods. It has the ability to convey, just through its physicality, the care and consideration placed in the design work.

Print Portfolio Types

This portfolio type is just what is says: printed on paper. There are many types of printed portfolios; below is a list with brief descriptions of the typical categories of printed portfolios. Keep in mind that the goals of portfolio output flexibility apply to these printed portfolio types. Design once and plan to output in multiple ways depending on the requirements of each specific portfolio application.

Cut Sheets

Printed cut sheets are usually submitted with a resume and cover letter and are formatted to match those text documents—letter-sized or A4. Each individual cut sheet is typically focused on one single project. It is appropriate to submit three to five cut sheets with each application. Consider the cut sheets to be an introduction to specific design abilities. The format is important; these documents should be easy to file, meaning they need to fit in a file cabinet. Outrageously sized documents that have been designed to get noticed can land the work in the trash bin if the professional organization being applied to can't properly store the material.

Leave-Behind or Mailer

Both the leave-behind and the mailer portfolio formats are usually less comprehensive than a full portfolio and can be considered similarly. The leave-behind is a portfolio that is literally left with the design firm after the interview and is considered a reminder to them of you and your work. The mailer is a portfolio that is sent in as part of an introduction package. It is considered a brief introduction to you and your work. The leave-behind, mailer and cut sheets could all be the same thing. However, consider a leave-behind or mailer as slightly more robust than the cut sheets but less comprehensive than the actual primary portfolio.

Primary Portfolio

A printed portfolio should be a reflection of the manner in which the designer produces a physical object. While similar in design task to any other portfolio format—including a digital portfolio—the printed portfolio is often requested so that the designer can be evaluated on the care with which this object was created. Paper selection, printing method, trim size, binding style, etc. all work together to deliver this message.

Interview Portfolio

The interview portfolio format is typically a larger format than any of the other printed portfolio formats. The printed interview portfolio is used—just as the title indicates—for an in-person interview. The size of the portfolio becomes an issue as the portfolio is being used to show another person, or persons, the work and it needs to be large enough for multiple people to review it at once. It is entirely possible to use a standard-sized portfolio (Letter or A4) for the interview portfolio; the thing to avoid is a miniature portfolio. Showing up for an interview with a 7" x 7" portfolio can be frustrating for the reviewers. Make sure to provide the best opportunity to show work in its best light during an interview.

Portfolio Dimensions and Orientation

Portfolio size and orientation has been discussed in detail in an earlier section, but it bears mentioning again. Keep these guidelines in mind:

1. Prepare the portfolio to meet required specifications.

2. Be aware that an oversized portfolio that will not fit in a standard file cabinet might get thrown away based solely on storage issues.

3. Either horizontal or vertical portfolio format is fine but make the decision with purpose.

4. Do not force the reviewer to rotate the portfolio between horizontal and vertical formats by changing the orientation of the portfolio from page to page.

Deciding on a Production Method

The primary decision to be made regarding the production of a portfolio is whether it will all be produced by hand, part of it will be produced by hand and part through a printing service, or if the entire portfolio will be produced through a printing service.

No matter which choice is made, it is prudent to do a series of test prints on the actual printer that will be used or through the actual printing service that will be used. It is very difficult—almost impossible—to get a print to completely match the color seen on screen. It is also important to understand how work will look once printed on different papers, etc. There can be radical color shifts depending on the paper selection and printing method so test early in the process and test often!

Printing in Color Models: RGB versus CMYK

There are two primary color models: RGB—red, green, blue for digital color—and CMYK—cyan, magenta, yellow and black for print color.

Keep in mind, CMYK is the color model for printing. RGB is the color model for digital files. If the portfolio material is in the RGB color model and the files are printed, there will be a noticeable color shift in the printed files. Typically when shifting from RGB to CMYK—going from digital to print output—colors will dull slightly. When shifting from CMYK to RGB—going from print to digital output—colors will increase in vibrancy.

It is not necessary to aggressively worry about these different color models, but it is important to understand the differences so that it is easy to recognize when a problem is present.

Printing Options

There are a variety of printing options available to output a portfolio. Each printing option has very different output qualities that should be taken into consideration.

Inkjet Printing

Inkjet printing can be successful on either a desktop inkjet printer or through a service bureau. Inkjet printing drops ink onto the page through ink cartridges that use combinations of cyan, magenta, yellow and black. With a good inkjet printer, astonishing results with a rich output of colors can be achieved.

Offset Printing

Offset printing is a printing process where an inked image is transferred—offset—from a plate to a rubber blanket and then to the paper. It is typically used for printing multiple copies of the same book and is the primary printing process used in professional printing.

Online Printing Services

There are several reputable online printing services that offer one-off offset printing services. Essentially, online printing services offer the quality of offset printing at a reasonable price without having to purchase a large quantity of books. Two good services are Blurb (blurb.com) and Lulu (lulu.com).

Color Laser Printing

Color laser printing is likely a printing process that most have easy access to. The truth of the matter regarding color laser printing is that it is not good enough quality for a professional portfolio. There is a chance that there is a service bureau that can produce a decent color laser print but in general it is problematic. Color laser printing uses toner instead of ink; the toner sits on top of the paper and often produces a shiny image whose tone lacks richness.

Binding the Portfolio

There are several things to consider when deciding what type of binding to use for a portfolio. Two things stand out as priorities: one is whether or not the portfolio will lay flat when open, and the other is what happens to images that bridge the gutter.

There will often be a trade-off between these two parameters. Weigh them against your specific objectives and make a decision. It is a good idea for the portfolio to be able to lay as flat as possible when it is open. This makes it easier for the reviewer to look at work. It is not an ideal situation if the reviewer has to fight the portfolio to keep the book open and prevent the pages from flipping. Often the bindings that permit a book to lay completely flat do not allow for images to bridge the gutter and remain a continuous image. When images are cut with a gap at the gutter of the spread it can cause legibility problems so be mindful of this issue.

Hard Bound: Sewn or Glued

Hard cover bindings include a stiff material for the front cover, the back cover and the book spine. A hard cover binding can have sewn or glued signatures—groups of pages folded together and attached at the spine. Pages that are sewn at the binding are more durable and more flexible than those that are just glued. Hard cover books with a sewn binding lay more flat than those with a glue binding. Hard cover books are much more durable than soft cover books but are also more costly to produce. Hard cover books allow images that span the gutter to be read as a singular image without a visual break at the gutter.

Soft Bound: Perfect Binding

Perfect binding is a soft cover method of binding that uses glue to attach signatures. Since the pages are attached in groups rather than separately, the pages are less likely to come loose from the binding edge one by one. Perfect binding gives a very professional appearance and, depending on the number of pages in a portfolio and the size of the pages, it can lay relatively flat. Soft cover books allow images that span the gutter to be read as a singular image without a visual break at the gutter. There are options for perfect binding single pages rather than signatures. This method works as

Determining Portfolio Format—The Printed Portfolio

hard bound—sewn or glued   soft bound—perfect binding   wire binding

Knowing how your portfolio will be bound will change decisions about the design of the layouts. Make this decision with purpose.

long as the book doesn't use particularly thick paper or get too thick at the spine. Either of these situations encourages pages to pop out of the glue binding.

Wire Binding

Wire binding is another great option for binding a portfolio. The biggest advantage to wire binding is that, since it is a coil, the portfolio will open completely flat and will stay open. It is also easy to find a print shop that has a wire binding machine. Be aware, however, that wire binding means a spread is physically split apart at the gutter so any images that span the gutter will be split. With particularly strong images, the gutter jump matters less because it is easy enough for the eye to stitch the image back together across the gutter.

Book Jackets and Extras

It is always possible to add things such as a full dust jacket to the portfolio—hard cover or soft cover—or a belly band—a partial dust jacket—to emphasize certain design elements within the portfolio.

Avoid These Bindings

Avoid any binding methods that are overly articulated. Avoid screw post attachments, nuts and bolts, ribbons, twine, etc. Stay away from plastic coil bindings: they look cheap and are not durable; portfolio pages will begin to slip out of the coil with very little use. If done poorly these bindings tend to look sophomoric and crafty.

Book Cloth Tutorial

If you feel compelled to create something handmade, here's something you can do that still looks professional. Make a hard cover for your portfolio that has been covered in book cloth. It is an effective way to make a wire bound portfolio more durable and it's easy to do!

Constructing the Persuasive Portfolio: the only primer you'll ever need

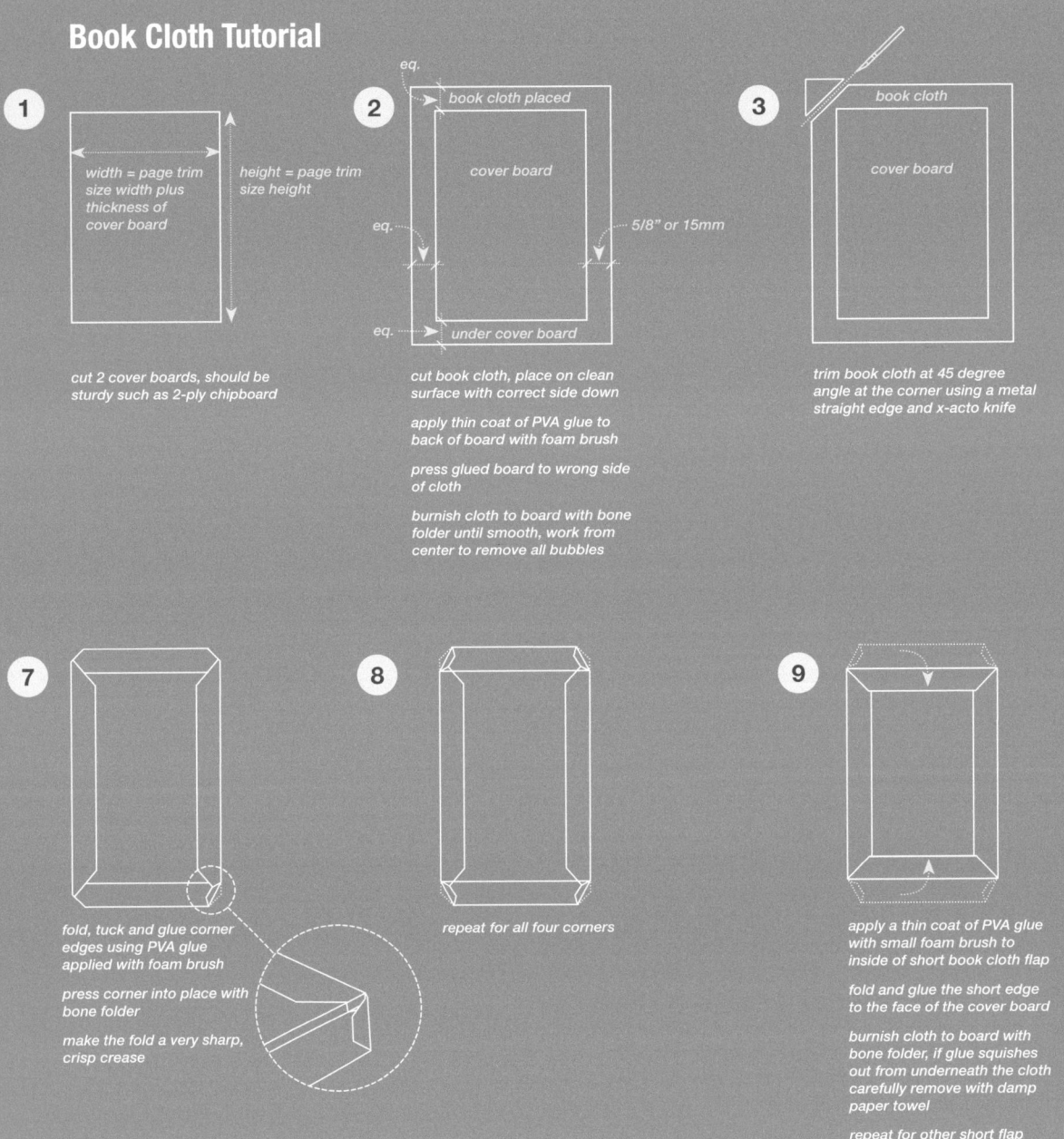

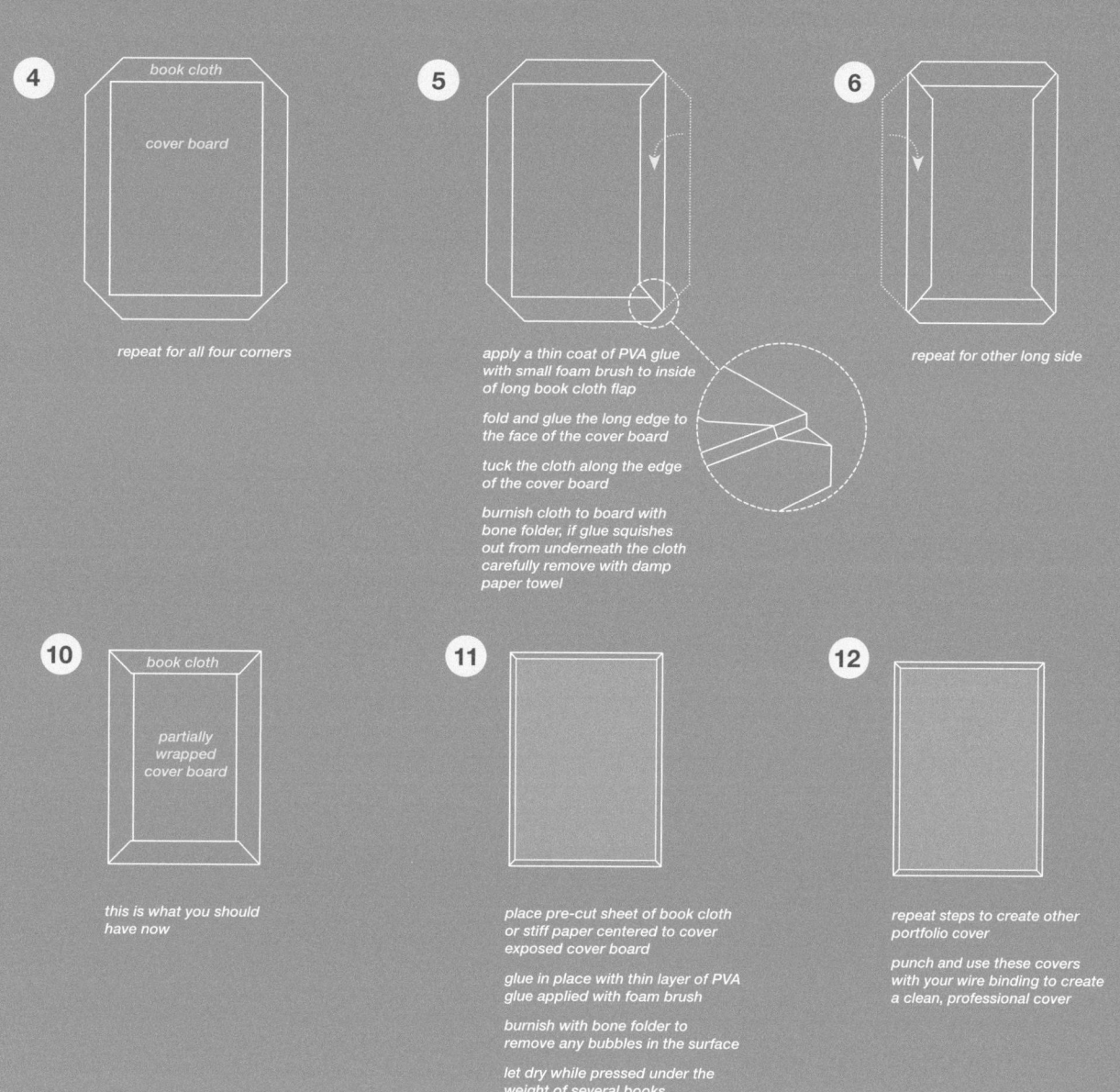

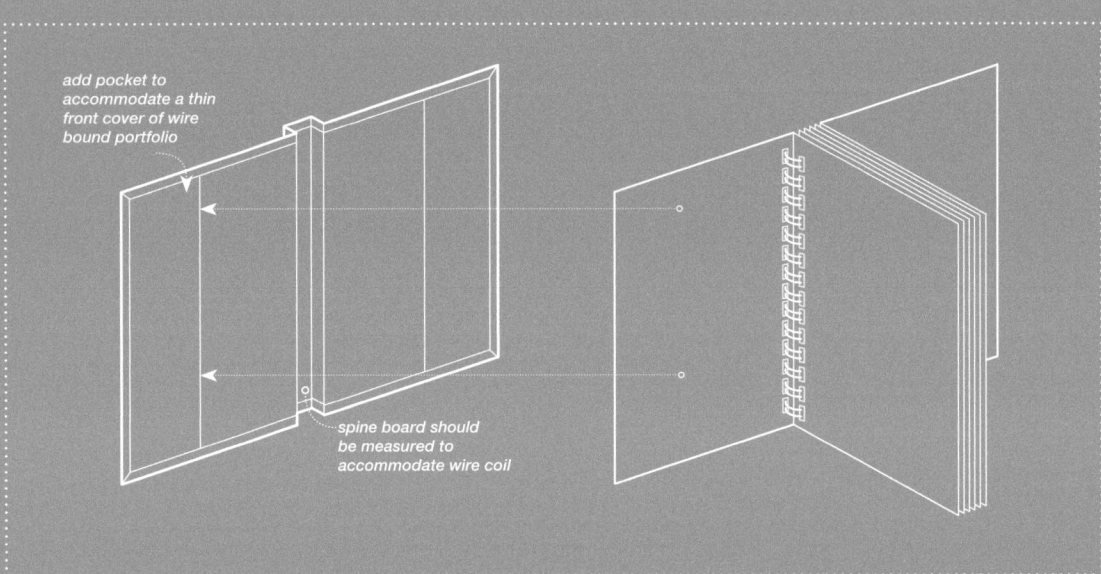

Make a full, three-panel cloth cover following the same methods in the book cloth tutorial. However, this time, use three book boards together—a front board, a spine board and a back board.

Material Choices

Material choices become very important for the tactile quality of a portfolio. These selections can greatly alter the look and feel of a portfolio.

The printed portfolio should also be designed with its durability in mind. Make material choices for the portfolio that have properties of durability and are not noticeably delicate. Solid colors on the cover with any sort of sheen will quickly show fingerprints. Soft bound portfolios without some thickness to the card stock on the cover will fray and get dented at the edges. Paper that is too thin on the interior of the portfolio will tear after several reviews. The list goes on but the point is clear: pay attention to these choices, they matter.

Cover

The cover of the portfolio is the first opportunity to make an impression on the reviewer of the portfolio. It is important that the cover sets the appropriate mood for the remainder of the portfolio. There are many options for a strong cover design and anything will work as long as it makes sense with the design of the remainder of the portfolio.

Hard Cover
Hard covers can be used for either hard backed portfolios with glued or sewn spines or for wire bound portfolios. If making it yourself, the hard cover is typically made from chipboard, black museum board or is wrapped in book cloth. Laser-cut windows can be cut into this surface to expose text located on the title page, but be careful not to go overboard with this technique. When using an online print service with a hard cover, there will likely be an opportunity to create a printed cover design often referred to as an image wrap.

Soft Cover
Soft covers can also be used in bound portfolios with a glued edge or for wire bound portfolios. Since they are more flexible by nature, they can be slightly less durable than a hard cover. If making it yourself, use a heavier weight yet flexible paper; this paper should be thicker than what is being used in the body of the portfolio. If using an online printing service for your soft cover, there will also likely be an opportunity to create a printed cover design often referred to as an image wrap.

Simple versus Overworked Cover Design
Be very mindful of the cover design. The majority of architecture portfolios have a very stately, minimalist cover design. This is absolutely fine and is seen as the normative condition. The cover design doesn't have to be this way. The cover could successfully have a powerful color or a simple band of images from the work found within the portfolio. The things to avoid when designing the portfolio cover really fall into the handmade, crafty or overdesigned category. So be careful not to overdesign and produce a cover that is too articulated. Excessively laser-cut covers or covers made from wood or Plexiglas should be avoided. Often with these portfolios, the overworked cover is seen as misguided indulgence to make up for the lack of well-designed content within the portfolio.

Paper

There is a wide variety of paper options that will greatly change the way images are represented in print. It is important to understand the choices and make purposeful decisions in the selection of these materials.

Opacity and Thickness
Paper thickness and its relative opacity go hand in hand. Select a paper that does not permit image bleed-through from one page to the next. To test this, print on both sides of a sheet of paper and lay the paper flat on a table. There should be no visibility of the image located on the reverse of the paper when it is positioned with no light coming through it.

Paper is measured in weight in pounds and is directly related to paper thickness. The higher the number, the thicker the paper. Keep in mind the weight allocations are relevant to specific individual paper lines. So weights may not translate across a variety of paper selections. 20# paper in one type of paper may not be the same thickness as 20# paper of another type.

Coated versus Uncoated Paper
Different paper finishes will produce vastly different image results. The first choice is to decide between coated and uncoated paper. Coated paper has been treated with a substance that acts as a sealant and alters the way the paper accepts and absorbs ink. Coated paper typically comes in a range of gloss, satin and matte. Be careful about using a high gloss paper; the reflection of light off the paper will make it more difficult to see the details associated with drawings and renderings found in an architectural portfolio. Satin paper is often a nice compromise between gloss paper and matte paper but make sure to see a sample since satin finishes vary widely between different paper types. A matte paper produces rich, deep colors because it accepts the ink more readily. Also there is no visible sheen apparent to images printed on matte paper and therefore it is easier to see the content without a reflective glare. Uncoated papers have no sealant on the surface; therefore the ink is absorbed into the paper. Uncoated papers tend to dull the printed colors. This may sound like a negative aspect but, in fact, printing on uncoated paper can produce a lovely softness to the printed inks.

Brightness and Whiteness
It is not important to understand the science between the ratings of brightness and whiteness of paper. It is important, however, to understand that they are two different ratings. Brightness relates to a paper's ability to reflect light. The higher the number, the more reflective—brighter—the paper will be. Whiteness refers to the color shade of a piece of paper. Suffice it to say that all "white" paper is not the same color at all and when placed side by side will likely vary incredibly. This can be very distracting in a print portfolio if you move between blue-white paper and warm-white paper. Make sure brightness and whiteness of all paper selections match or at least coordinate.

Determining P[ortfolio]

Design Actions

(46) *Match your goals and objectives for creating a digital portfolio to the value of each digital portfolio option before embarking on a separate digital portfolio exercise.* page 173

(47) *Review and implement issues related to presenting architectural work digitally.* page 177

(48) *Review and implement basic web guidelines.* page 178

Portfolio Format

The Digital Portfolio

Determining Digital Portfolio Goals

It is important to take some time and think through the value of each digital portfolio type and match and align the overall portfolio goals prior to embarking on the specific design of a digital portfolio. The goals and function of a digital portfolio will likely be directly related to a specific request from an organization that is being applied to. As discussed below, there are a variety of digital portfolio types. Do not spend time designing a digital portfolio that only has a life as a digital portfolio unless that is the only goal to be achieved. As mentioned before, it is best to design one portfolio system that can accommodate a variety of outputs.

Typically digital portfolios are requested to accommodate the portfolio review needs of the organization requesting it. For example, a scholarship program may wish to review portfolio applications through digital projection so that a large committee can review the material together. Other organizations may wish for something to arrive via email so they do not have to physically store all of the print portfolios they might receive.

Think through the objectives of the organization requesting a digital portfolio; it can help determine which output makes the most sense to produce.

There will probably be a point in any designer's career when it makes sense to have a website that comprehensively describes their work. This is certainly the case when owning your own design firm or trying to make a presence as a legitimate company; a website makes sense in this case. But for application purposes, energy is better spent designing one system with multiple output opportunities.

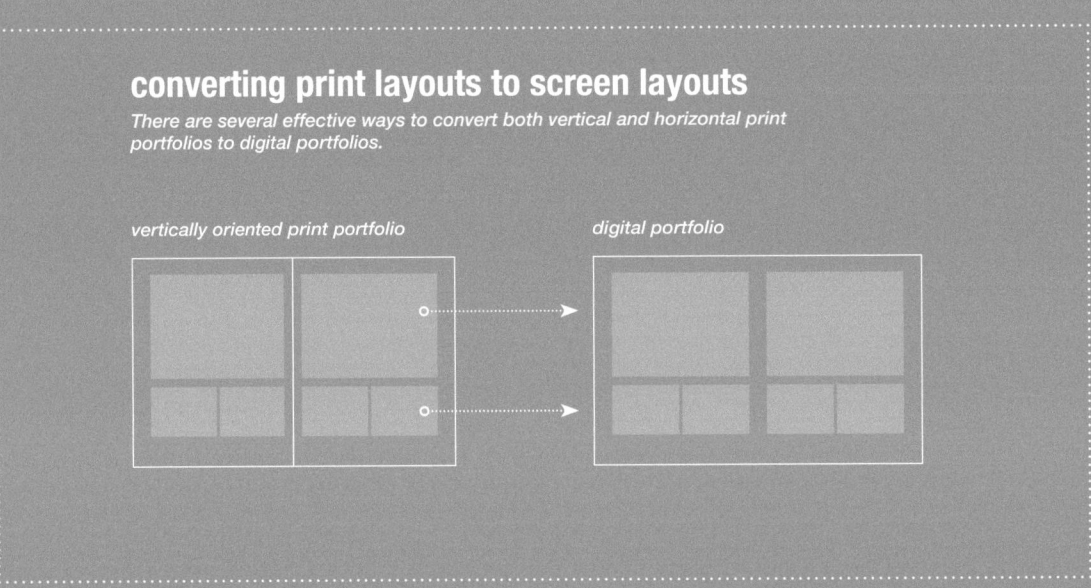

Two spreads of a vertical print portfolio convert seamlessly to a digital portfolio that takes advantage of the horizontal format of a digital screen.

Digital Portfolio Types

Just like the print portfolio, digital portfolios have a variety of formats. They are largely organized in two categories: web portfolios and portable digital documents—typically PDF files.

Web Portfolio
Having the ability to provide some version of a web-based portfolio is critical. At some point in a designer's academic or professional career, an organization will request a URL for the review of work. The ultimate trick is to figure out how to prepare this information without having to embark upon the redesign of an entirely new portfolio system.

Architectural web portfolios are typically designed around a standard gallery website that provides navigational content around links such as: About the Designer, Projects, Resume, Awards, etc. Since the portfolio resides online, it is very easy to send out the URL to get material easily seen by a large variety of people. However, there are some negatives to consider with this kind of portfolio. A web portfolio simply is not very flexible. It is a one stop, one look, one message presentation of work and does not necessarily provide the flexibility of designing a single system that can have multiple outputs. The other drawback with a web portfolio is that since the navigation system is a digital interface, it is more difficult to develop a project narrative that unfolds in the designed and desired manner. Below are several types of web portfolios each with their own pros and cons.

Self-Coded Website
A self-coded website is exactly as it sounds and requires extensive knowledge of coding language and web design strategies in order to be successful.

Determining Portfolio Format—The Digital Portfolio

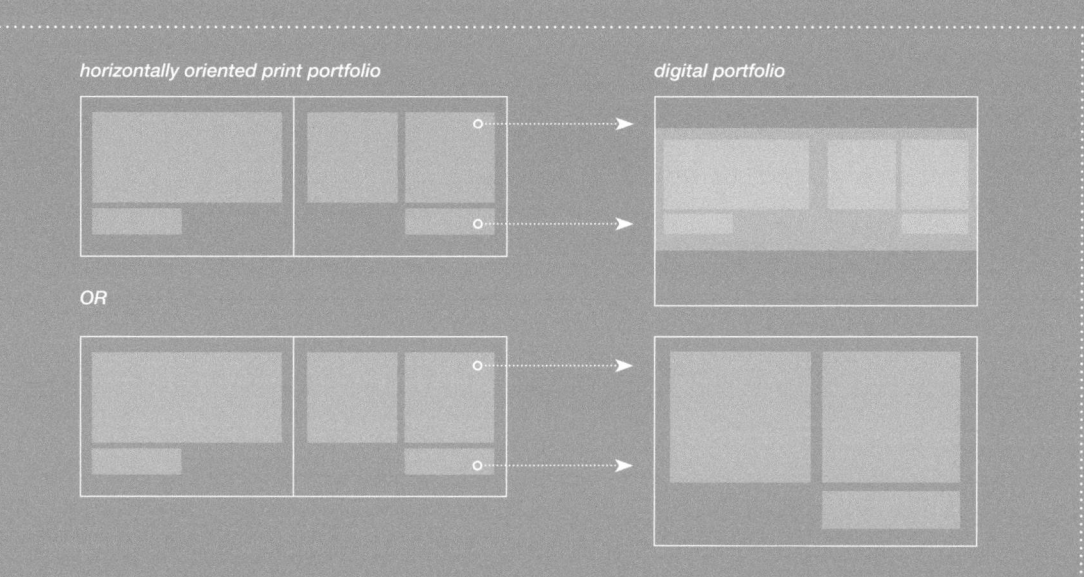

Horizontally formatted portfolios offer two easy options for digital conversion. You can take the entire long, skinny horizontal layout and reduce it to a band of material that spans the screen thus keeping the relationships developed for the print spreads true. Alternately, you can export each individual page as a separate screen.

Pros: The pro to this type of website is that there is an opportunity to build something from scratch that is representative of exactly how the work should be organized. Of course, this is also one of the clear opportunities offered with a print portfolio.

Cons: The con to this type of website is that it requires extensive knowledge of coding language and web design strategies. There is a significant risk of the web design looking sophomoric if the designer doesn't know what they are doing. An additional con to this type of website is that it requires regular maintenance to keep up with browser updates, software updates, etc.

Pre-Coded Portfolio Template Website: Gallery Website
A pre-coded portfolio template website—also known as a gallery website—is one that is already coded and the designer can add images and text to the template. There are often some choices that can be made regarding the look and feel of the template.

Pros: The primary pro for a gallery website is that it produces a professional looking website with minimal understanding from the designer of how the coding works. There are literally hundreds of vendors that offer this service so there are a significant amount of options from which to choose.

Cons: With a gallery website there are limitations to the layouts provided by each vendor, with minimal ability to change the primary functionality of the website.

Blog Website
The typical blog website—something like WordPress—is a relatively persuasive solution to the development of a website. A blog website operates on the premise of

making daily updates in both text and word and typically organizes posts in this manner.

Pros: The pro for a blog website is that even though it was developed for daily post updates, it is relatively easy to understand the organization of a blog site to adapt it to specific needs. It is possible to make more of a gallery style website with a blog website but it requires some time to figure out how to adapt it.

Cons: The primary con for a using a blog site for a portfolio website is that it does require significant time to figure out how to adapt it to individual needs. It is possible, but it does take time. If aiming for a gallery site anyway, why spend this extra time figuring out how to adapt blog software?

Web-Based Book Portfolio
A web-based book portfolio—something like ISSUU.com—is a website that allows the designer to upload a PDF of a printed book-style portfolio. The book gets embedded in a URL and it operates by essentially "flipping" through the portfolio as if it were a printed book.

Pros: The best thing about this type of website is that it uses a PDF output of an already designed print portfolio. Then the portfolio operates online as it was designed to in print.

Cons: Frankly, there are no cons in terms of students or young professionals who need to have a web location for their portfolio.

PDF Output: Email it, Put it on CD, or Upload it

A PDF (portable document format) is often a reasonable solution for a digital portfolio. A PDF can be easily exported from an already designed print portfolio. This format affords a wide range of options for dispersing a portfolio and can accommodate a variety of format requirements from different organizations. After generating a PDF of the portfolio, the file can be optimized thus reducing the size of the file so that it becomes appropriate to email the portfolio in its entirety for a digital review. The PDF can also be burned onto a CD to mail to an organization. And lastly, there are several online websites that present a print portfolio in a digital format by uploading and reading the PDF; see the previous section on web-based book portfolios.

How to Best Export a PDF from Adobe InDesign
There are several methods to export a PDF from Adobe InDesign. One particular method is recognized by most printing services and publishers as the preferred method to achieve the best results. This is the process: in Adobe InDesign navigate to the top menu bar, select File / Adobe PDF Presets / High Quality Print. The pop up menu will provide a wide range of options: compression settings, crop marks, bleed settings, print page settings of single page or spread output, etc.

Optimizing PDF Files: How to Manage Resolution and PDF Output
One of the most challenging things about outputting a portfolio as a PDF is that since the portfolio was designed for print, image resolution and file size reflects this output. Once a PDF is exported, the resultant file size is too big to be practical and useful. There is a fine balance between adjusting the output quality of the images and the file size. Reduce the file size so that the file can be emailed or uploaded but make sure not to sacrifice image quality in the process of optimization. There are some tricks.

To optimize a PDF file, do the following: open the PDF in Adobe Acrobat Pro; select File / Save As or Save As Other / Optimized PDF; in the pop-up window under Image Settings, ensure that all ppi settings are below 300ppi; select Discard User Data in the left window; select Discard Private Data of Other Applications; select Discard Hidden Layer Content and Flatten Visible Layers in the main window. Click OK.

Ultimately determine what the required file size limitations are for the PDF submission—this will be provided by the organization being applied to—and work toward those specifications.

Issues Presenting Architectural Work Digitally

For any of the digital portfolio options, there are issues that are specific to the presentation of architectural work that should be considered to ensure the absolute best quality results.

Digital Color Models: RGB versus CMYK

These color models were discussed in a previous section but are worth mentioning again to ensure understanding relative to your digital output. There are two primary color models: RGB—red, green, blue for digital color—and CMYK—cyan, magenta, yellow and black for print color.

RGB is an additive color model where red, green, and blue light are added together in various ways to reproduce a broad array of colors. The RGB color model is used for the digital display of color.

CMYK is a subtractive color model that describes the actual color printing process and references four colors used in color printing: cyan, magenta, yellow and black.

Remember, when a file is swapped between color models, shifts will happen in the color profiles. Don't worry too much about this shift, just be aware of it so a problem can be recognized when it arises.

Line Weight Challenges

Maintaining proper line weights in digitally viewed files can be a challenge. When working in a print portfolio, clear line weights are easier to manage because the actual prints are available to review and adjust as needed. While it is not possible to simulate and predict every way a digital file will be viewed, it is possible to make some best guesses regarding what will happen to line weights as they are viewed digitally. Typically, line weights that look perfectly legible in print will be too light when digitally projected. More times than not, this is the direction of degradation of line weights. In most cases, it is best practice to increase the weight of line work if it is going to be viewed digitally.

Typeface Size and Scale

Similar problems happen with the legibility of typefaces when viewed digitally. Typefaces that are perfectly legible in print can often feel completely out of scale when viewed digitally. It is usually the case that typefaces that are comfortable to read at a print scale are too small to be read comfortably digitally. Increasing typeface size and scale might be necessary in order to make the text legible digitally. Remember, if any of the typefaces are changed for digital legibility, it may be necessary to reestablish proper hierarchy on the page by adjusting other typefaces or even their physical relationship to other objects on the page.

White on Black versus Black on White

Rules of typeface legibility indicate that placing black text on a white background is the most legible of any color combinations. This fact is the case in both print and digital outputs. However, particularly with architectural model photography with standard black backgrounds, there are quite a few instances when it is necessary to use white text on a black background. Typically in print, it is necessary to increase the size of the typeface for legibility reasons when placing white text on a black background because a printer does not drop white ink. A printer will drop black ink and the black will begin to encroach on the white area thus making the text appear smaller. There is a similar print issue when using white line work on a black background.

However, this also occurs in digital files but for different reasons. While there is no worry about black ink encroaching on the white text or lines in digital files, there is a visible legibility problem when it comes to white text or lines on a black background. Pay attention and make sure that there is enough visible contrast so the eye can pick up the differences between background color and foreground color. Again, it may be necessary to increase line weights and typeface sizes.

Color Vibration

There are certain color combinations that vibrate uncomfortably—particularly in digital files—when they are located in an adjacent location. While some of these color combinations may seem vibrant and powerful, if their use makes it uncomfortable for someone to read text or review portfolio materials, then it seems to defeat the purpose! Avoid these color vibrations. Determine if colors will vibrate against one another by placing them in an adjacent relationship and if a spatial shift between them is perceived—one seems to hover in front of the other—they are vibrating. It's called chromostereopsis and it should be avoided. Don't pair pure hues of red, green and blue on a page and expect anyone to be able to look at it long enough to read it!

Basic Web Guidelines

There are a slew of web guidelines that are important to be aware of if building a portfolio website. Most of the template, pre-coded websites embed the majority of these rules within the parameters of their sites and will do conversions or issue warnings about problems as needed. If coding your own website, there are some basics to be aware of before getting started. There is plenty of information online to help but this should give some guidance regarding the things to watch out for.

Web Image File Formats

GIF, JPEG and PNG files are the most common image file formats consistently used on the web. It is important to understand the differences between these three image types and to understand when to use each format.

GIF

A GIF file (Graphics Interchange Format) is typically one of the most popular image file formats for the web largely because of its small size. Since a GIF can only display a maximum of 256 colors, it is most appropriate to use a GIF for simple graphics with large areas of a single color. It is not appropriate to use a GIF format for an image of photographic quality because of the limited color range. GIFs can also be animated and can be interlaced so that they load in layers giving the illusion of a faster load time.

JPEG

A JPEG file (Joint Photographic Experts Group) can display 16.8 million colors and therefore is great for photographic representations. JPEGs permit the application of different degrees of compression that can result in the loss of certain data in the file. However, there is a definitive relationship between compression—and thus data loss—and image quality. There is a sweet spot in this relationship that results in a relatively high quality image that is small in file size—perfect for the web.

PNG

A PNG file (Portable Network Graphics) has a combination of the features provided by the GIF and the JPEG. There are two PNG formats: PNG-8 and

PNG-24. PNG-8 operates similar to a GIF in that it displays a maximum of 256 colors. The PNG-24 can display millions of colors but has a larger file size. PNG images can contain a short text description embedded in the image file that will allow Internet search engines to locate it. A drawback to the PNG is that not all browsers support the PNG format.

Web Safe Colors

Back when most computers could only display 256 colors, a set of 216 web safe colors was developed that all computers could display. At the time, only these web safe colors could be used without running the risk of the color on a website not displaying properly. Now that most computers can display millions of colors, it is not quite as much of a problem as it used to be but is definitely something to be aware of. Sticking to web safe colors for large implementations of color on your website is still a good idea and not difficult to do.

Image Resolution and the Internet

There is a long-standing idea that all images that are to be displayed digitally should be 72 ppi or 96 ppi. The history behind this idea is lengthy and tedious, but suffice it to say that all images to be displayed digitally do not have to be 72 ppi or 96 ppi. However, it is important to understand that image resolution is tied to pixels per physical inch and that it is quite important to get the resolution correct for printing. For digital display and particularly for the Internet, it is important to get the highest image quality with the smallest file size. As it turns out, 72 ppi or 96 ppi works perfectly for this issue.

File Size and Upload Time

As mentioned above with image resolution and the Internet, aim for a balance between image quality and file size. The ultimate goal regarding image resolution and the Internet is upload time. If an image needs to be 400 pixels by 400 pixels, make it that size. Don't worry so much about the physical dimension in inches. Pixels are the dimension on the screen. However, the smaller the file size, the quicker the upload. Don't lose viewers because they are waiting for large files to upload.

Browser Compatibility

When working on any type of website, browser compatibility becomes a well-discussed topic. The basic issue is that different browsers on different computer platforms will display the same website differently; in some cases, very differently. What should be remembered is that it is a good practice to periodically review what is being designed on different computer platforms using different browsers to understand how things are behaving across the various systems. It is impossible to make a website look exactly the same across all of these variables and some design compromises will have to be made to achieve a high visual standard across the majority of browsers.

| 182 | **Case Study 01**
Will Gregory | 226 | **Case Study 06**
Jia Joy Hu |

| 194 | **Case Study 02**
Adarn Kernes | 232 | **Case Study 07**
Nikki Hall |

| 202 | **Case Study 03**
Wei Xia | 236 | **Case Study 08**
Annie McCarthy |

| 208 | **Case Study 04**
Ryan Tyler Martinez |

| 218 | **Case Study 05**
Derek Pirozzi |

Case Studies

As a descriptive analysis, case studies provide one of the most robust ways to learn about portfolio design. These case studies allow you to fully understand the design of the visual narrative, content narrative and project narrative as they are implemented across an entire portfolio.

Looking at a range of portfolios and understanding how each portfolio achieves its specific goals provides a qualitative, descriptive, visual understanding across a variety of examples. Use these case studies to better understand the principles outlined in this text and to better understand how to achieve your own portfolio goals.

Constructing the Persuasive Portfolio: the only primer you'll ever need

Case Study 01
Will Gregory—*Auburn University*

Specifications
size: 8" x 10", 203mm x 254mm
orientation: vertical page, horizontal spread
length: 108 pages, 5 project sections with miscellaneous section that includes 7 additional projects

Strengths

portfolio organization
visual narrative

portfolio uses white space coupled with a full bleed image to announce new project sections

portfolio maintains complementary color palette throughout

portfolio uses full bleed images to break visual pace of portfolio

grids and margins

horizontal datum in both text and image provides an organizing principle between all spreads—reduces the need for a clear grid

page margins are standardized and maintained throughout

image organization

portfolio does not overpack images on a page—images have enough room to breathe on the page

hierarchical variation of images directs the viewer's eye to the most important image(s) on a spread

large images allow the viewer to insert themselves visually into the images

portfolio maintains simple margins between images and does not employ a four-square grid image arrangement and therefore avoids a bullseye white 'plus' on the pages

text and
typeface strategies

text boxes fall on similar hangline creating secondary horizontal band

there is a clear organization of typeface hierarchy

typeface size and selection does not impede visual legibility of graphics

Case Studies

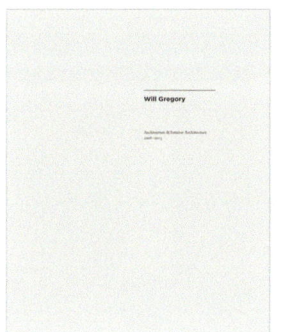

table of contents

project introduction page

white space

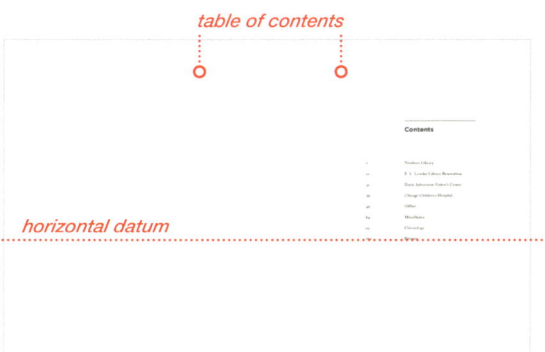
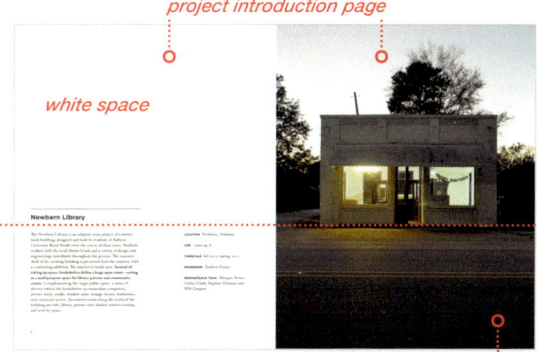

horizontal datum

full bleed

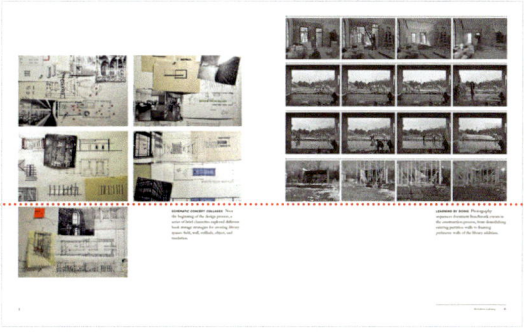

Constructing the Persuasive Portfolio: the only primer you'll ever need

full bleed

full bleed

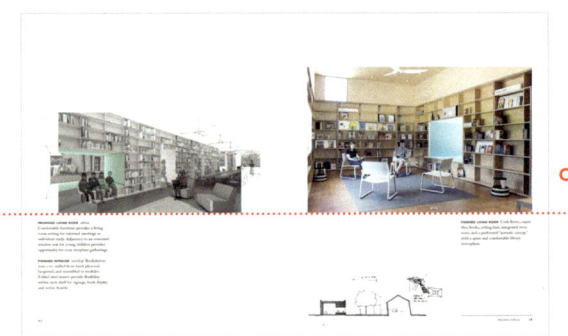

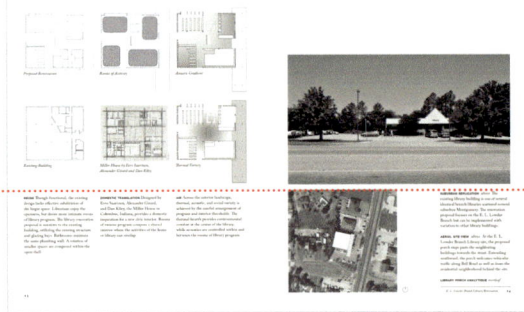
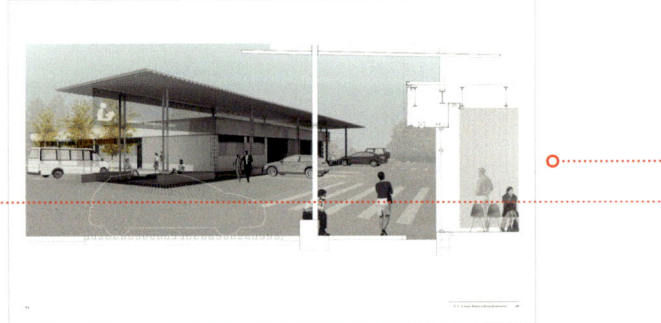

184

Case Studies

full bleed

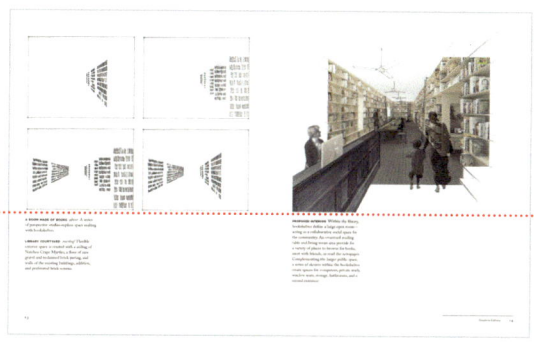

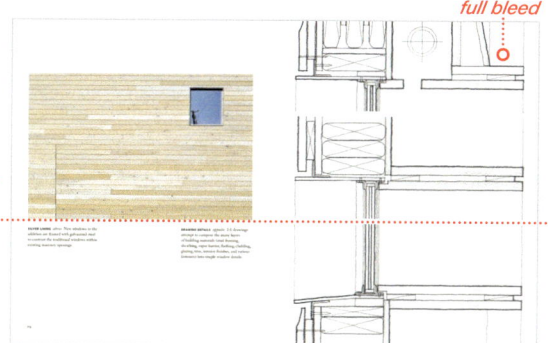

full bleed

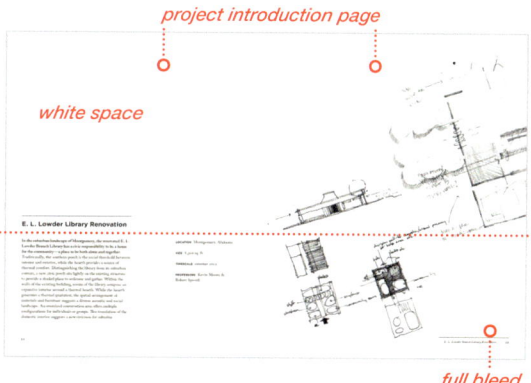

project introduction page

white space

full bleed

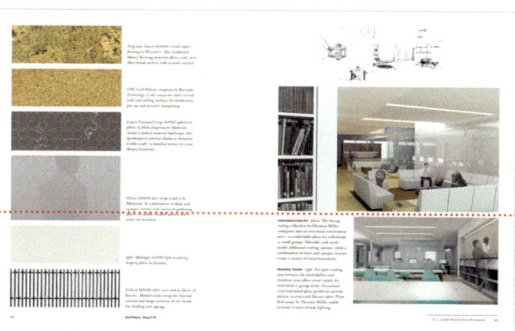

185

Constructing the Persuasive Portfolio: the only primer you'll ever need

Case Studies

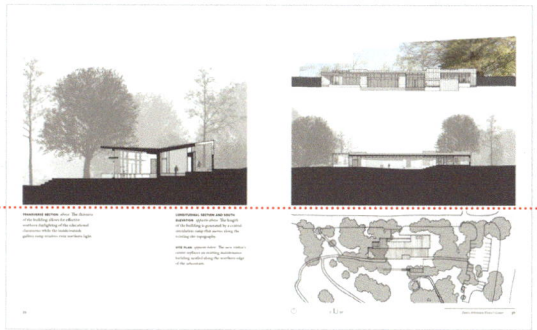
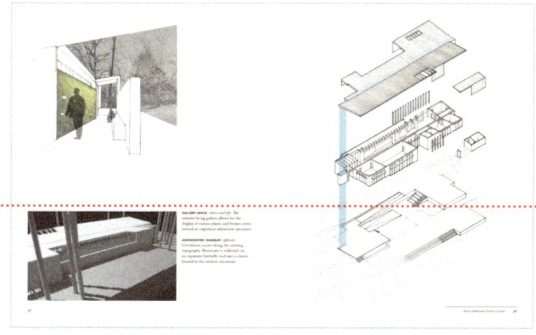

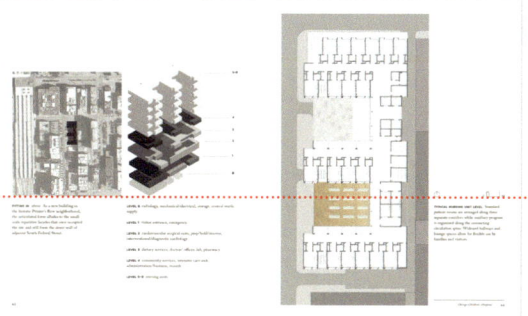
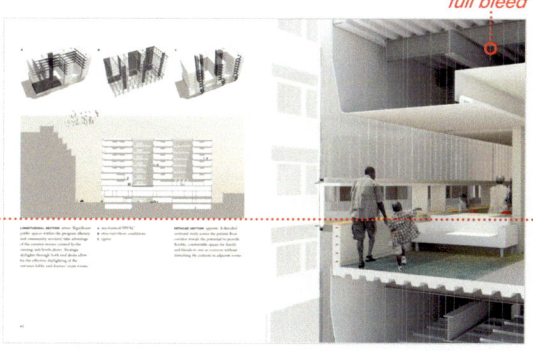

full bleed

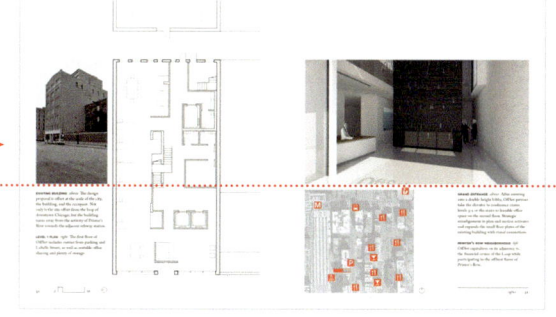
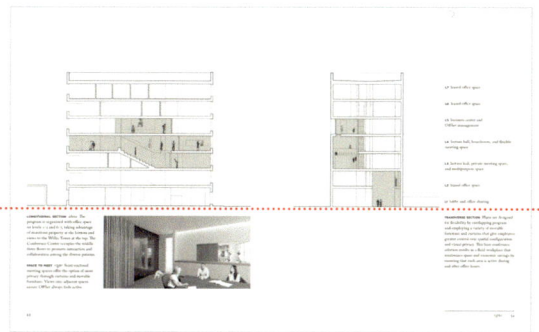

187

Constructing the Persuasive Portfolio: the only primer you'll ever need

full bleed

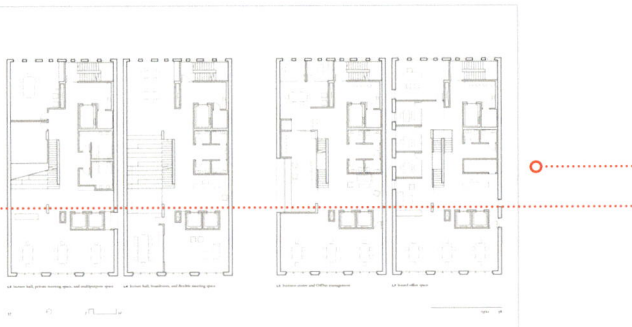

section divider

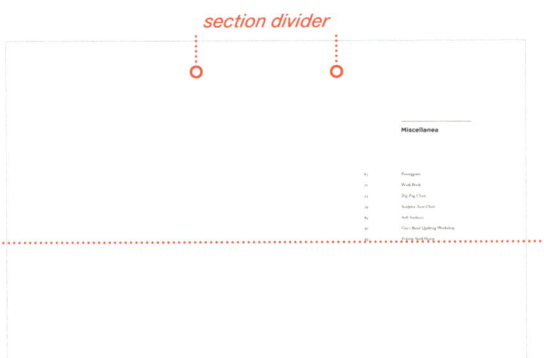

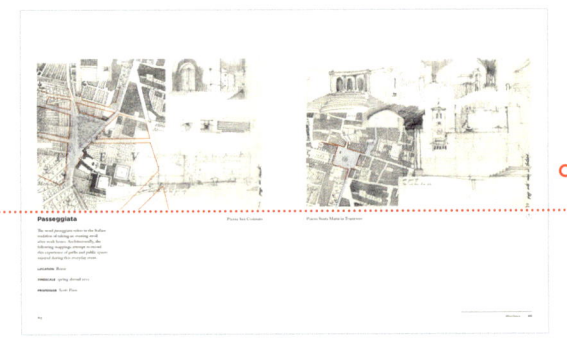

Case Studies

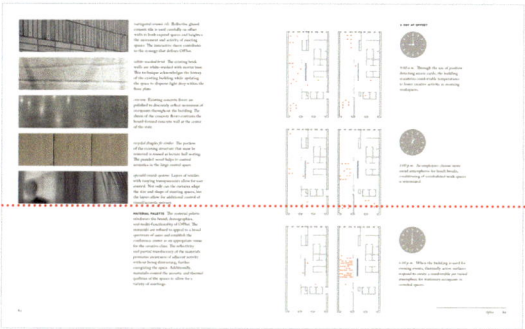

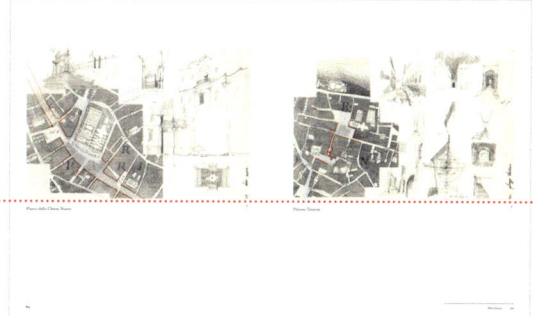

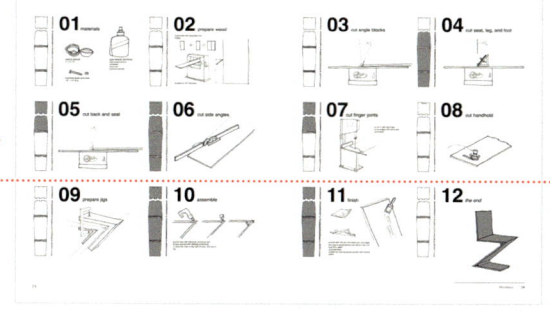

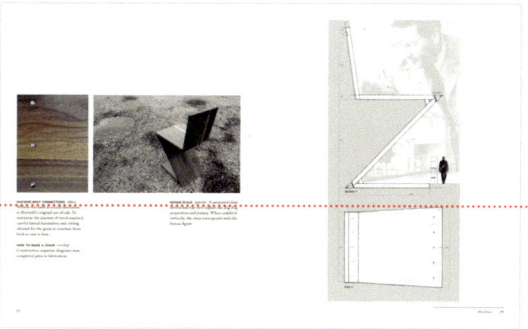

189

Constructing the Persuasive Portfolio: the only primer you'll ever need

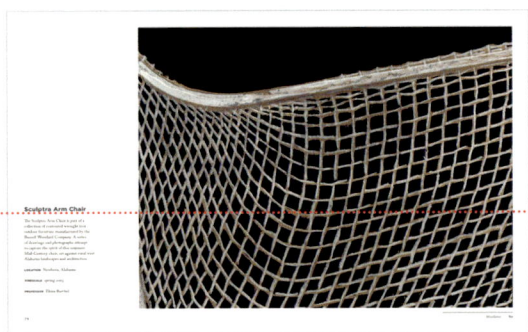

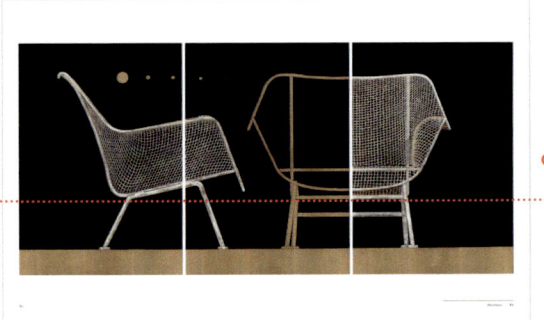

full bleed

full bleed

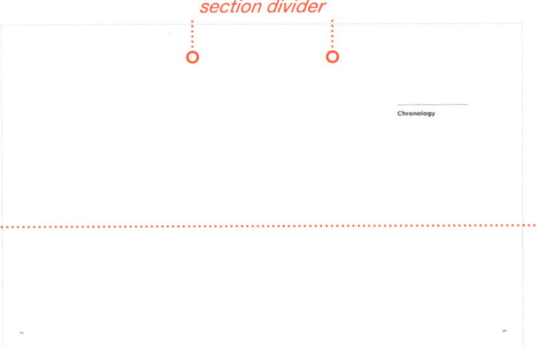
section divider

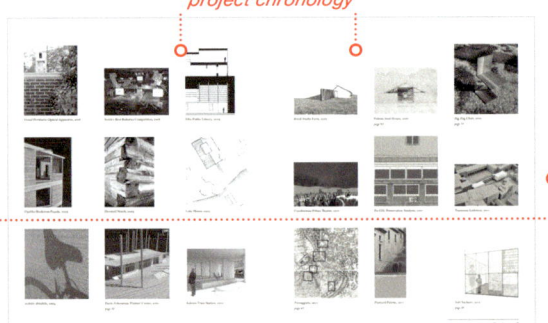
project chronology

Case Studies

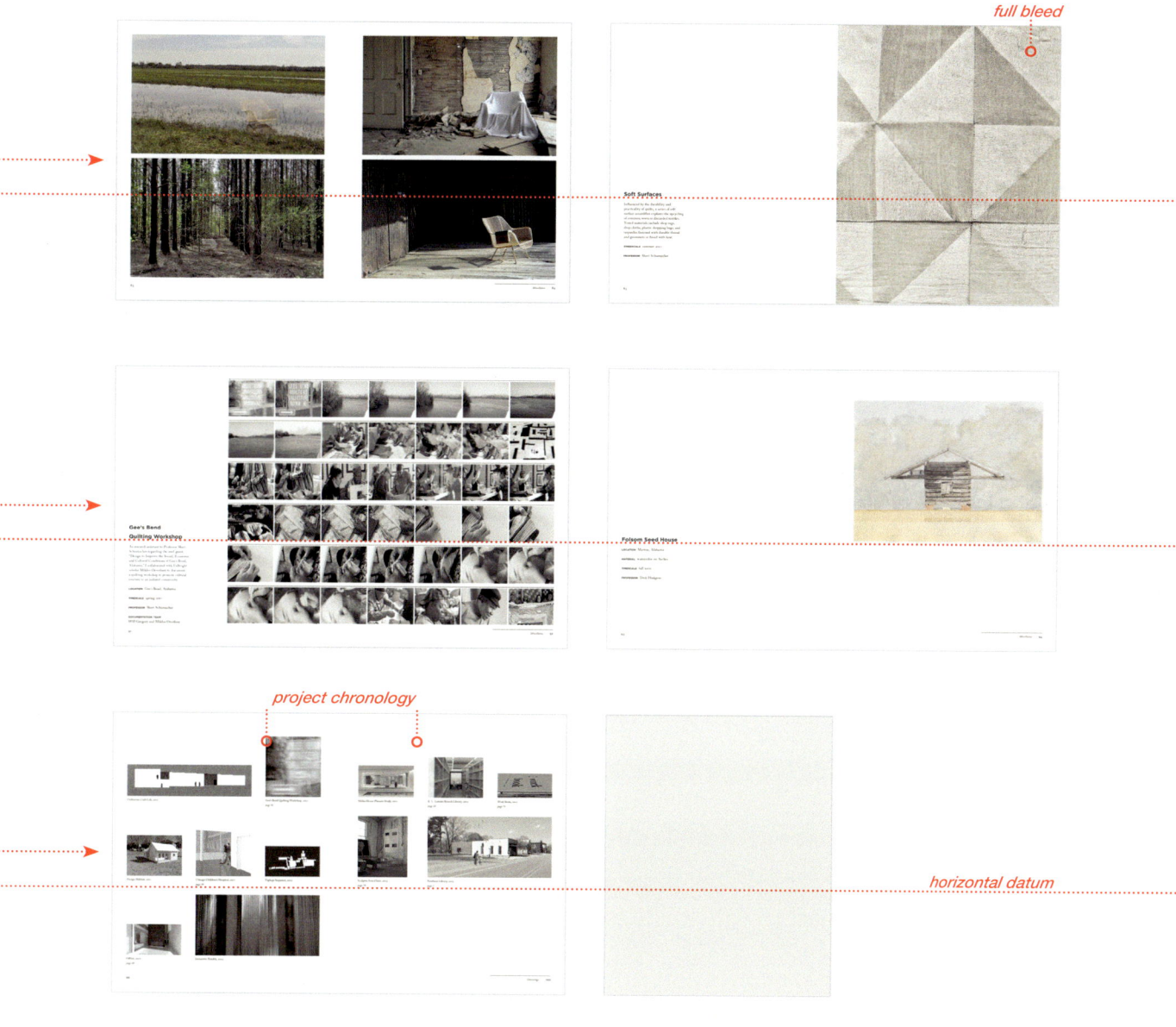

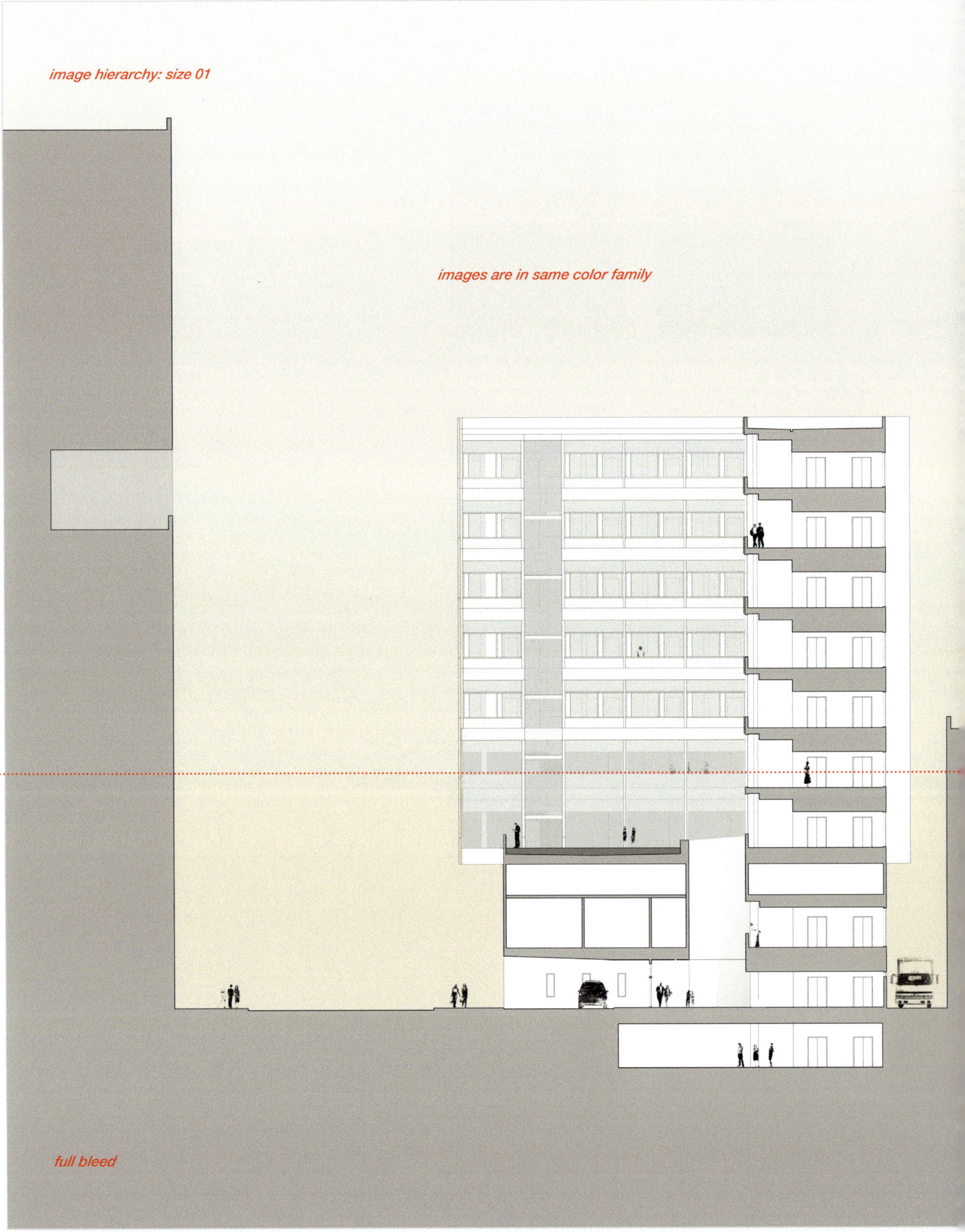

image hierarchy: size 01

images are in same color family

full bleed

image hierarchy: size 04

white space gives breathing room to images on spread

standard image margin

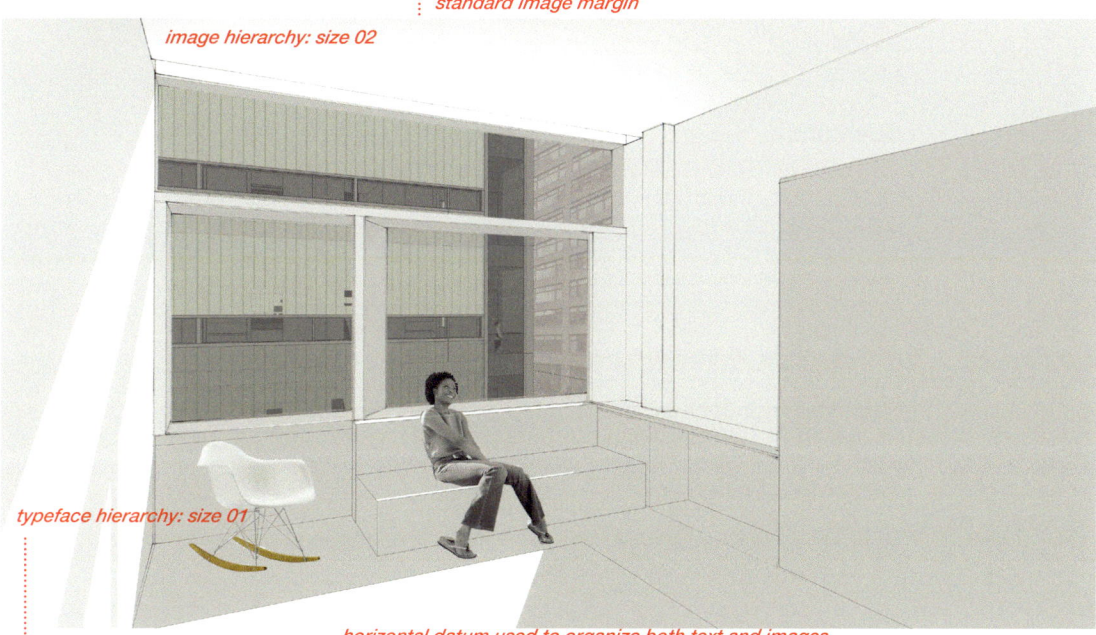

image hierarchy: size 02

typeface hierarchy: size 01

horizontal datum used to organize both text and images

CAREFUL VIEWS Various vignettes explore visual connections on nursing levels: gathering in the oversized hallways, a patient's window view, and arrival in elevator lobby. Views across the exterior space are carefully controlled for each situation. From the widened patient hall, blurred views across are permitted through translucent channel glass. Patient room views are directed towards the street while allowing visual access to adjacent hospital activity.

TRANSVERSE SECTION *opposite* Narrow floor plates allow for maximized daylighting of circulation corridors. A large light well penetrates from terrace to lobby, relating users to their location within the hospital. *typeface hierarchy: size 02*

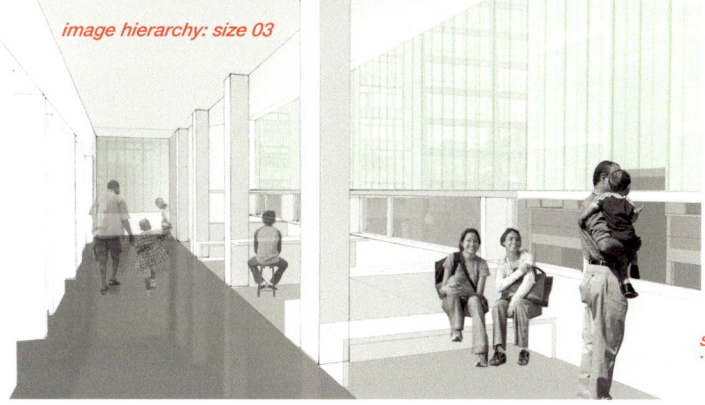

image hierarchy: size 03

standard margin

typeface hierarchy: size 03

Chicago Children's Hospital 48

standard margin

Constructing the Persuasive Portfolio: the only primer you'll ever need

Case Study 02
Adam Kernes—*California State Polytechnic University, Pomona*

Specifications
size: 14.25" x 10.5", 362mm x 267mm
orientation: horizontal page, horizontal spread
length: 45 pages*, 6 project sections

Strengths

portfolio organization
visual narrative

table of contents utilizes super graphics for project titles and page numbers with a secondary table of contents for specific architectural representation project deliverables

parallel project introduction pages include project title, location, year completed, studio critic and large contextual or overview image

grids and margins

all image pages are full bleed and engage the entire page as active area

margins are established and maintained for text blocks throughout

image organization

images are all large and full bleed allowing the reviewer to immerse themselves in the imagery

all images included have similar unique quality that makes them appear remarkably tangible for two-dimensional representations

images are pictorial and have their own narrative quality in rendering style thus reducing the need for additional explanatory text

special care is taken with each individual visual artifact included

text and
typeface strategies

parallel project introduction pages provide the only text and contain project specifications and one descriptive paragraph about the project

text is right justified with a rag left which maintains a strong vertical edge adjacent to the full bleed introductory images

*some pages of this portfolio were not included for issues of space allocation

table of contents

project introduction page

Constructing the Persuasive Portfolio: the only primer you'll ever need

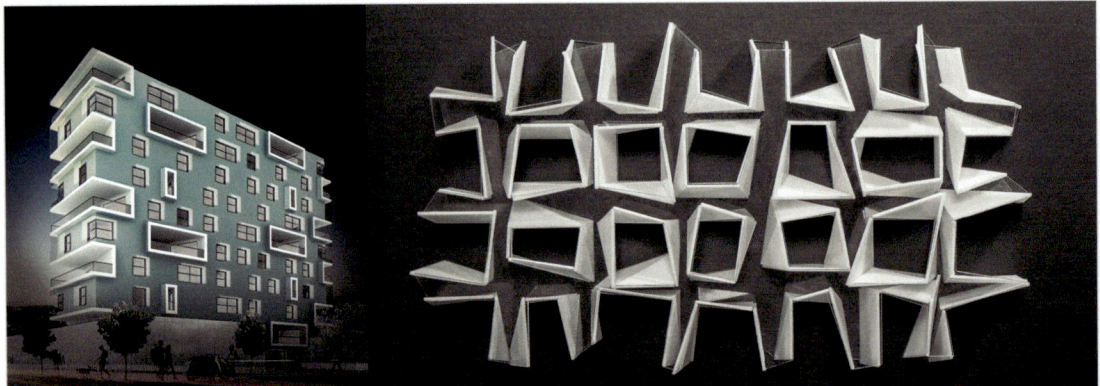

Case Studies

project introduction page

SUNSET BLVD. TOWER
Silver Lake, Los Angeles, CA

The mixed-use project is situated in a young and creative part of Los Angeles, requiring a design as unique and diverse as the individuals of the neighborhood. With 16 two-bedroom apartments, ground-floor community center, 10,000 square feet of retail space, and subterranean parking garage with capacity for 48 vehicles, the development aims to introduce attractive and affordable housing, while investing in the local economy. The project investigates some of these social and cultural issues, and challenges the benefits of more traditional multi-family residential spaces.

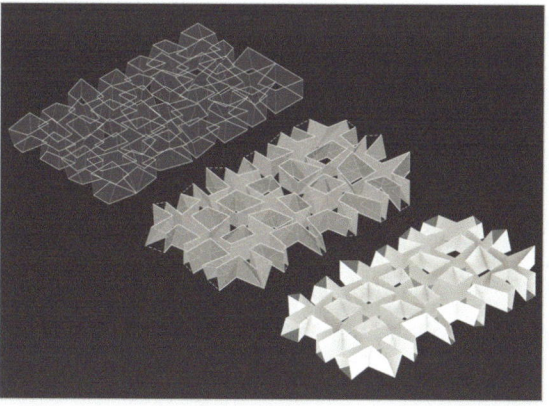

Constructing the Persuasive Portfolio: the only primer you'll ever need

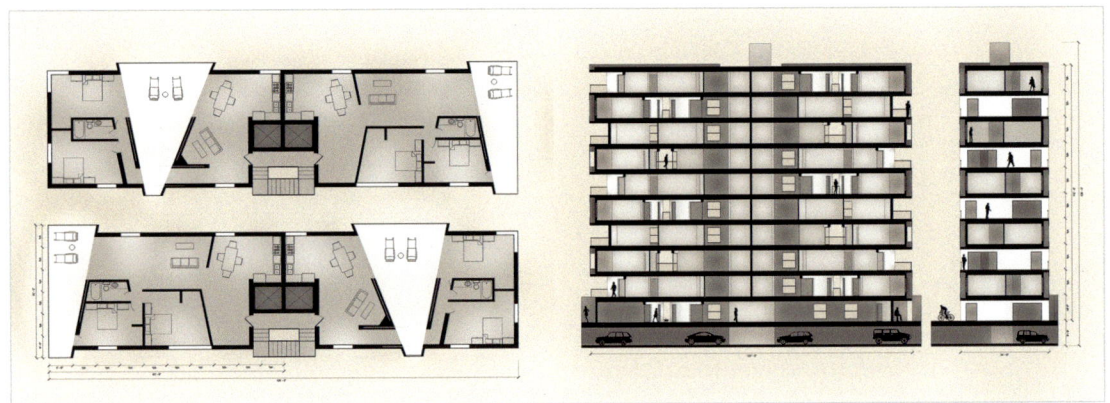

project introduction page

Case Studies

199

Constructing the Persuasive Portfolio: the only primer you'll ever need

project introduction page

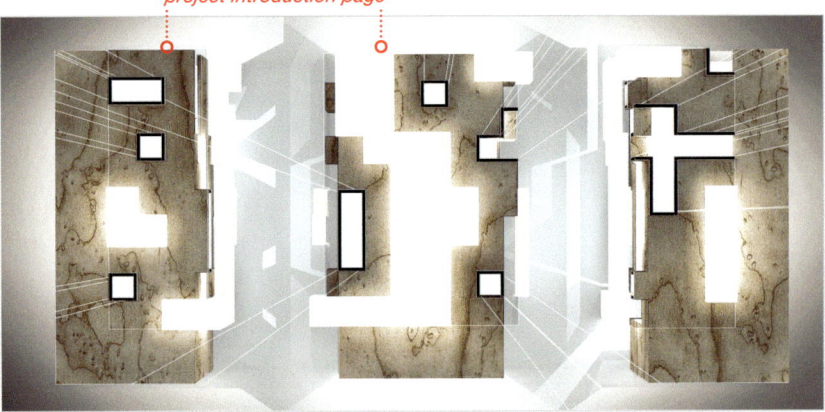

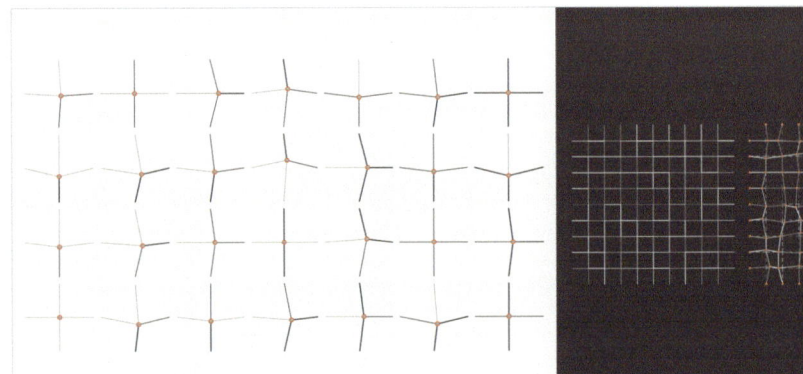

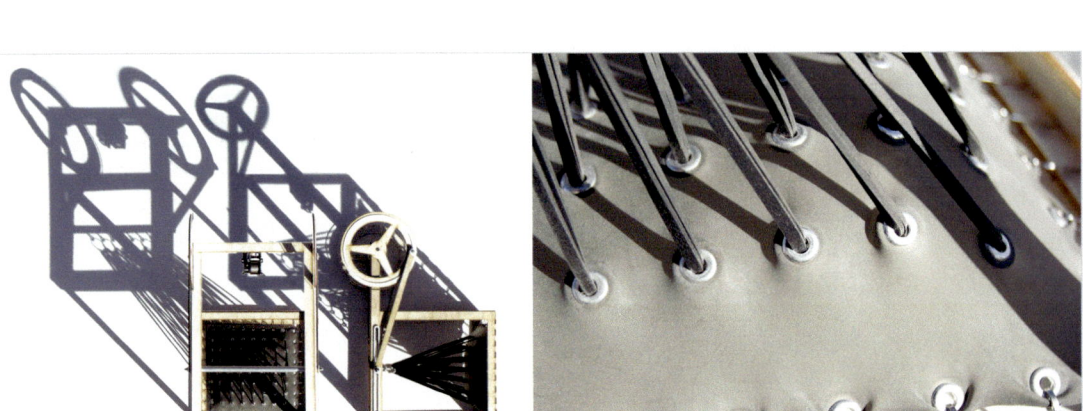

Case Studies

project introduction page

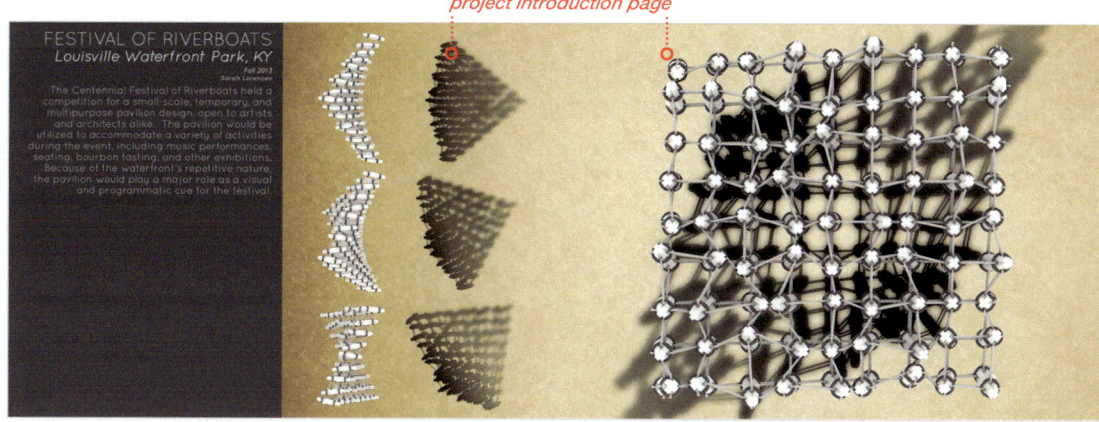

FESTIVAL OF RIVERBOATS
Louisville Waterfront Park, KY
Fall 2012
Sarah Lorenzen

The Centennial Festival of Riverboats held a competition for a small-scale, temporary, and multipurpose pavilion design, open to artists and architects alike. The pavilion would be utilized to accommodate a variety of activities during the event, including music performances, seating, bourbon tasting, and other exhibitions. Because of the waterfront's repetitive nature, the pavilion would play a major role as a visual and programmatic cue for the festival.

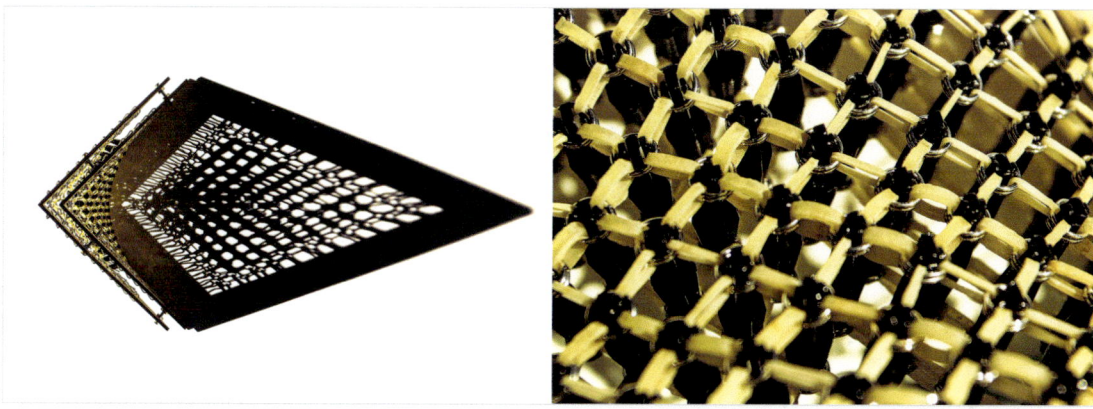

project introduction page

#CPPENV CHINA PROGRAM
NCUT, Beijing, China
Summer 2013
Andy Wilcox

The 5 week study abroad program at the North China University of Technology was unreal. The journey focused on the rich architectural history of the Chinese, and the future of the country. It was our task to document the social and cultural aspects of travel through both written and visual media. We experimented with photographic techniques and quick sketches to create a personal narrative of the experience, from Beijing, to Shanghai, and Hong Kong.

201

Constructing the Persuasive Portfolio: the only primer you'll ever need

Case Study 03
Wei Xia—*University of Nebraska–Lincoln*

Specifications
size: 8.5" x 11", 216mm x 279mm
orientation: vertical page, horizontal spread
length: 32 pages, 3 project sections with 1 additional works spread

Strengths

portfolio organization
visual narrative

table of contents is text-based and includes project title, subtitle and location

parallel project introduction pages have strong vertical image on left with text block on right and include project title, subtitle, studio name, studio critic and brief project description

headers are utilized: on the left is student name, on the right is project title and specifics of that spread

footers are used with page numbers on the left and right

consistent color families are used for each spread

grids and margins

portfolio is organized around single column grid

active area is defined by headers, footers and tight page margins

primary images at parallel project introduction pages are always framed with a consistent margin

image organization

full bleed images expand past defined active area and provide visual respite

portfolio makes good use of diagram sets and series to explain project fundamentals

clear use of image hierarchy principles orders visual artifacts on the page

text and
typeface strategies

establishes and maintains appropriate typeface hierarchy throughout

project titles on project introduction pages are clear but not overpowering

captions and small sub-texts are used to direct reviewers to the specifics of project artifacts

Case Studies

project introduction page

table of contents
full bleed

strong vertical

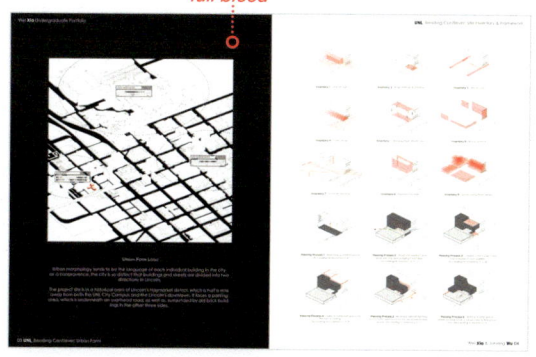

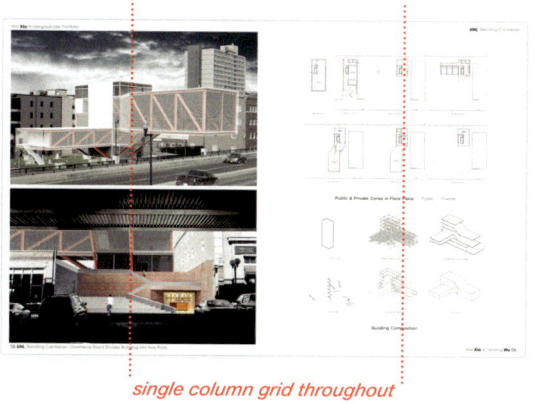
single column grid throughout

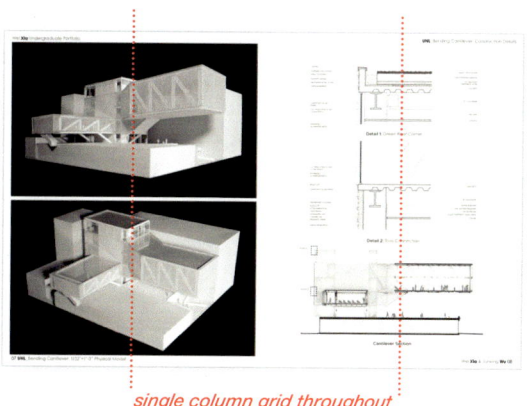
single column grid throughout

203

Constructing the Persuasive Portfolio: the only primer you'll ever need

full bleed

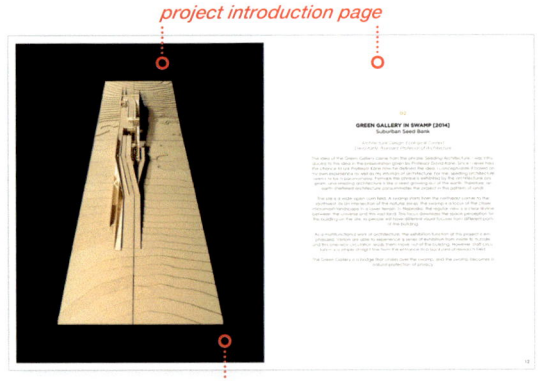

project introduction page

strong vertical

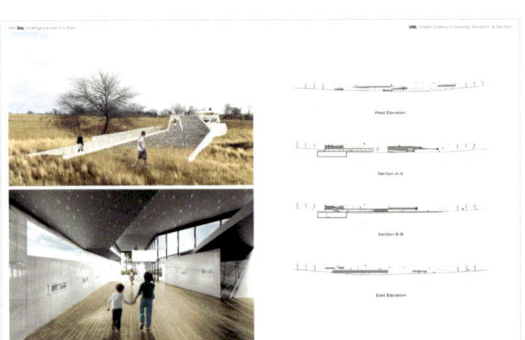

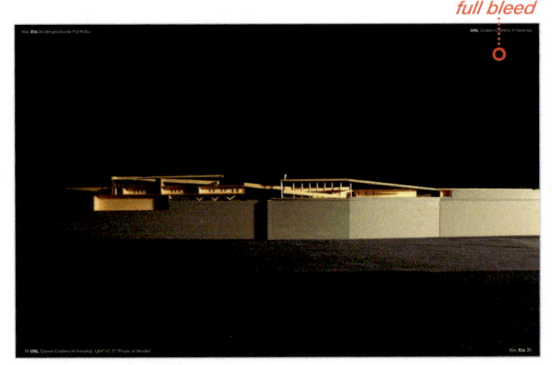

full bleed

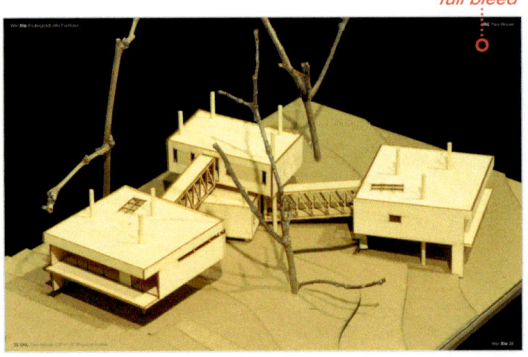

full bleed

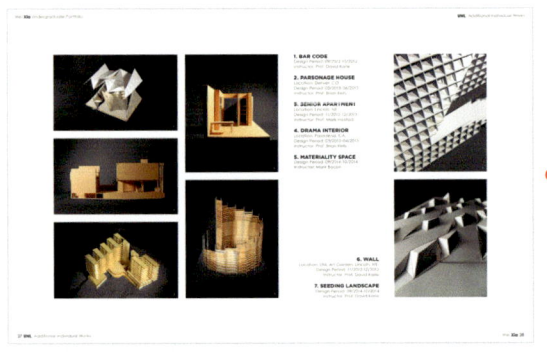

Case Studies

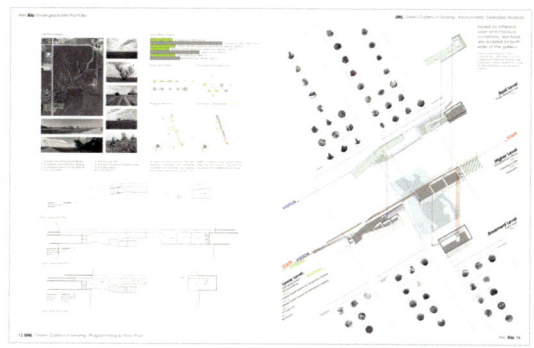

project introduction page

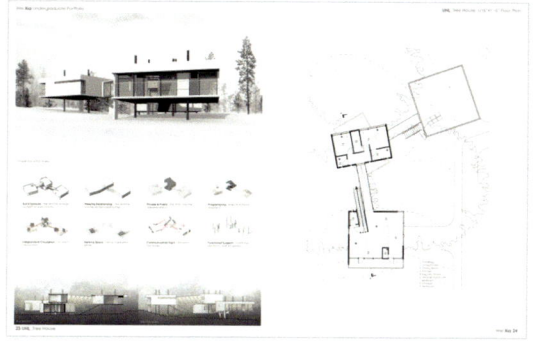

strong vertical

205

Wei **Xia** Undergraduate Portfolio

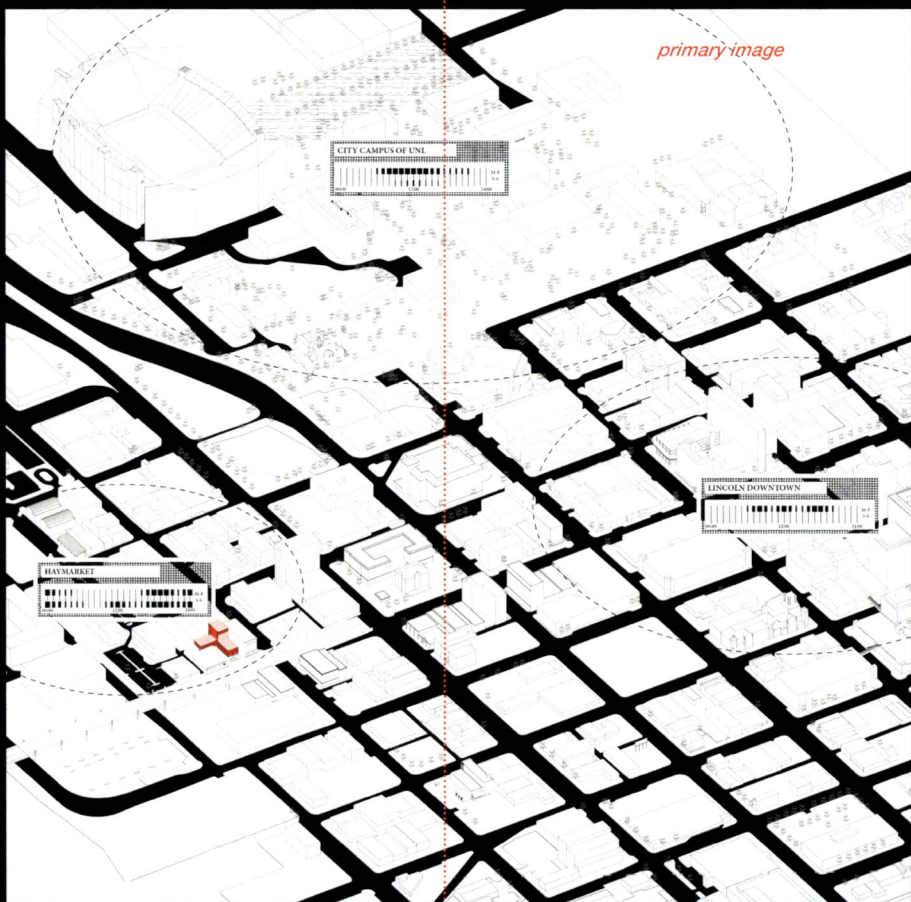

URBAN FORM LOGIC

Urban morphology tends to be the language of each individual building in the city, as a consequence, the city is so distinct that buildings and streets are divided into two directions in Lincoln.

The project site is in a historical area of Lincoln's Haymarket district, which is half a mile away from both the UNL City Campus and the Lincoln's downtown. It faces a parking area, which is underneath an overhead road, as well as, surrounded by old brick buildings in the other three sides.

03 **UNL**_Bending Cantilever: Urban Form

UNL_Bending Cantilever: Site Inventory & Framework

support images

headers and footers define active area

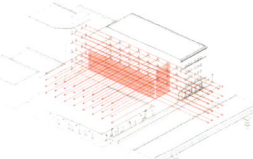
Inventory 1 - *Line of Sight*

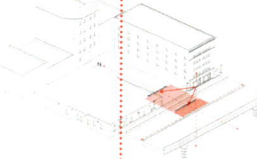
Inventory 2 - *Solar Altitude & Shadow*

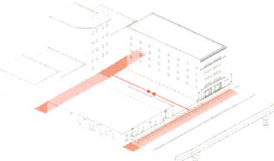
Inventory 3 - *Site Access*

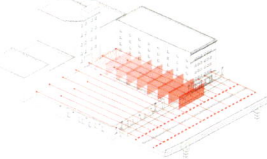
Inventory 4 - *Trafic Noise*

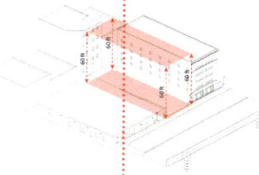
Inventory 5 - *Building Hight Restriction*

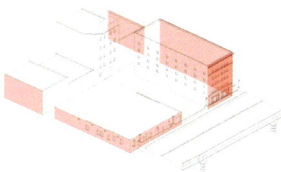
Inventory 6 - *Block Surface*

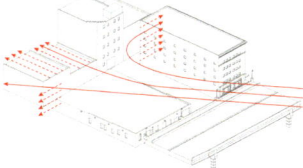
Inventory 7 - *Summer Monsoon*

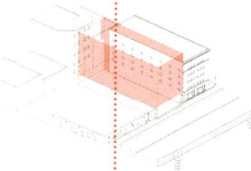
Inventory 8 - *Exposed Facade*

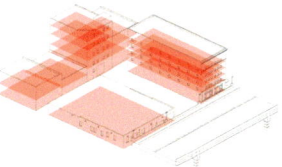
Inventory 9 - *Surrounding Floor Levels*

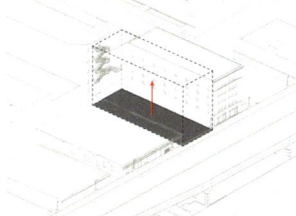
Massing Process 1 - *Maximize potential space. (According to Inventory 3,5)*

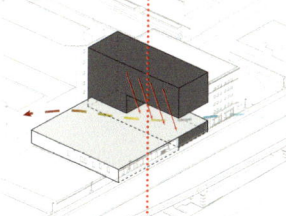
Massing Process 2 - *Avoid the viaduct and level with the next building's roof line. (According to Inventory 4, 6, 9)*

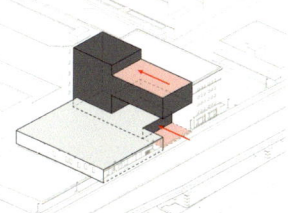
Massing Process 3 - *Create a front courtyard and a research roof garden. (According to Inventory 2, 3, 8)*

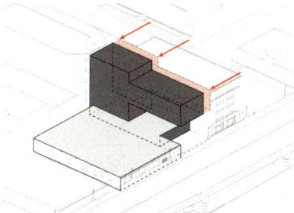
Massing Process 4 - *Keep a natural lit space for the next building. (According to Inventory 1, 7, 9)*

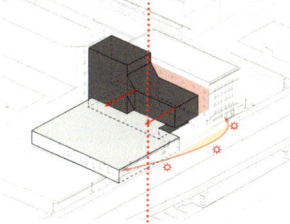
Massing Process 5 - *Increase natural lighting and control west sunshine for the lower exterior space. (According to Inventory 2, 7)*

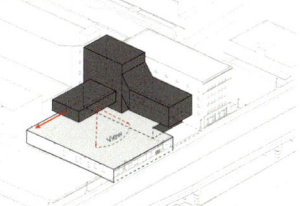
Massing Process 6 - *Build a quality space where people have a closer view to the green roof. (According to Inventory 9)*

diagram series uses exact base drawing with incremental design moves layered on top

content organized about a central axis

Wei **Xia** & Junxing **Wu** 04

Case Study 04

Ryan Tyler Martinez—*University of North Carolina at Charlotte, Southern California Institute of Architecture*

Specifications

size:	7.75" x 9.75", 197mm x 248mm
orientation:	vertical page, horizontal spread
length:	78 pages, 9 project sections with additional section of drawing, photography and graphic design*

Strengths

portfolio organization / visual narrative

table of contents organizes portfolio as: design statements, information about Ryan Tyler Martinez, architectural projects and art endeavors

storyboard graphics are established with table of contents and used throughout as page number way-finding system

section dividers use blue color to establish these pages as part of overall visual narrative

grids and margins

primarily a one column grid with intermittent two and three column grids

active area is defined by generous page margins as well as the header

header includes project title, year of completion, studio critic, content information and digital programs used to produce artifacts

image organization

each spread has clear image hierarchy with primary images supported with secondary and tertiary graphics

images are dramatic with clear contrast and focus

full bleed images on single vertical pages and entire spreads break the portfolio pace and provide moments of pause for reviewer to visually enter the image

image series are employed for visual impact

text and typeface strategies

typeface hierarchy is clear and maintained throughout portfolio

text blocks are two shades of blue simultaneously allowing text to recede and come to the foreground

typeface hierarchy and text placement allows images to have primary visual role on page

*portfolio case study is designer's undergraduate portfolio

Case Studies

table of contents   design statement

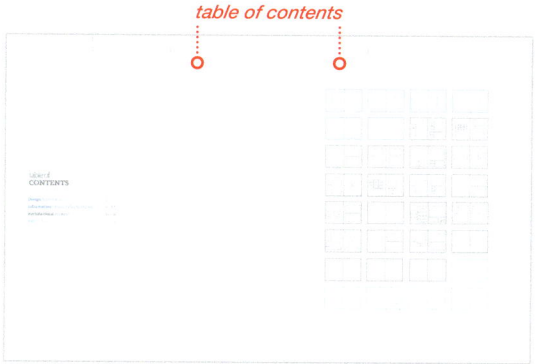
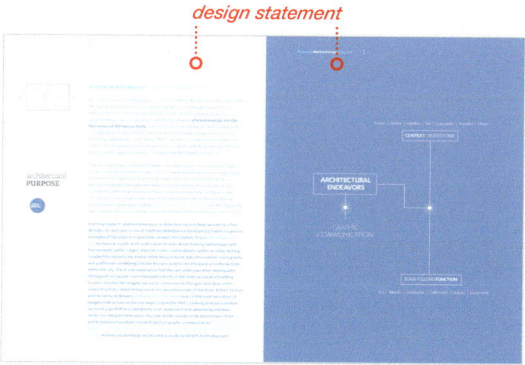

                                  about the author

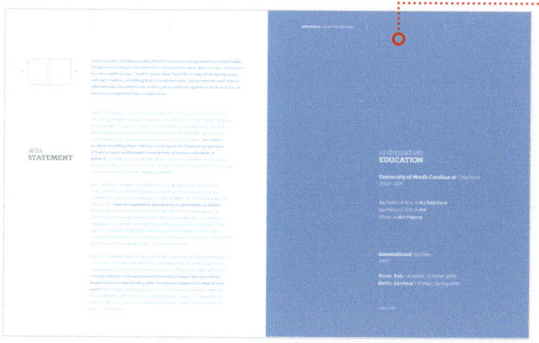

209

Constructing the Persuasive Portfolio: the only primer you'll ever need

about the author

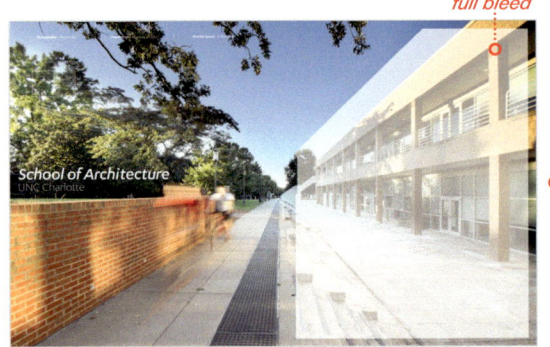

full bleed

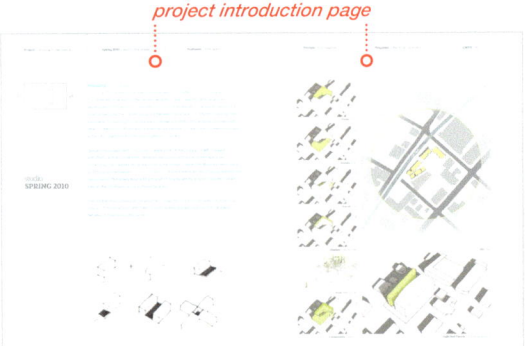

project introduction page

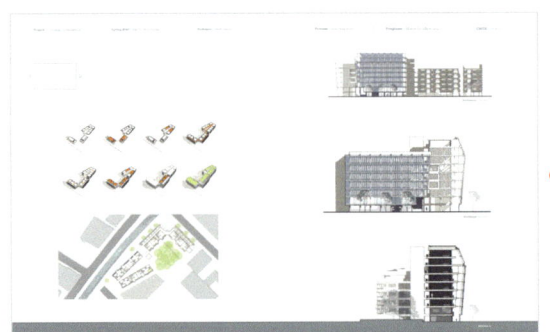

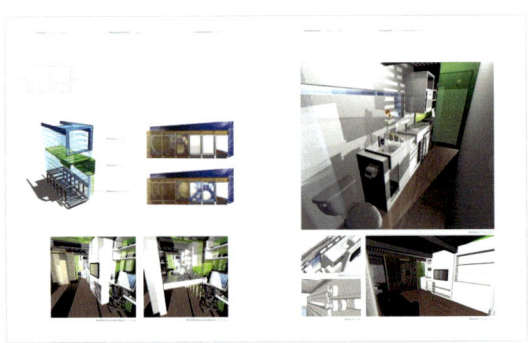

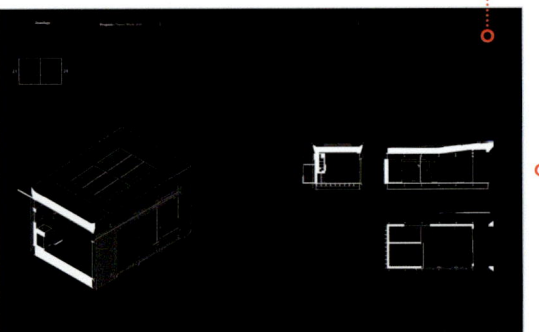

full bleed

Case Studies

full bleed   *section divider*

 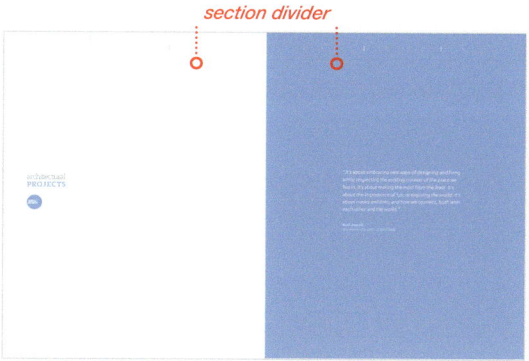

project introduction page

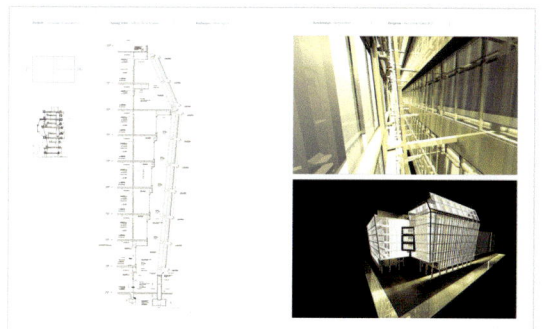 

project introduction page   *full bleed*

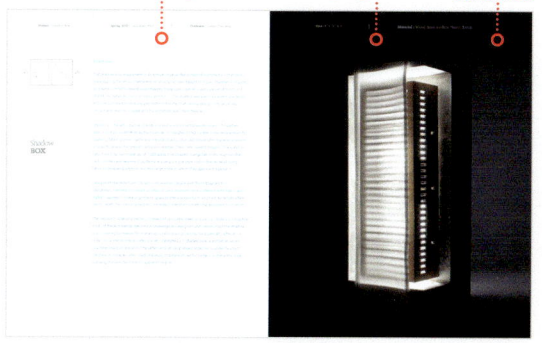 

211

Constructing the Persuasive Portfolio: the only primer you'll ever need

project introduction page

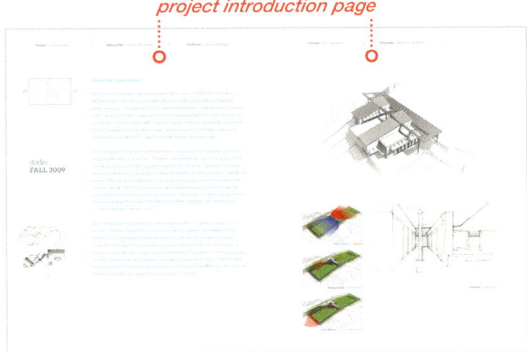

project introduction page

project introduction page   *project introduction page*

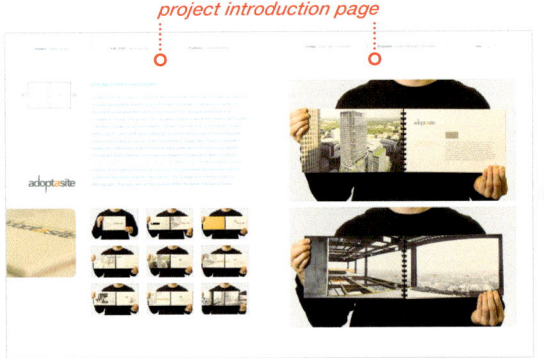

Case Studies

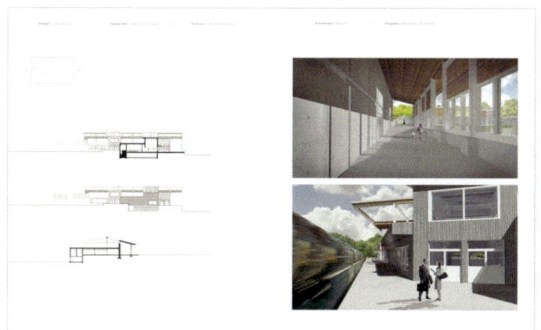

full bleed

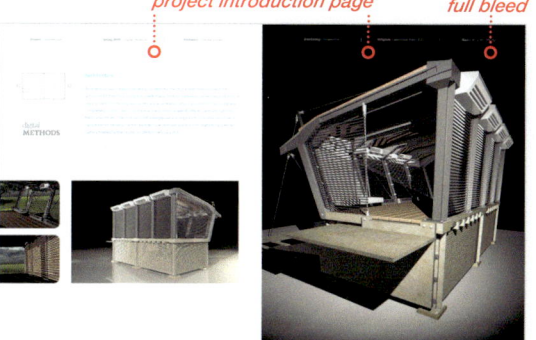

project introduction page   *full bleed*

project introduction page   *full bleed*

Constructing the Persuasive Portfolio: the only primer you'll ever need

full bleed  *full bleed*

Case Studies

full bleed   *section divider*

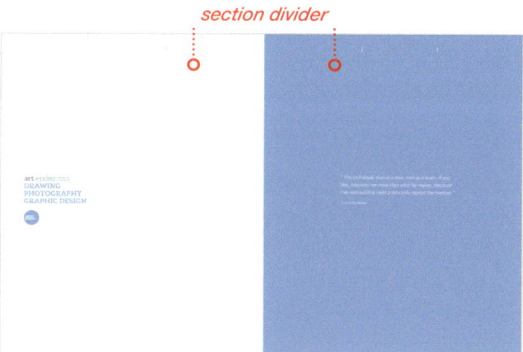

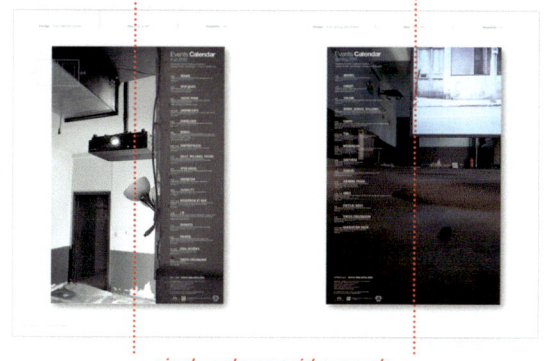
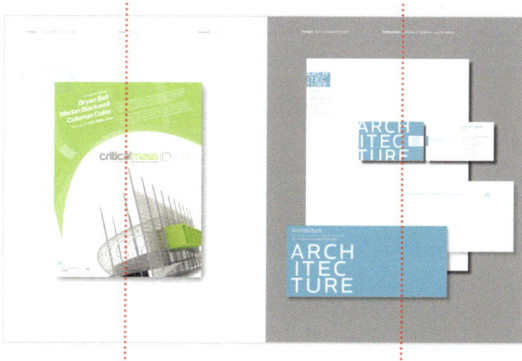

single column grid example   *single column grid example*

215

Project: Train Station | **Spring 2010:** ARCH 3101 Studio | **Professor:** Michael Williams

storyboard graphic used as page number way-finding system

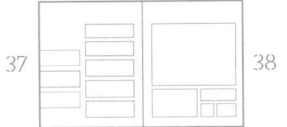

image hierarchy: size 03

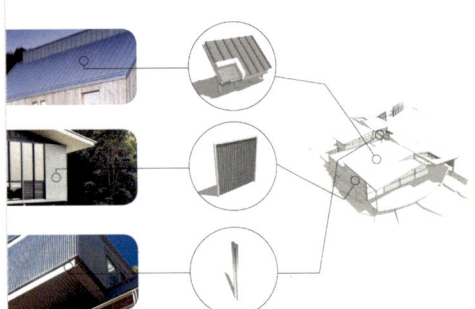

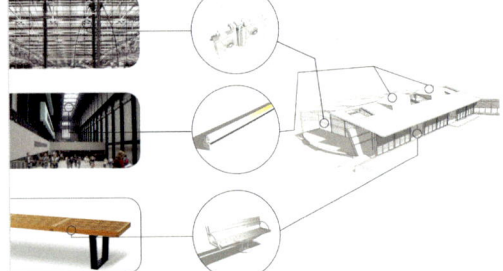

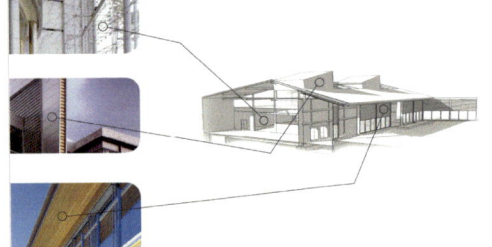

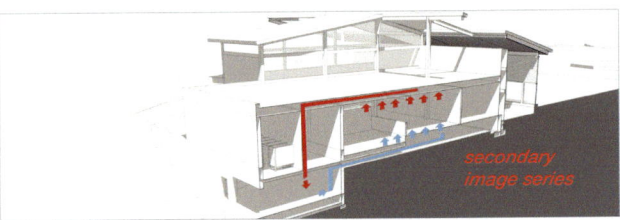

secondary image series

Heating + Cooling

Heating + Cooling

precise and consistent image margins

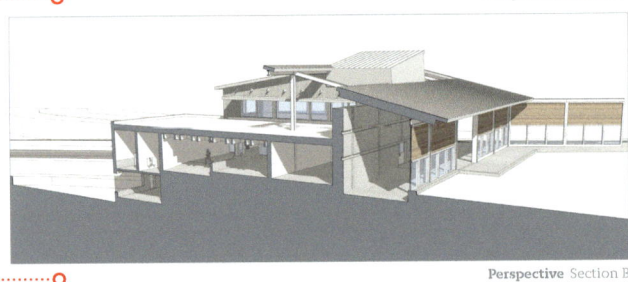

Perspective Section A

Perspective Section B

Perspective Section C

consistent page margins

Model : 1/4" Structural Section | **Materials :** Bass Wood, Chip Board, Cardboard, Rockite

margins and headers define active area

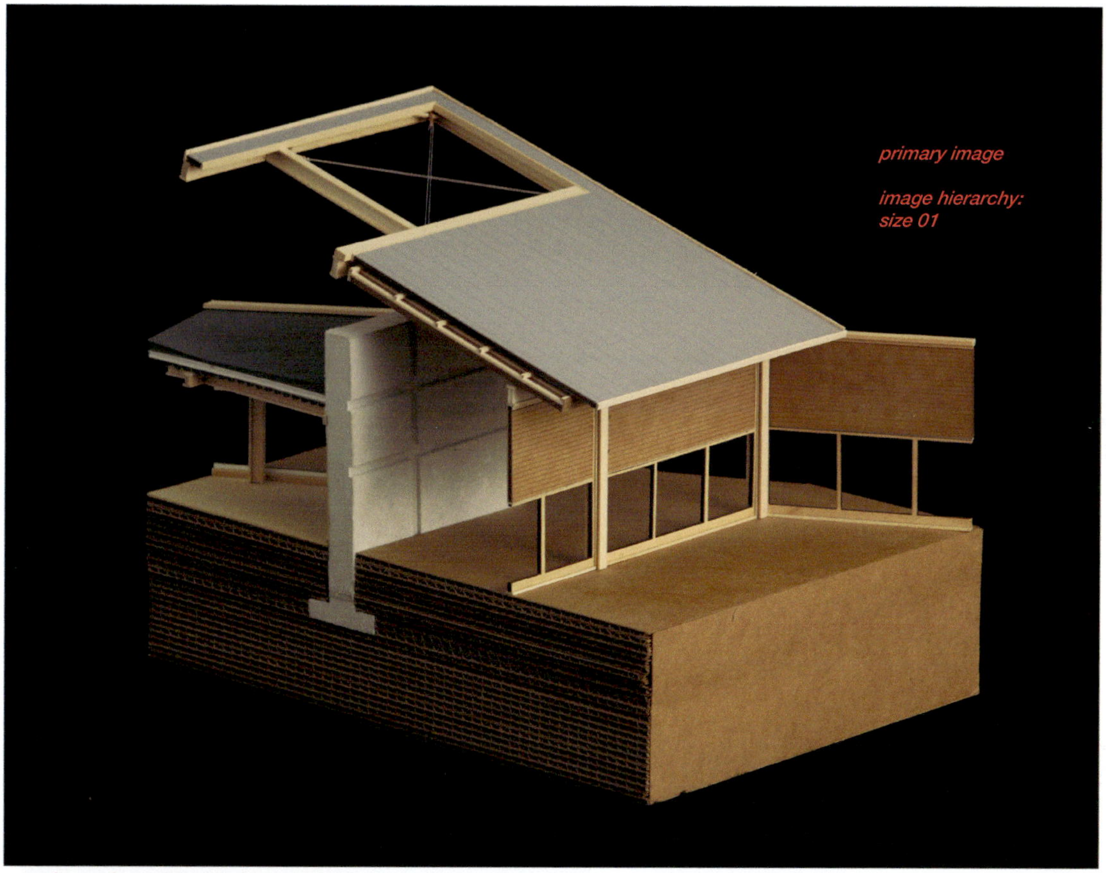

primary image

image hierarchy: size 01

precise and consistent image margins

image hierarchy: size 02

consistent page margins

Constructing the Persuasive Portfolio: the only primer you'll ever need

Case Study 05

Derek Pirozzi—*University of South Florida School of Architecture and Community Design*

Specifications

size: 6.875" x 6.875", 175mm x 175mm
orientation: square page, horizontal spread
length: 188 pages, 14 project sections plus additional photography section*

Strengths

*portfolio organization
visual narrative*

table of contents is text-based and gives page number, project title, subtitle

each project has a section divider project lead-in page with project title, subtitle, completion date and brief one sentence project description

parallel project introduction pages have project title, studio name, duration of project and studio critic

page numbers at lower right act as consistent graphic indicator and way-finding system

grids and margins

portfolio spreads have three different organizational strategies—either one full image across the entire spread, a spread split in half or the layout utilizes a vertical column to break the horizontal spread into a different proportion

spreads are predominantly full bleed and establish page margins through consistent placement of text

image organization

utilizes primarily full bleed images to allow viewer to visually enter the images

consistently uses unusual photography angles to add dynamic quality

good use of drawings and diagrams to support understanding of the projects

*text and
typeface strategies*

typeface hierarchy is established and consistent throughout portfolio

typeface hierarchy on section divider spreads is particularly successful

subtle insertion of color in text application

portfolio uses direct and adjacent captions, diagram titles and call-outs to clearly direct reviewer to pertinent information

*some pages of this portfolio were not included for issues of space allocation

Case Studies

vertical column

table of contents

vertical column

section divider project page

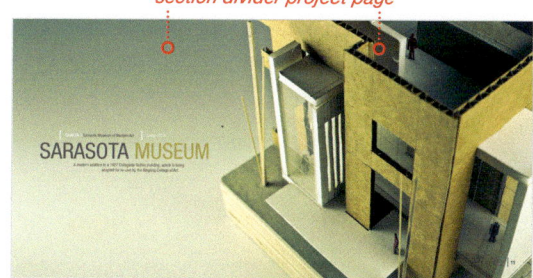

project introduction page

vertical column

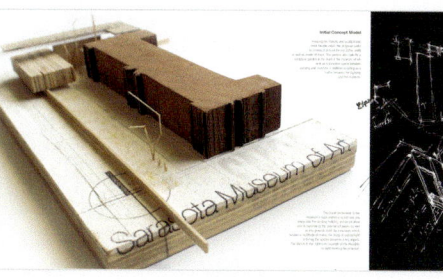

219

Constructing the Persuasive Portfolio: the only primer you'll ever need

vertical column

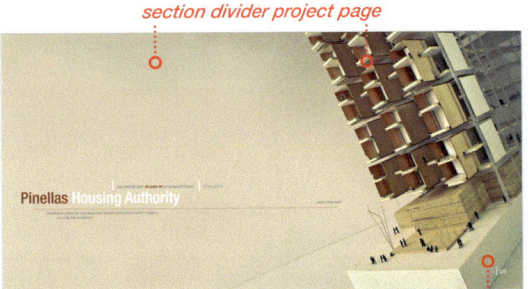
section divider project page

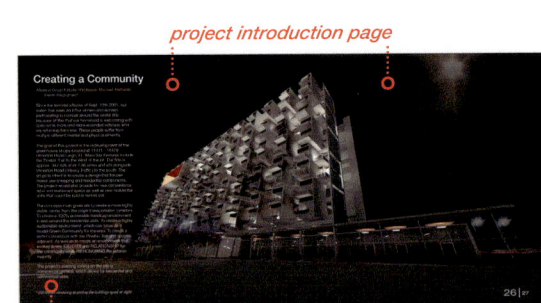
project introduction page

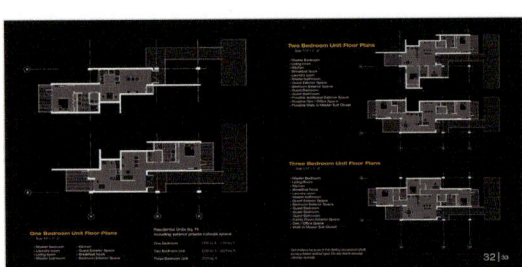
vertical column

vertical column

vertical column

vertical column

vertical column

220

Case Studies

vertical column

vertical column

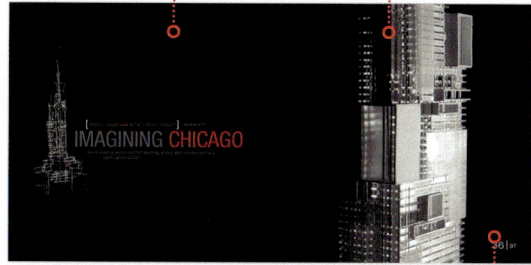

section divider project page

project introduction page

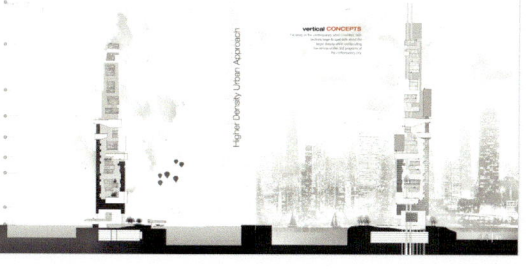

vertical column   *vertical column*

221

Constructing the Persuasive Portfolio: the only primer you'll ever need

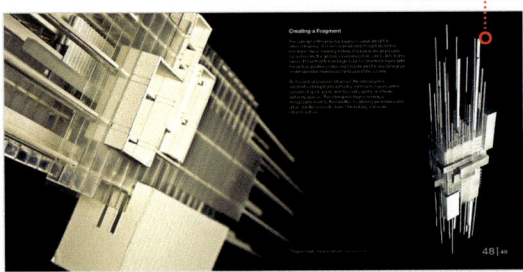
vertical column

vertical column

vertical column

section divider project page

portfolio break

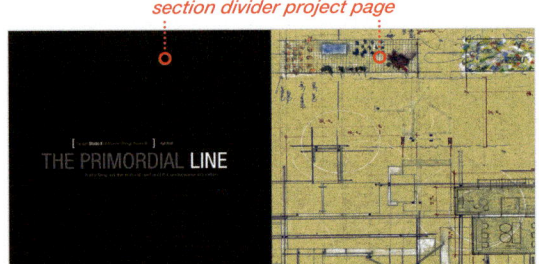

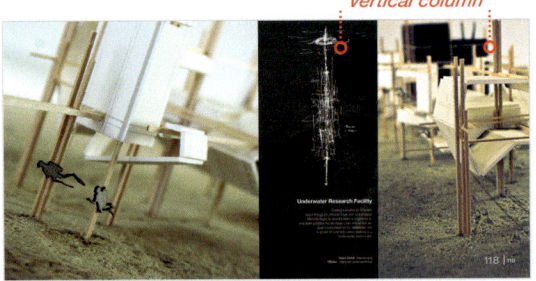
vertical column

Case Studies

section divider project page *project introduction page*

vertical column

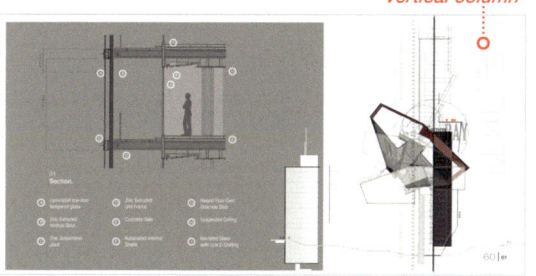 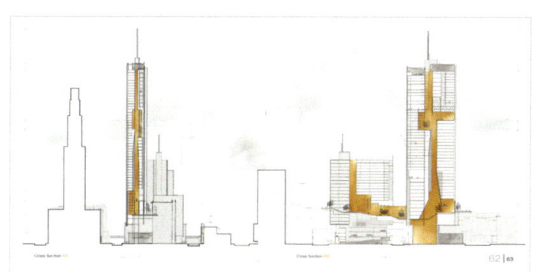

project introduction page

vertical column *vertical column*

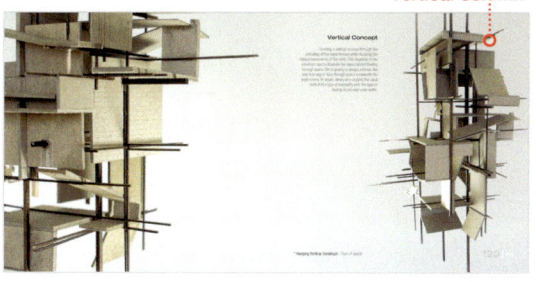 

223

image hierarchy: size 02

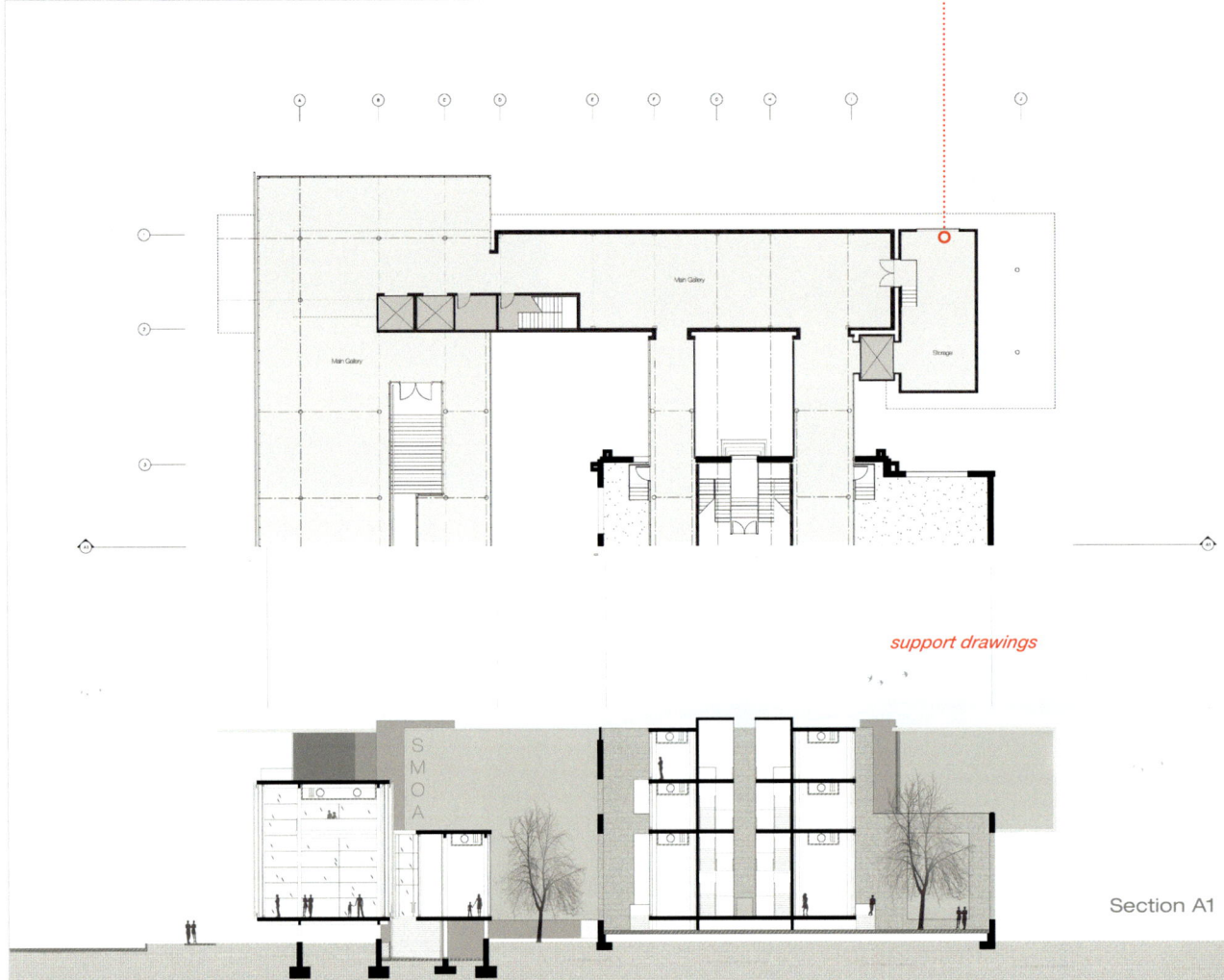

support drawings

Section A1

Relationship

Upon entering the Sarasota Museum of Art, the visitor becomes immediately conscious of the relationship between old and new. Utilizing the existing brick exterior as a detached skin system, this proposal explores the potential of the heavy brick facade acting as protective element to the new layer of interior glass. This transition between modern adaptation and original intent becomes a celebrated relationship, enhancing the visitors experience as they move through each threshold. As indicated in the section model seen to the right, visitors transitioning from central to west galleries will find themselves enveloped by a glass volume which extrudes through the old facade's window bay. As one crosses this boundary, visitors can't but help realize their relationship within the constructed context.

*Final Section Model - A section cut portraying the relationships in scale between the large gallery space and the transitional spaces.

image hierarchy: size 01

primary image

portfolio is characterized by full bleed images photographed from dramatic points of view

page number way-finding system in footer

Constructing the Persuasive Portfolio: the only primer you'll ever need

Case Study 06
Jia Joy Hu—*University of Virginia, Harvard Graduate School of Design*

Specifications
size: 10" x 10", 254mm x 254mm
orientation: square page, horizontal spread
length: 43 pages, 7 project sections plus additional photography, painting and drawing sections

Strengths

portfolio organization
visual narrative

table of contents is primarily text-based with small image icons and includes project title, professional or academic project and studio critic if academic

image icons are used on parallel project introduction pages as consistent graphic indicator

parallel project introduction pages include icon, project title, location, studio, studio critic and project collaborators

color families are unified per spread and throughout entire portfolio

footers contain page numbers only

grids and margins

hangline and baseline are used throughout portfolio to establish central horizontal band that organizes all content

content can either respond to both the hangline and baseline or just to one

margins are larger at top and bottom of page thus supporting the horizontal nature of the image organization

image organization

every spread employs image hierarchy to focus reviewer on primary material

right and left bleeds are used to emphasize the horizontal structure set up by the hangline and baseline system

images on each page are ordered to support the horizontal nature of spreads

text and typeface strategies

typeface hierarchy is established and consistent throughout

content spreads often have titles at upper left that define the graphic content

captions, diagram labels and call-outs are succinct and clear and have appropriate adjacency relationships to the content they support

Case Studies

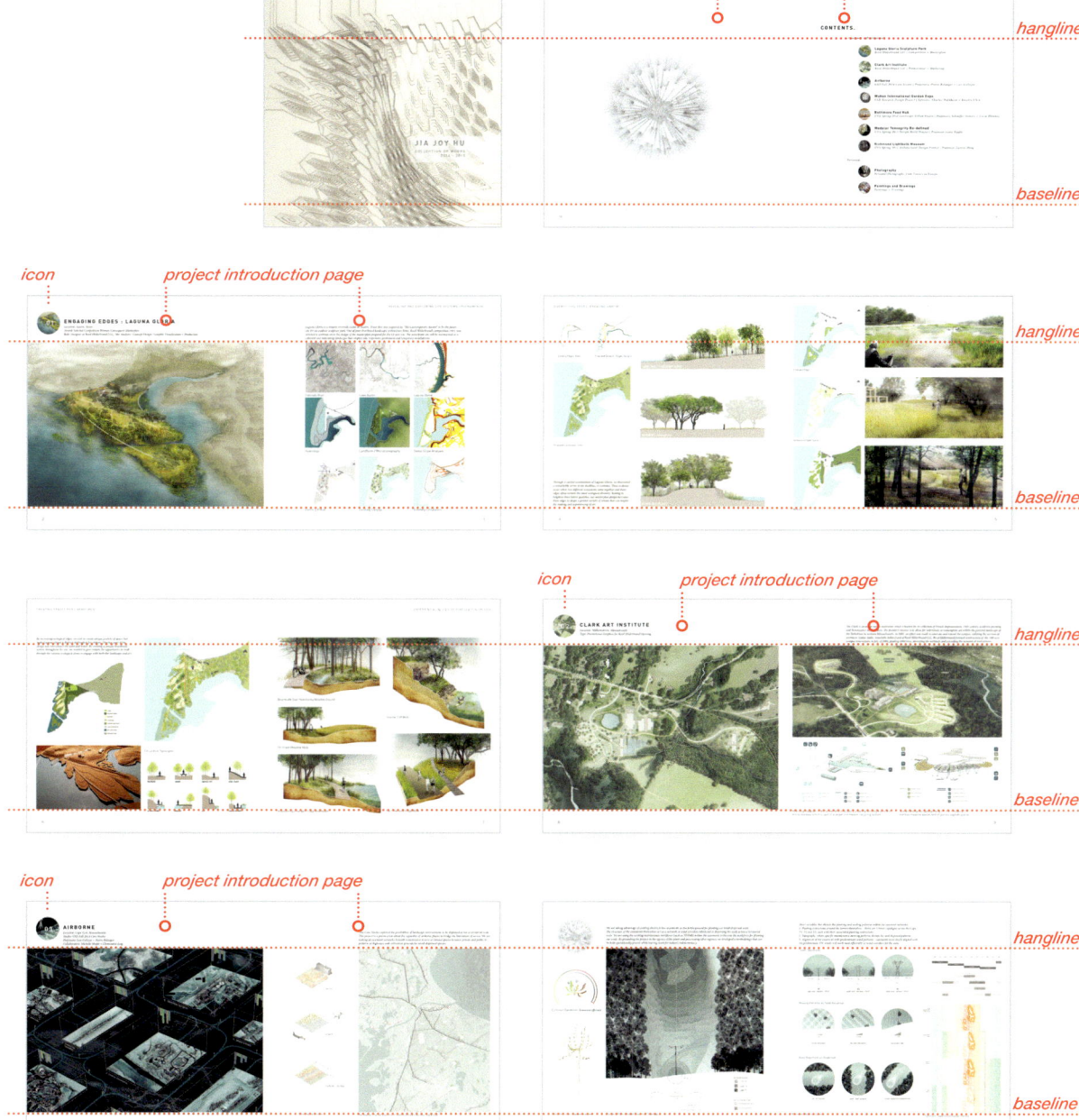

227

Constructing the Persuasive Portfolio: the only primer you'll ever need

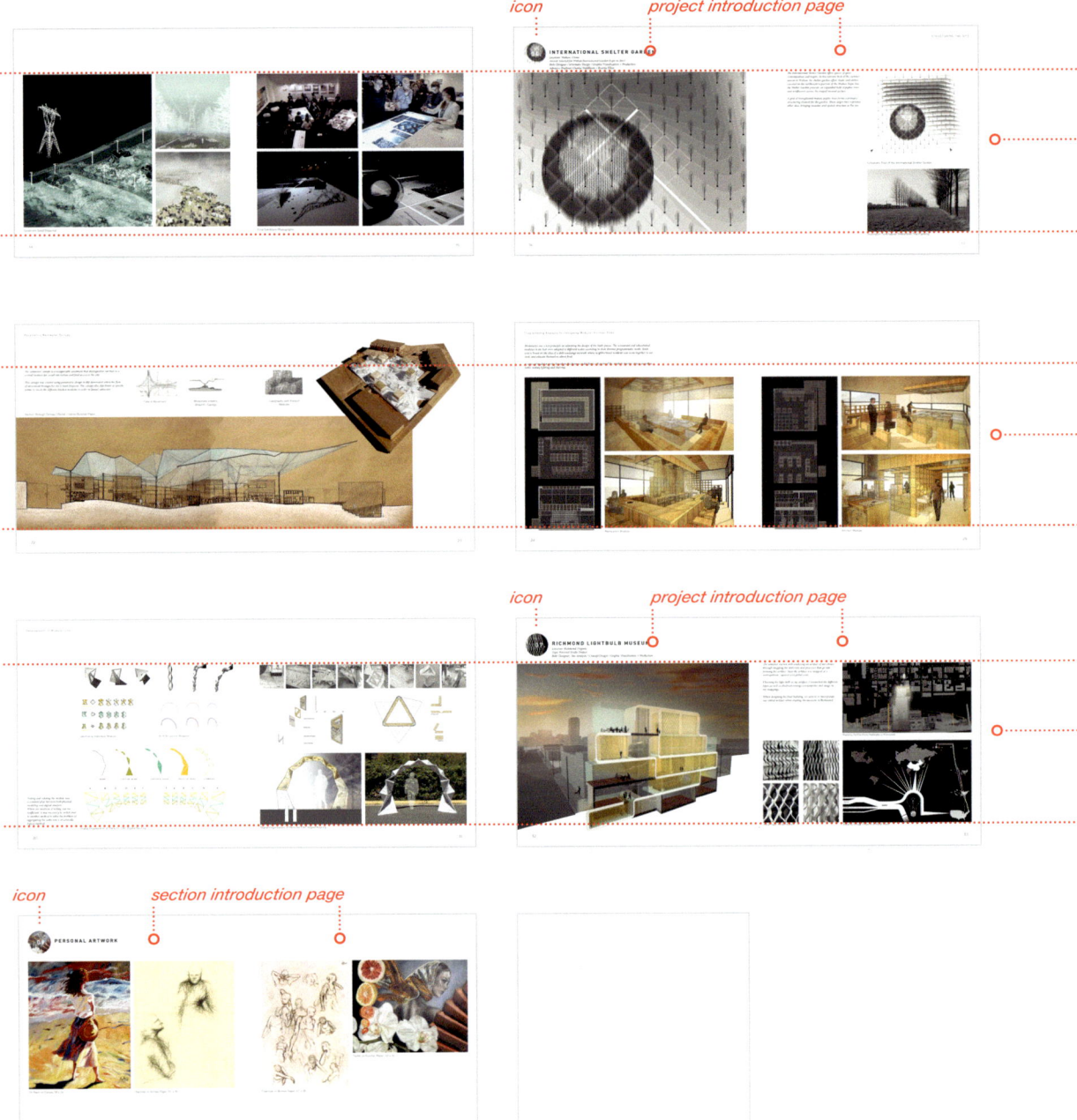

Case Studies

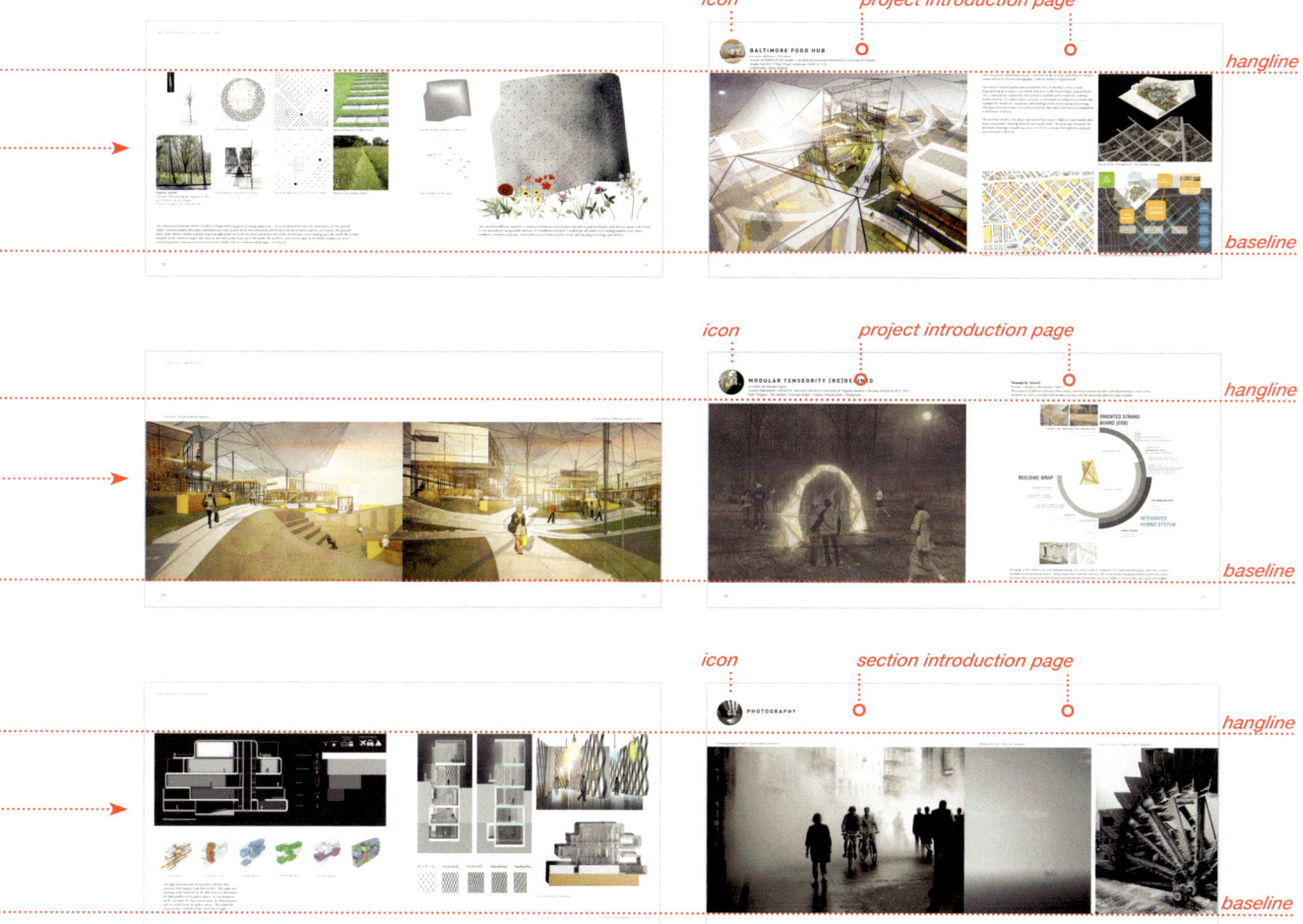

229

way-finding icon also located on table of contents

RICHMOND LIGHTBULB MUSEUM *typeface hierarchy: size 01*

Location: Richmond, Virginia
Type: Personal Studio Project
Role: Designer: Site Analysis / Concept Design / Graphic Visualization + Production

image hierarchy: size 01

hangline

The semester started with analyzing an artifact of our choice through mapping the materials and processes that go into forming the artifact. Next the artifact was mapped at a metropolitan, regional and global scale.

Choosing the light bulb as my artifact, I researched the different types as well as electricity/energy consumption and usage in my mappings.

When designing the final building, we were to re-incorporate our initial artifact when creating the museum in Richmond.

typeface hierarchy: size 02

image hierarchy: size 02

Mapping the Electricity Networks in Richmond   *typeface hierarchy: size 03*

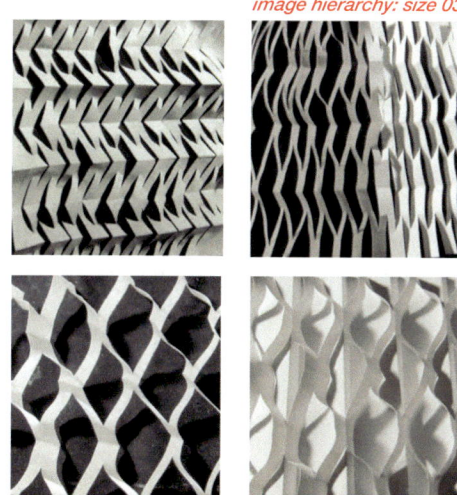

image hierarchy: size 03

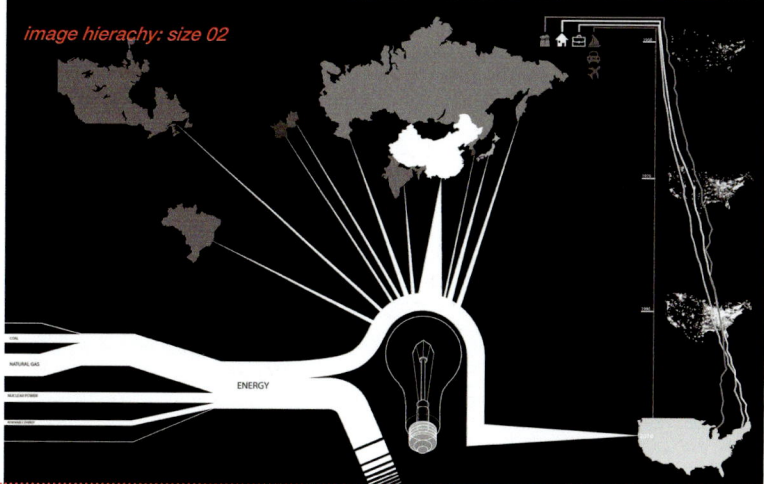

image hierarchy: size 02

Initial Paper Model Studies

Mapping Energy Usage on a Global Scale

baseline

Constructing the Persuasive Portfolio: the only primer you'll ever need

Case Study 07
Nikki Hall—*University of Arizona*

Specifications
size:　　　　　8.5" x 11", 216mm x 279mm
orientation:　　vertical page, horizontal spread
length:　　　　36 pages, 7 project sections

Strengths*

*portfolio organization
visual narrative*

table of contents is text-based with project number and project title

parallel project introduction pages include project title, subtitle, descriptive paragraph and introductory graphics

title on parallel project introduction pages is red and acts as a consistent graphic indicator to announce the beginning of each new project

footers include page number and project title on left and page number and year of project completion on the right

grids and margins

active area is defined by hangline and baseline

all layouts respond to both hangline and baseline on each spread

top and bottom margins are larger than side margins to support the horizontal nature of the image arrangement

image organization

images are primarily organized through horizontal banding

portfolio makes good use of primary images with secondary support images

image sets and series are used throughout portfolio

*text and
typeface strategies*

typeface hierarchy is established and maintained throughout portfolio

text blocks are justified to maintain strong text column edges

*for larger images of this portfolio, see page 55.

Case Studies

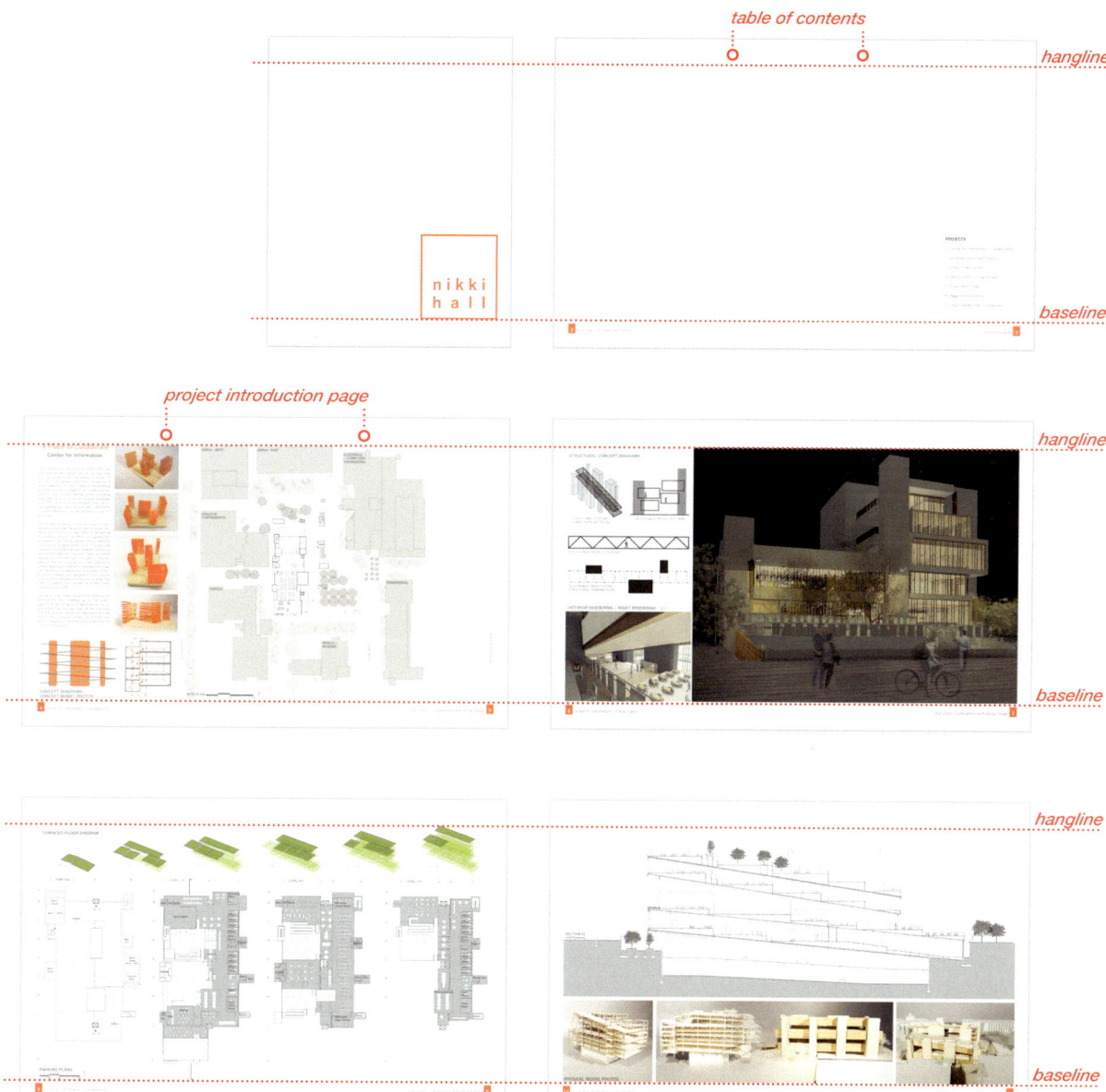

233

Constructing the Persuasive Portfolio: the only primer you'll ever need

Case Studies

235

Case Study 08
Annie McCarthy—*Georgia Institute of Technology*

Specifications
size: 8" x 8", 203mm x 203mm
orientation: 4 square booklets open horizontally
1 square booklet (case study) opens vertically
length: 130 pages across 5 individual project booklets

Strengths

portfolio organization
visual narrative
portfolio is organized across five booklets that operate as a set; each booklet begins with project introduction page and includes project title, subtitle, year of completion, studio critic and descriptive text

grids and margins
the case study booklet flips vertically to accommodate the vertical nature of the tower project and maintains a predominantly single column grid throughout

image organization
vertical spreads alternate between full bleed images, image pairs and image sets

text and typeface strategies
descriptive text is set as rag right with careful attention to have no word breaks at the end of each line of text

Case Studies

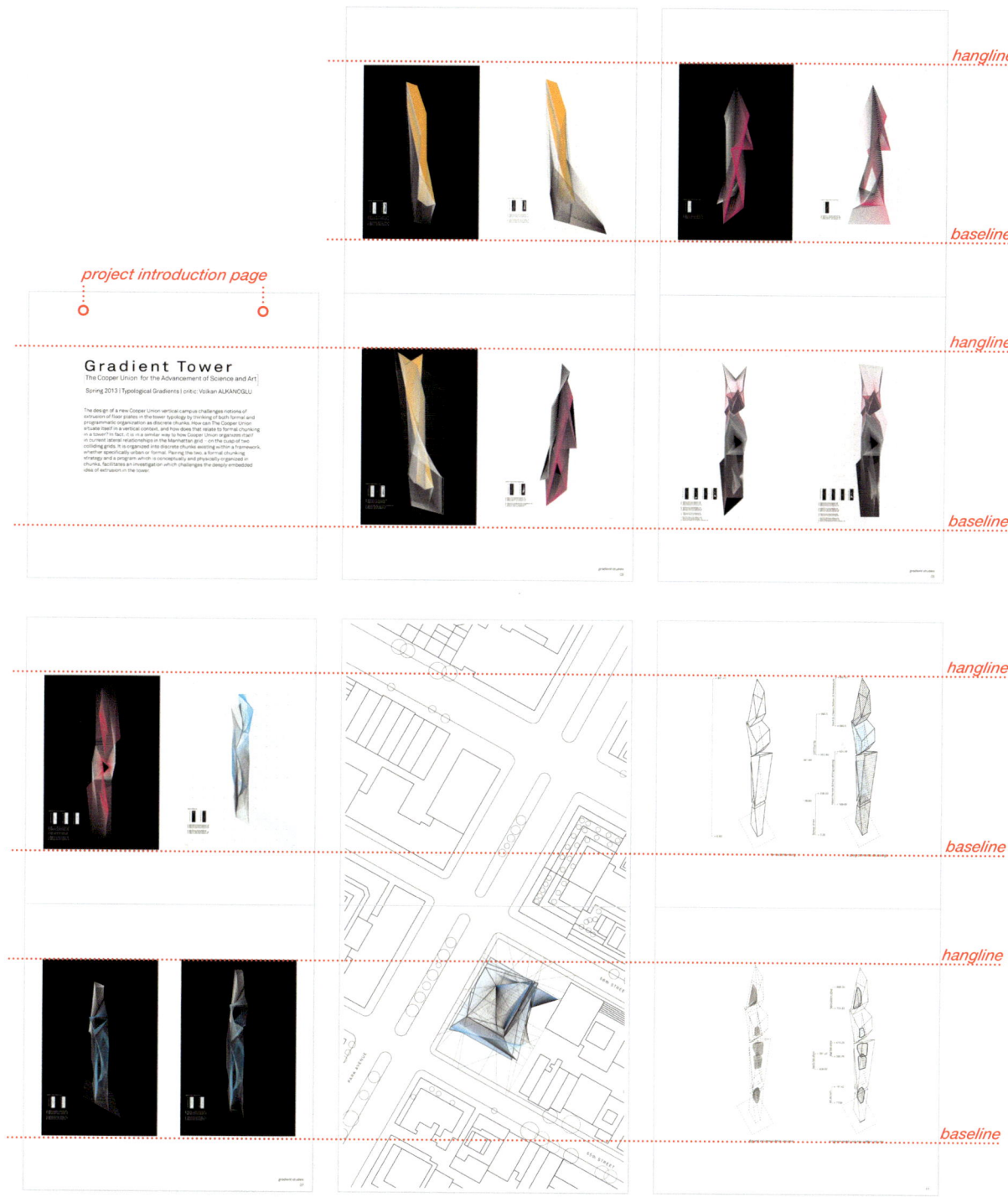

237

Constructing the Persuasive Portfolio: the only primer you'll ever need

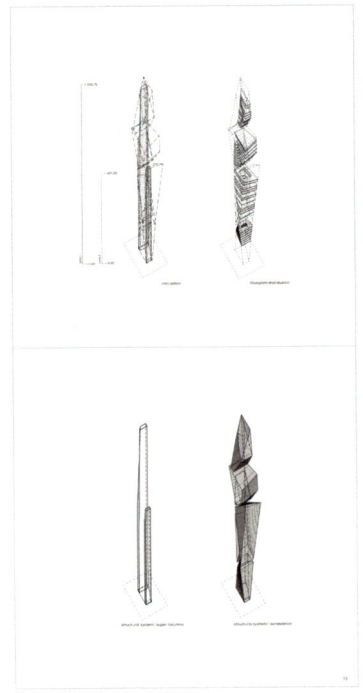
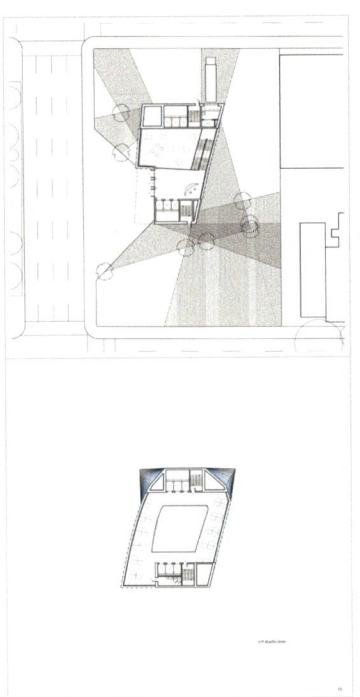
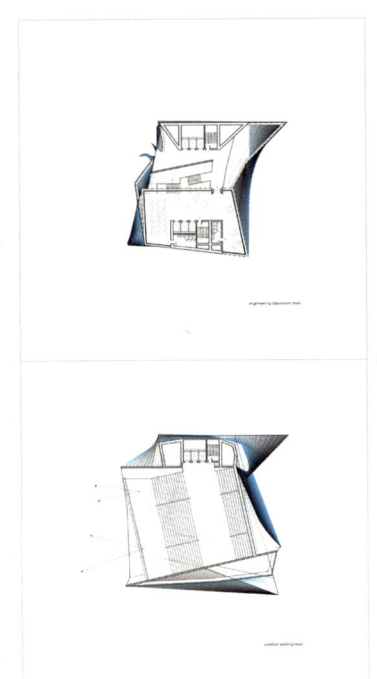
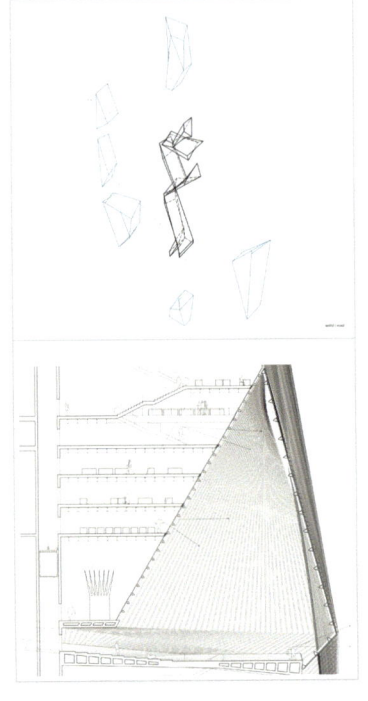
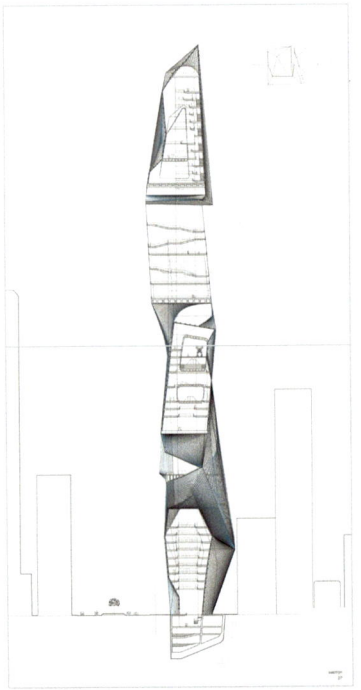
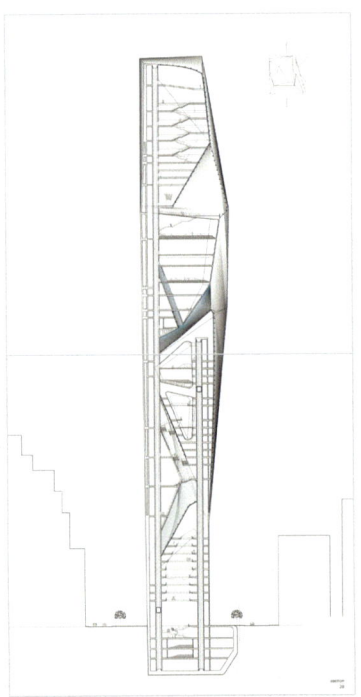

Case Studies

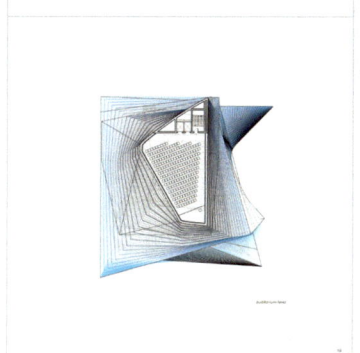
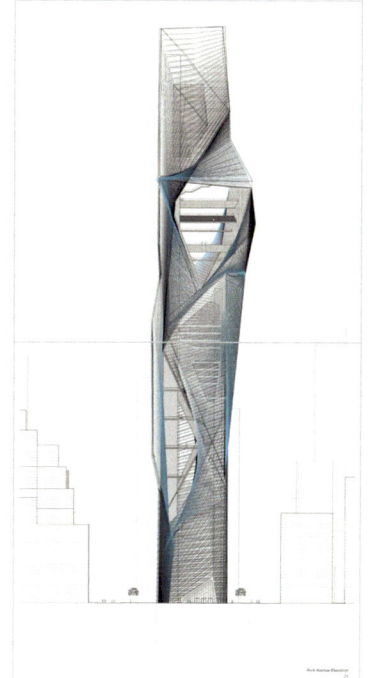
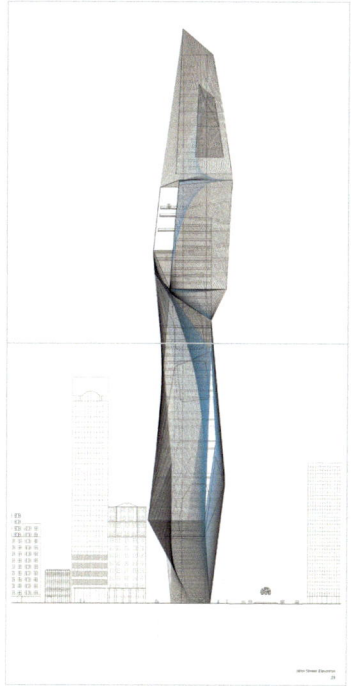
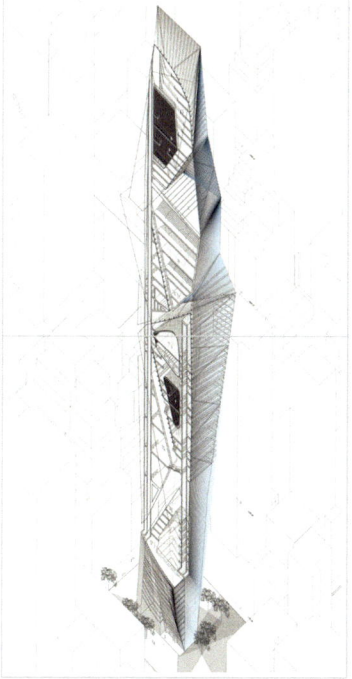
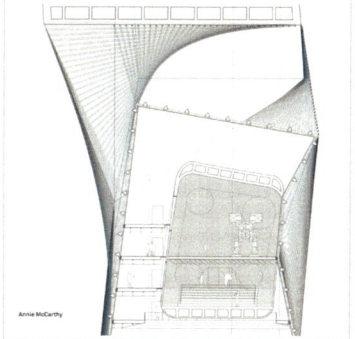

Annie McCarthy

239

Illustration Credits

Shawn Backstrom 44–5
Cynthia Baker 37, 153
Eric Barr 72–3
Christopher G. Beck 88
Sean Burns 43
Erin M. Butler 60
Ashley R. Claussen 151, 154–5
Jeffrey Collins 133
George Criminale 46, 123 (diagram thumbnail)
Karolina Czeczek 91
Phillip Denny 68–9, 132
Devin Dobrowolski 98
Callie Eitzen 79, 99, 123 (diagram thumbnail)
Xavier Encerrado 138
Nico Forlenza 43, 118–19
Timothy Fuerst 123 (diagram thumbnail), 136
Madeline Gonzalez 12
Will Gregory 182–93
Nikki Hall 55, 232–5
See Jia Ho 82–3
Ahmed Hosny 76
Jia Joy Hu 226–31
Pavan Iyer 117
Thomas Johnston 107, 152
Chase Jordan 62–3
Rasem Kamal 106
Chris Kay 105
Adam Kernes 194–201
Brian Kerr 126
Katherine Lynch 96, 142
Annie McCarthy 236–9
Mack Scogin Merrill Elam Architects 141
Flavio Sciaraffia Márquez 59
Ryan Tyler Martinez 77, 81, 208–17
Marrisa Jena Meeks 49
Saurabh Mhatre 41
Ethan Miller 104, 125
Andrea Moore-Lewis 11
Angela Ng 138
Fani Christina Papadopoulou 101
Derek Pirozzi 50–1, 218–25
Joseph Pucci 134–5
Joshua Riek 42
Curtis Roth 70–1
Ibrahim W. Salman 100, 132
Alberto Embriz de Salvatierra 127

Israel B. Sanchez 97, 136
Alena Savera 52–3
Natacha Schnider 130
Ciera Shaver 40
Michelle Shofet 102–3
Liz Szatko 149
Casey Tucker 86, 137
Oliver Vranesh 61, 86
Vonn Weisenberger 47
Scott Wooten 129
Wei Xia 202–7

Carnegie Mellon University—Gates Center for Computer Science and Hillman Center for Future Generation Technologies courtesy of Mack Scogin Merrill Elam Architects. Project Design Team: Mack Scogin, Merrill Elam, Lloyd Bray, Kimberly Shoemake-Medlock, Alan Locke, Jared Serwer, Jason Hoeft, Clark Tate, B Vithayathawornwong, Dennis Sintic, Carrie Hunsicker, Misty Boykin, Barnum Tiller, Matt Weaver, John Trefry, Margaret Fletcher, Helen Han, Ben Arenberg, Brian Bell, Trey Lindsey, Francesco Giacobello, Daniel Cashen, Jeff Collins, Janna Kauss, Patrick Jones, Cayce Bean, Jeff Kemp, Anja Turowski, Bo Roberts, Matthew Leach, Gary McGaha, Ted Paxton, Britney Bagby, Jacob Coburn, Amanda Crawley, Reed Simonds.

Cover Art: *azureus novalis 9:14* by Margaret Fletcher, encaustic and dry transfer on braced panel. Courtesy of Sandler Hudson Gallery, Atlanta, Georgia. Photograph by Mike Jensen.

All other illustrations by Margaret Fletcher.

Acknowledgments

This publication would not have been possible without the enthusiasm of the team at **Routledge / Taylor & Francis**. In particular, I would like to thank **Louise Fox** for her interest in the project when it was just an idea, **Wendy Fuller** for her invaluable advice shepherding this project forward, **Grace Harrison** for her patience as we moved through the writing and design process and **Alanna Donaldson** for her expertise in guiding me to completion.

The **College of Architecture, Design and Construction at Auburn University** saw enough merit in this project in its very early phases to award me a SEED Grant to begin the research. My sincere thanks go to **Vini Nathan**, Dean and McWhorter Endowed Chair; **Rebecca O'Neal Dagg**, Associate Professor and former Associate Dean for Research and Academic Affairs; and the entire **SEED Grant Selection Committee**. Special thanks also go to **David Hinson**, FAIA, Head of the School of Architecture, Planning and Landscape Architecture at Auburn University, for his continued support of this project. **Steven K. Wall** and **Stephanie Stratton** were an incredible help setting up and maintaining the submission website for the National Portfolio Call. Without their help, I wouldn't have received so many fantastic portfolios. Thanks go to **Tina Maceri**, for her early research assistance and to **Will Gregory** for his willingness to let me use his portfolio as the initial example that accompanied my publication proposal. Also, special thanks go to Associate Professors **Rusty Smith** and **Kevin Moore** for their review of the publication design. Their insightful comments helped polish the graphic organization of the book.

It's a funny thing to contemplate all the ways people have influenced a project like this one. I have been working on issues related to the communication of architectural ideas since before my undergraduate education. When I consider the many people who have had impact on the way I think about these ideas, there are a few folks who stand out and bear mentioning. To **Sambo Mockbee** for my first official portfolio review 25 years ago at the Strutting Duck; thank you for your good natured laughing at my efforts and explaining to me that there was an entire area of communication studies that I had yet to understand. That one conversation directed me to a profound interest in the topic. At Harvard Graduate School of Design, **Nigel Smith** opened my eyes to all of the possibilities and **Brooke Hodge**, **Darell Fields**, **Eve Blau**, **Marco Steinberg**, **Christine Smith**, **James Ackerman** and **Preston Scott Cohen** allowed me to hone my skills on their projects.

Ten years of working in collaboration with **Mack Scogin** and **Merrill Elam** provided a fantastic opportunity to work through the visual communication of extraordinarily complex architectural ideas in a straightforward and clear manner. This work was a vehicle for us all to not only be able to explain the work to others, but also to be able to better understand it ourselves.

To my brother, for his thoughtful care packages of strange, foreign treats. Your kindness and support made me too big for my britches.

And finally. . . many, many thanks go to my **friends** and **family**—Mom, Eric, Alex, Dad who always said, "Nothing worthwhile is easy!," **Jean** and all the **Ragons**—for their patience with and support of this project. Your constant enthusiasm and attention helped me hang in there to finish even when the refrain of "Is the book done yet?" nearly sent me into a tailspin because, alas, it wasn't done then. But it is now!

And to my dear husband, **Russ**, for his cheerful willingness to constantly rearrange our lives so I had time to work on this project.

To all who have contributed to this success, a heartfelt thank you!

Acknowledgments

I would like to thank all of the designers who responded to my National Portfolio Call and submitted their portfolios for inclusion in this book. Without their enthusiasm for this project, I wouldn't have had so many wonderful design examples. In particular, I would like to thank the following designers whose work is included in this volume:

Shawn Backstrom—Clemson University
Cynthia Baker—Auburn University
Eric Barr—University of Cincinnati, University of Virginia
Christopher G. Beck—University of Maryland, College Park; Rhode Island School of Design
Sean Burns—Kent State University, University of Pennsylvania
Erin M. Butler—Rensselaer Polytechnic Institute
Ashley R. Claussen—University of Missouri, University of Kansas
Jeffrey Collins—The Ohio State University, Georgia Institute of Technology
George Criminale—Auburn University
Karolina Czeczek—University of Technology, Kraków, Poland; Yale School of Architecture
Phillip Denny—Carnegie Mellon University, Princeton University School of Architecture
Devin Dobrowolski—St. Lawrence University, Maine College of Art, Harvard Graduate School of Design
Callie Eitzen—Auburn University
Xavier Encerrado—Texas Tech University
Nico Forlenza—Auburn University
Timothy Fuerst—Auburn University
Madeline Gonzalez—Auburn University
Will Gregory—Auburn University
Nikki Hall—University of Arizona
See Jia Ho—National University of Singapore, Harvard Graduate School of Design
Ahmed Hosny—American University of Sharjah, Harvard Graduate School of Design
Jia Joy Hu—University of Virginia, Harvard Graduate School of Design
Pavan Iyer—Georgia Institute of Technology
Thomas Johnston—University of Colorado at Boulder, Auburn University Rural Studio, University of Texas at Austin
Chase Jordan—Emory University, Harvard Graduate School of Design
Rasem Kamal—University of Jordan, Rice University
Chris Kay—Auburn University
Adam Kernes—California State Polytechnic University, Pomona
Brian Kerr—Pennsylvania State University
Katherine Lynch—Auburn University
Annie McCarthy—Georgia Institute of Technology
Flavio Sciaraffia Márquez—Universidad Católica de Chile, Harvard Graduate School of Design
Ryan Tyler Martinez—University of North Carolina at Charlotte, Southern California Institute of Architecture
Marrisa Jena Meeks—Texas Tech University; University of California, Los Angeles
Saurabh Mhatre—Balwant Sheth School of Architecture, NMIMS University, Mumbai, India; Harvard Graduate School of Design
Ethan Miller—Texas A&M University, Washington University in St. Louis
Andrea Moore-Lewis—Auburn University
Angela Ng—Ryerson University, University of Illinois at Urbana-Champaign
Fani Christina Papadopoulou—National Technical University of Athens, Harvard Graduate School of Design
Derek Pirozzi—University of South Florida School of Architecture and Community Design
Joseph Pucci—Northeastern University
Joshua Riek—University of South Florida School of Architecture and Community Design
Curtis Roth—Portland State University, Massachusetts Institute of Technology
Ibrahim W. Salman—University of Illinois at Urbana-Champaign
Alberto Embriz de Salvatierra—Cornell University, Harvard Graduate School of Design
Israel B. Sanchez—University of South Florida School of Architecture and Community Design
Alena Savera—The University of Texas at Austin
Natacha Schnider—California Polytechnic State University, San Luis Obispo
Ciera Shaver—University of Idaho
Michelle Shofet—University of California, Berkeley; Harvard Graduate School of Design
Liz Szatko—University of Nebraska–Lincoln, University of Michigan Taubman College of Architecture
Casey Tucker—The University of Texas at Arlington, The University of Texas at Austin
Oliver Vranesh—University of Virginia
Vonn Weisenberger—Pennsylvania State University
Scott Wooten—Texas Tech University
Wei Xia—University of Nebraska–Lincoln

Index

A active area 75–7
adjacency relationships 84
  captions and titles 87
  chronology 85
  cinematic 85
  pairs 84–5
  series 85
  sets 84
  timeline 85
Adobe Illustrator 26, 139
Adobe InDesign 26, 32, 113, 116, 139, 143, 176
Adobe Photoshop 13, 26, 143
  tool descriptions and use 15–17
alignment systems 65, 74
  hangline and baseline 67, 69, 73
architectural conventions 128
architectural symbols 128
arrows 140
audience
  differences 04
  identify 04
  research 04

B back matter 31, 57
Backstrom, Shawn 44–5
Baker, Cynthia 37, 153
balance 106–7
Barr, Eric 72–3
bar scale 128–30
Beck, Christopher G. 88
binding
  to avoid 167
  hard bound 166–7
  soft bound 166–7
  wire 167
bleeds 80–3, 91
Blurb.com 28, 166
bold lettering 110
book cloth tutorial 167–70
Burns, Sean 43
Butler, Erin M. 60

C captions 149
case studies 182–239
cataloging digital files 17
Claussen, Ashley R. 151, 154–5
CMYK 16, 165, 177
collecting artifacts 08
Collins, Jeffrey 133
colophon 31
color 102–5
  laser printing 166
  vibration 178
color models
  CMYK 16, 165, 177
  grayscale 16
  RGB 16, 165, 177
compound line edits 140
consistent graphic indicators 62–3
content narrative
  goals and purpose 24–5
  as organizing system 35–6
content pages 30, 56–7
contour lines 139
cover of portfolio 29, 166–71
Criminale, George 46, 123
curriculum vitae (CV) 31
Czeczek, Karolina 91

D dashes 115
Denny, Phillip 68–9, 132
design
  actions x–xi
  knowledge viii
  narratives 24
  thinking viii, 124
diagram labels 149–50
diagram titles 149
digital file
  cataloging 17
  organization 17, 19
digital image editing
  Adobe Photoshop tools 15–17
  best practices 15
digital portfolios 172–9
  determining goals 173

PDF 05, 176
web portfolio 05, 174–6, 178–9
digital storage 19
Dobrowolski, Devin 98
documentation
    best practices 09–10
    list of 08
    presentation 09
    reference 08–9
door swings 142
drawing labels 131–3, 149–50
drawing titles 149

E editing 156–9
    checklists 158–9
    copy editing 159
    graphics 158
Eitzen, Callie 79, 99, 123
em dash 115
Encerrado, Xavier 138
en dash 115

F file formats 16–17
file nomenclature 19
flexibility
    of content 05
    of grid 67
    of portfolio 05, 26, 163
    of typeface 147
Forlenza, Nico 43, 118–19
front matter 29–30, 56
Fuerst, Timothy 123, 136

G GIF file 178
Gonzalez, Madeline 12
graphic
    design 94
    icon systems 58–9
    layout 94
    punctuation 115–16
    scale 128–30
grayscale 16
Gregory, Will 182–93
grid systems 65

modular or compound 67, 71
multi-column 66–7, 70–1
single column 66, 68–9, 106
six column 72–3
gutter, content crosses 89

H Hall, Nikki 55, 232–5
hatch 140
headers and footers 48, 150
hierarchy 152–5
    image 126
    typeface 117–19, 147–8
Ho, See Jia 82–3
Hosny, Ahmed 76
Hu, Jia Joy 226–31
hyphen 115
    settings 116

I image
    focus 143
    primary 96–7
    quality 143
image resolution
    internet 179
    print 13
including other work 38–9
inkjet printing 166
ISSUU.com 176
italics 110
Iyer, Pavan 117

J Johnston, Thomas 107, 152
Jordan, Chase 62–3
JPEG file 16–17, 178

K Kamal, Rasem 106
Kay, Chris 105
Kernes, Adam 194–201
kerning 111
Kerr, Brian 126

L labels
    diagrams 149–50
    drawing 131–3, 149–50

laser printing, color 166
line weight 139
list style 116
leading 112
lowercase letters 110
Lulu.com 166
Lynch, Katherine 96, 142

M McCarthy, Annie 236–9
Mack Scogin Merrill Elam Architects 141
margins 75, 78–9
Márquez, Flavio Sciaraffia 59
Martinez, Ryan Tyler 77, 81, 208–17
measure 74, 112
Meeks, Marrisa Jena 49
Mhatre, Saurabh 41
Miller, Ethan 104, 125
Moore-Lewis, Andrea 11

N Ng, Angela 138
north arrows 128

O offset printing 166
online printing 166
optical edge 79
order of projects 36–9
orphans 114
overlapping content 89

P page numbers 54–7
Papadopoulou, Fani Christina 101
paper selection 171
paragraph
  alignment 112–14
  indentation 116
PDF 04, 05, 27, 174, 176
  optimizing 176
photography
  at desk 11
  flat work 12
  models 11–12
  outdoors 10
  in studio 10

Pirozzi, Derek 50–1, 218–25
pixels per inch (ppi) 13
PNG file 178–9
poché 139
portfolio
  components of 29, 56–7
  digital types 05
  flexibility 05, 26, 163
  format 163
  organization 35
  orientation 28–9, 165
  planning 23
  print types 05
  review process 04
  size 28, 165
  visual review 158
presentation drawings 139–43
printing options 166
print portfolios 05, 162–71
  binding 166–7
  cut sheets 05, 27, 164
  interview portfolio 05, 27, 164
  leave-behind 05, 27, 164
  mailer 05, 27, 164
  material choices 170–1
  printing 166
  production method 165
project introduction spread 31, 56–8, 60–1
project narrative 120–1
  holes in 122
  goals and purpose 24–5
  order of 124
project(s)
  chronology 31
  number to include 123
  order of 36–9
PSD file 17
Pucci, Joseph 134–5

R representation, complexities of 07
resume 31
RGB 16, 165, 177
rich black 143

Riek, Joshua 42
rivers 111
Roth, Curtis 70–1
runts 114–15

S Salman, Ibrahim W. 100, 132
Salvatierra, Alberto Embriz de 127
Sanchez, Israel B. 97, 136
sans serif 109
Savera, Alena 52–3
scanning 12
   best practices 14
   large format 14
   small format 14
Schnider, Natacha 130
section cut lines 128, 131
section divider spread 30, 48–53
serif 109
Shaver, Ciera 40
Shofet, Michelle 102–3
simplicity, of layout 116–17
sketchbook 08, 14, 40
storyboard 32–3
subtitles 148
symmetry 107
Szatko, Liz 149

T table of contents 30, 42–7
text
   graphic presence 147–50
   types 124–5, 145
TIFF file 16
titles 148
   diagram 149
   drawing 149
tracking 111
Tucker, Casey 86, 137
typeface
   consistency 54
   hierarchy 108, 117–19
   range 109
   selection 108
typography 108
   alignment 112–14
   graphic rules 108

U underlining 110
uppercase letters 110

V visual
   hierarchy 94–107
   order 94–107
   pace 90–1
   structure 65
   weight 100–1
visual narrative
   goals and purpose 24–5
   as organizing system 35, 42–63
Vranesh, Oliver 61, 86

W web guidelines
   browser compatibility 179
   file formats 178–9
   resolution 179
   upload time 179
   web safe colors 179
website portfolio
   blog website 175–6
   converting print to 174–5
   self-coded 174–5
   template 175
   web-based book 176
Weisenberger, Vonn 47
white space 88–9, 98–9
widows 114
Wooten, Scott 129
writing tips 146

X x-height 110
Xia, Wei 202–7

Colophon

Futura designed by Paul Renner, 1927.
Helvetica Neue originally designed by Max Miedinger, 1957; redesigned by D. Stempel AG, 1983.
Gill Sans designed by Eric Gill, 1928.